My Brother Is a Hairy Man

AN EXTRATERRESTRIAL VIEW
ON BIGFOOT AND HUMAN GENESIS

Ida M. Kannenberg
Lee Trippett

Atlantis Phoenix
Missoula, Montana

Atlantis Phoenix
Missoula, MT
www.atlantisphoenix.com

Ordering Information: Quantity sales. Special discounts are available on quantity purchases by corporations, associations, and others. For details, contact Atlantis Phoenix at phoenix@atlantisphoenix.com.

Fourth Edition 2017

My Brother Is a Hairy Man: An Extraterrestrial View on Bigfoot and Human Genesis. Ida M. Kannenberg and Lee Trippett

ISBN 978-0-9837051-4-7

Cover design by Radiant Arts
Painting of Bigfoot © Hartmut Jager 2014

Contents

Contents

This book is dedicated to Marlys Trippett. Her consistent patience and generous support are deeply appreciated.

Other books by Ida M. Kannenberg

PROJECT EARTH FROM THE EXTRATERRESTRIAL PERSPECTIVE

TIME TRAVELERS FROM ATLANTIS

UFO INITIATION: ULTRATERRESTRIAL TIME TRAVELERS

RECONCILIATION

THE ALIEN BOOK OF TRUTH: WHO AM I?
WHAT AM I DOING? WHY AM I HERE?

A human being is part of a whole, called by us 'Universe,' a part limited in time and space. He experiences himself, his thoughts and feelings as something separated from the rest — a kind of optical illusion of his consciousness. This delusion is a kind of prison for us, restricting us to our personal desires and to affection for a few persons nearest us.

Our task must be to free ourselves from our prison by widening our circle of compassion to embrace all living creatures and the whole of nature in its beauty.

Albert Einstein

Painting of Bigfoot © Hartmut Jager

Genesis 27:11

And Jacob said to Rebekah his mother,
Behold, Esau my brother is a hairy man,
and I am a smooth man.

The Arcturians

So now we had three strains of nearly fully Earth humans: Bigfoot, a borderline human; *neanderthalensis*
[Neanderthal], a *Homo sapiens*; and Cro-Magnon type
Homo sapiens sapiens. These three were all together on
the continent you call Lemuria.

Most of the cross-bred humans were brought back to
Lemuria, as their original purpose had been to help us
colonize our new country. These new "citizens" were
mostly from the Levantine corridor and were several
strains in the neighborhood of *Homo erectus*. (November
1998)

Nature journal of science

The ancient genomes, one from a Neanderthal and one
from a member of an archaic human group called the
Denisovans . . . suggest that interbreeding went on between the members of several ancient human-like groups
in Europe and Asia more than 30,000 years ago, including
an as-yet-unknown human ancestor from Asia. . . ."we're
looking at a *Lord of the Rings*-type world — that there
were many hominid populations," says Mark Thomas, an
evolutionary geneticist at University College London . . .
("Mystery Humans Spiced Up Ancients' Sex Lives," Ewan
Callaway; *Nature* international weekly journal of science,
November 19, 2013).

Foreword

KRSANNA DURAN

Time travelers from Atlantis revealed to Ida Kannenberg their origin and objectives in her first book, *Project Earth from the Extraterrestrial Perspective,* in 1978:

> We travel through a time differential. I am not at liberty to reveal our propulsion system, except to say it is something akin to anti-magnetic forces.
>
> Our purpose is friendly and for the mutual benefit of both planets, and other planets and worlds, for we are of a con- federation of planets. Great events are coming that you must be prepared to meet, and we are here to help you be- come alert, to prepare and to understand what is happening. It is vital to our welfare that you are successful.
>
> Because you are so primitive technologically and so unde- veloped psychically, we greatly underrated your capacities of understanding and learning. . . . Now we know we have only to explain and teach and help you develop yourselves along the necessary lines.

The time travelers recommended research and tutored Ida's study. They repeatedly advised they provided only outlines – the bare bones – for Ida to pursue and make her own discoveries. It is not, and has never been, the time travelers' intent to dictate a bible of hard and fast scriptures. In *Time Travelers from Atlantis* Ida observed that they had never corrected her on anything except time. They take time seriously and will correct errors about it. They encouraged her to think – to look beneath the words – and correct her own course.

In seventy years of experiences with UFOlk, Ida found that each and every element of an encounter is planned and orches- trated with intent to reach an objective. The time travelers cannot afford to squander an iota, a dot or a tittle. Time is short and resources are not unlimited.

In the beginning, Ida reported, she had little actual interest in Bigfoot, "just a general curiosity when the subject was brought up in conversation." She and I had discussed our mutual UFO experiences at length in seven years of friendship. Neither of us had mentioned Bigfoot until 1998, when she embarked on a search for the elusive species with Lee Trippett. Soon after Trippett sparked Ida's interest in Bigfoot, Maez, the representative of an Arcturian council, began speaking to her. On several occasions Maez and the time travelers explained that they cannot discuss a topic until it has taken root in our thought. (Albeit, they seem to feel free to hint wildly in arousing interest.)

Maez explained Bigfoot's reason for being on Earth, his human nature, mind of the species, journey of soul, relationship with modern humans and threatened wilderness home. Responding to Ida's repeated requests to arrange a meeting with Bigfoot for evidence of the species' existence, Maez commented on December 11 1998:

> "Yes, of course, we could do all this for you, even deliver the bones of a Bigfoot right to your door by United Parcel Service. But you would miss out on a vital experience that would prove necessary for future and successful research. You are building a complete but slow road to obtaining proof of Bigfoot's nature and existence in ways that cannot be denied."

The Arcturian spoke about numerous special interests he juggled, and emphasized that Bigfoot's survival, desires, free choice and culture were foremost concerns. He could encourage Bigfoot to meet with Ida and Trippett, but could not force a meeting. On one occasion Maez said he would send a car to drive Trippett to a meeting with Bigfoot, but neither the car nor the meeting materialized. The false start challenged the researchers' expectations, intent and methods. Maez defined his role as advocate for Bigfoot and provided guideposts for future and successful research of lasting value.

In *My Brother Is a Hairy Man*, the last book Ida wrote with the time travelers, Maez reviewed passages from her first book, *Project Earth from the Extraterrestrial Perspective*. He explained the larger context of comments about Bigfoot and human origins made twenty years earlier in 1978. With her new understanding, Ida made critical observations about objectives, methods and differences between extraterrestrials, ultraterrestrials and spiritual teachers.

Maez's outline of Bigfoot's birth and history has proven remarkably close to new discoveries made a decade and more after discussions with Ida in 1998-2000. Bigfoot's human DNA (The Erickson Project Press Release) and mystery ancestors identified in DNA (*Nature* journal of science) are among the groundbreaking discoveries.

I had first encountered Bigfoot's physical reality at a sun dance with Native American elder Wallace Black Elk at Ashland, Oregon in 1988. We were aware of the Bigfoot family presence, could hear them moving in the brush at night, and had seen their nest. I made no extraordinary effort to communicate with the Bigfoot that curiously watched from the woods. In 2009 I was again in proximity of a Bigfoot that appeared in the presence of UFOs on Native American land in Montana. Again, I made no effort to "habituate," or actively mingle with Bigfoot. Like Ida, I had no focused interest in Bigfoot. I viewed them as highly psychic, intelligent and sentient beings, deserving privacy and good neighbors.

Maez's explanation of the transition from ape to human evolution, which echoed information from my UFO contact in 1963, inspired my strong interest in Bigfoot. After the UFO contact when I was fifteen years old, my life changed in ways that are common for UFO experiencers, and telepathic contact commenced. When doing a special project on evolution for tenth grade biology, my telepathic confidant explained that human souls mingling with apes altered the anthropoid and initiated human qualities. Imagery of human souls cohabiting with apes to engender human features and intelligence was so clear and profound that it spoke at the deepest levels of intuition. Years later I read Edgar Cayce's description of virtually the same scenario. Maez's explanation of human souls commingling with apes was the third iteration of the theme.

After acquiring publishing rights for Ida's books, I struggled with making two small corrections in the new edition of *My Brother Is a Hairy Man*. At that late date, I could not review the changes with Ida and had no way of identifying the origin of the data, but facts are facts. The facts ruled. I made minor changes with no concern about how the errors had crept in the book, as long as the information was corrected. Then I moved on to the next project.

Several days later Maez spoke to me, much as he had first spoken to Ida, and made a startling comment:

"I see that you found my errors. I gained a colleague."

How Maez knew I had made the changes is one of the mysteries of the time travelers' communications system. He knew. He owned the errors. And he recognized me as a "colleague."

Collaboration between the time travelers and modern humans is the stated objective of their presence among us. They challenge, tease, taunt and cajole to bring us to our feet with awakening and expanding the mind of the species.

Exploring the state of Earth's sciences, the time travelers recommended and discussed literature with Ida. Veteran Bigfoot researcher Lee Trippett provided valuable insights gleaned from decades of experience on the ground in search of Bigfoot. The time travelers mentor the expanding species mind.

Krsanna Duran
March 22, 2014

Introduction

IDA KANNENBERG

In the beginning I had very little actual interest in Bigfoot, just a general curiosity when the subject was brought up in conversation.

Then, in October 1998, I was introduced to the Trippetts — Lee; Marlys; and Ben, Lee's father.

Lee and Ben had been on the trail of Bigfoot for nearly forty years. Ben, who was 87, left us too soon. He sat down one morning to catch his breath before starting on his morning walk and gently went to sleep. He is greatly missed.

Lee and Marlys, his wife, have become my guides, friends, inspiration and direction-pointers ever since. I had no idea how involved I was to become in the study of Bigfoot, so I took no notes at first. I shall have to shake out my memory bins. Lee had an excellent plan for getting a memento of Bigfoot. All he needed was a cooperative one. I mentioned I had some experience in map dowsing although I had never followed it very far. Lee brought some local maps and we dowsed several places where Bigfoot might be found, all within the Coast Range of Oregon.

Just about there a telepathic voice broke into our discussion to give us some specific directions. I have been steadily interacting with such voices since 1977. This was a new one. He introduced himself as Maez, the head of the Council that monitors Bigfoot. From the planet Arcturus yet! That would explain the UFOs that have been seen in the vicinity of our subject.

You may shrug or grimace at the mention of UFOs, but when reports keep coming in about seeing Bigfoot in conjunction with such a craft, none of the reporters known to each other, you cannot just shrug them off. They are part of the total picture and are to be considered as legitimately as any footprint.

Until you know Bigfoot in all his characteristics, including his relationship to such craft, you don't know him well enough to find him.

And that is how, why this book came to be written. If you don't like me bringing up the subject of UFOs, go away, but you will miss some very revealing and important information. You don't have to believe everything, just be willing to listen. I am writing this as a service to Bigfoot hunters everywhere. Personally, I wouldn't know what to do with a Bigfoot if I caught one. I do not dream about it.

I have never sworn fealty to any current scientific paradigm. My Irish won't let me. My mind must be free to poke into the forbidden corners and give each discovery at least a chance to be heard.

There are two major and conflicting belief systems about Bigfoot.

Positive	Negative
Bigfoot has a significant role toward our own safety and welfare.	Bigfoot is a useless species and expendable.
Bigfoot is borderline human.	Bigfoot is pure animal.
Bigfoot's environment must be protected and he must have clean water, air, food, and proper living space.	Bigfoot is fair game. We have no responsibility for him.
Bigfoot must be protected by law.	We must get evidence of Bigfoot's reality at any cost for the sake of personal glory and gain.

The purpose of this story is to make the above facts known with evidence of his reality and worth through

- photos,
- footprints,
- record of Maez's information, and
- record of communication with Bigfoot through Maez or more closely with BF, and other physical evidence.

Whole Person Profile

Until we know Bigfoot completely for what and who he really is, we cannot hope to have any profitable interaction with him. Any reporter studies the one to be interviewed thoroughly before he calls upon him. So let us study the whole person of Bigfoot before we go tromping through the forest hoping to scare one up. That means gathering all the material we can from books, stories, conversations, website, and imagination.

Every thought, idea, quest starts with imagination, and that does not mean fantasy. Imagination works itself up into a speculative premise. We ask, "Why do we think this?" And we line up our ducks (facts, observations) all in a row and proceed to shoot them down one by one. Those that do not fall under the force of our critical study are what we have left to work with; they form the basis of further investigation.

In this study of Bigfoot we are fortunate to have an extra and certainly knowledgeable source of information — the UFO people who created him, represented by Maez, the head of the council that monitors Bigfoot in his earthly career.

Is this idea too rich for your blood? Then go away, we won't want your nagging. Or does it make your heart pound and your ears ring? Then come along for a true adventure in ferreting out the real Bigfoot. I tell the story as it was given to me and as I lived it day by day. To me it is all as true as sunshine and rain.

Lay aside your skepticism and doubt and come along. All you will need to bring is what the poet Samuel Coleridge called "the willing suspension of disbelief". This story is not only true. It is some pretty serious stuff.

Our speculative premise: Bigfoot is a borderline *Homo sapiens*, derived from *Australopithecus africanus* and with a genetic input from true humans (the Masters of Arcturus).

I am sure the proponents of the "Bigfoot is an Ape" theory will cuss me up one side and down the other for intruding this story among the "serious literature". I have to do it because it is true and it gives a full picture of the real creature and explains a lot of the mysteries that surround him. I promise not to insert anything but what I believe — after great consideration and struggle — to be true.

Along with me on this unplanned and unanticipated excursion are Mr. and Mrs. Lee Trippett. Lee Trippett has brought along his observations, thoughts and questions that resulted from nearly forty years of Bigfoot research in the field. He has shared the results of his experiences generously for this book. His input is valuable and adds a realistic background — forty years' worth.

Mrs. Lee (Marlys) Trippett has collated incidents from some of the better-known books which indicate Bigfoot has human qualities. Without these two this book never would have been written.

I appreciate also the loan of their books, and their patient reading of my daily output of pages, and the comments that sometimes pointed firmer directions for my thoughts to follow. I needed help as Bigfoot was a new subject to me. I started as a blank sheet of paper back there in October 1998.

Getting involved in the study of Bigfoot was something I had never anticipated or thought of doing. I sort of fell into it, or lunged. My telepathic mentors, Thoth and Tres, told me it was a forerunner to my next book that will concern the genetic interference with our own human development that was engineered by the same experimenters from Arcturus, at least in part.

I did not have much confidence that such a story would be readily received until I read about Zacharia Sitchin's and Monsignor Balducci's conversation on that subject that took place on April 1, 2000 in Bellaria, Italy. Balducci was a Vatican appointee chosen to deal with the issue of UFOs and E.T.s. He expressed to Sitchin that it was quite probable that there were sentient beings on other planets and that there had been genetic interference with our race. Whew! With acceptance of these ideas by a Vatican official, who am I to hesitate? But that is to be the subject of my next book for which the study of Bigfoot is to prepare me. So I dig hopefully into the inquiry of the source and characteristics of Bigfoot.

I am not going to rehash all the old Bigfoot stories here. You can read them better in the original books. But I have made a complete list of the most often cited physical characteristics that I think reveals the "average" Bigfoot of the Pacific Northwest. The books of John Green are invaluable here, especially

Sasquatch, The Apes Among Us. Mr. Green rejects any suggestion of Bigfoot being human. As a counter-balance, read Jack Lapseritis' *The Psychic Sasquatch*; and as a right-on sensible and sensitive correlative read anything you come across by the Russian, Dimitri Bayanov.

A brief résumé of some personal characteristics culled from written reports of those who have had close observation/contact with Bigfoot.

Personal Characteristics

Height	Average 7 to 8 feet tall. Others have been reported 5 and even 12 feet tall.
Weight	Average 350 to 500 pounds. There are higher estimates.
Hair	Covers body except for clear patches on palms of hands and soles of feet. Most often hair is black or shades of brown or reddish brown. Also noted are red, white, gray, or bluish. Sometimes hair is tipped with silver or white. Hair on body averages 2 to 4 inches, in some places as back of arms, 6 inches. Hair on head is sometimes longer. A few seem to have the appearance of a mustache or even a beard.
Body Build	Stocky, sturdy, muscular, robust, huge.
Skin	When it shows through the hair, it is most often described as black or brown, more rarely as white or beige.
Teeth	Like ours but larger.
Ears	Usually hidden by the hair, but when seen, described like ours.
Mouth and Lips	Mouth usually described as wide with thin lips.
Face	Flat, no snout.
Chin	Wide jaw but minimal chin.
Neck	Practically none. From front view head seems to sink into the shoulders.
Shoulders	Huge, 36 to 48 inches broad.

Arms	Very long. Hands seem to hang in vicinity of knees when Bigfoot is standing. Upper arms are especially bulky, enormously strong. He swings arms briskly in rhythm to stride.
Nose	Large, flat, snub, big nostrils.
Head	Sometimes described as dome shaped, or pointed with crest. Sometimes mentioned as seeming small in comparison to rest of body. He has a low forehead that slopes up to back.
Hands	Comparable to ours but much larger. Thumb seems to be set lower down and thumb is not fully opposable. Bigfoot wraps his whole hand around an object, does not use thumb as we do. No hair on palms.
Nails	Like ours but strong and tough!
Eyes	Small, dark, deep set, and close together. Reflects a light source, usually with a red glow, sometimes greenish instead.
Torso	No noticeable waistline. Form tapers downward from shoulders to hips. Well-padded bottom. A few reports mention a prominent belly.
Feet	Big! Average reports length 15 to 18 inches, width 5 to 8 inches, sometimes broader. Lengths have been reported at 22 to 25 inches.
Toes	Are long also, some might be webbed.
Stride	40 to 60 inches. Prints are 2 to 5 inches deep, depending on soil, mud, or snow. Runs 40 (and more) miles per hour. Leans forward from waist when walking. Keeps knees slightly bent.
Sounds	Screams, whistles, howls, growls, gibbers, chatters.
Odor	Stinks.
Activities	Swims and goes under water, twists branches and saplings, throws stones, rips bark off trees, tears rotten logs apart for grubs, likes to rock vehicles and shake corners of cabins and houses, is inquisitive and curious and looks in windows; many sightings are of Bigfoot crossing a road;

	the majority of sightings are at night; does not meander around objects, goes over them; piles rocks.
Emotions	He has been reported to giggle, and even to sing and shed tears.
Play	Wrestling, swimming, tossing rocks, enjoying water, building rock towers
Other	It seems certain he does not have tools other than sticks or stones. He beats sticks together as a warning signal. He uses them to dig roots. He uses stones in simple, natural ways. He will eat just about anything that is raw, even spoiled food. A few reports have him wearing an article or piece of clothing, a vest or belt or piece of hide. His personal hygiene does not deserve the name. His sleeping nests are not permanent.

For more than 40 years researchers have been tabulating such physical facts with impressive repetition. But what does it tell us about the inner Bigfoot? No one wants to stick his neck without analyzing what Bigfoot's behavior reveals. For one thing, the reporter doesn't have anything to compare Bigfoot to except himself and Bigfoot's brethren and cousins. Well, that's a start. It's a place to begin, a strong and secure place, uncontaminated by any other species.

We can start with the material at hand by asking questions such as: What has Bigfoot been witnessed doing on many occasions? How has he reacted to specific situations time after time? What has he done to reveal his emotions? How has he indicated his distress, displeasure, humor, his reluctance to be seen? The answers to questions such as these are hidden in the stories of sightings. Even a momentary glimpse of Bigfoot tells us something, observing the time, the place, the weather, the degree and extent of contact. *And don't think for a moment that all those brief sightings are accidental!*

The stories told in a number of excellent books about Bigfoot are a good place to begin our questioning. All of that work has been done for us, the value and importance and veracity of the stories have been sifted by the sincere and watchful writers of the past 40 years. We do not, ourselves, need to spend sleepless, cold, wet, pneumonia-inviting nights in stake-outs, or go to lengthy and expensive expeditions to the ends of the earth except for fun and adventure.

An invalid, tied to a convalescent bed, has as much opportunity to analyze the known physical data as a man or woman in the hunter's field. A little knowledge of anthropology and general psychology is a great help. Some experience in combating human nature will also prove its worth. One does not have to be a PhD or a Doctor of this or that. These poor souls are tied into a knot by their own paradigm, by their own learning and reputation. They dare not risk their credibility by thinking too far from the general consensus of their peers. It takes a brave man to contradict his peers, and there are few brave enough. The fact that they are who they are is as constrictive to their actions as a live boa around their middle.

I am therefore glad I have no reputation except for honesty, sincerity, and good intentions, and that is easy to maintain; just be myself.

So that is the general situation when I pick up my pen in the dark hours of the night and write with sleepy abandon. I am not even positive these are my own original thoughts; someone may be feeding them to me, a muse perhaps, or an angel, an alter-ego, a doppelganger. Such fellows do get around, and as I so often repeat, "I need all the help I can get!" Thank you Inspirators!

Introduction

LEE TRIPPETT

My search for Bigfoot has been a unique adventure for almost forty years. It has opened doors to travel, exploration, interviews, and research beyond the ordinary.

It all started in the early 1960s when a relative shared his personal experience with Bigfoot activities in northern California. The published Bigfoot reports of that time and my personal interest of outdoor activities led to a serious hobby and the question of the century, "How could something so big survive and stay hidden for so long?"

The initial quest for adventure was the possible honor of making a modern unique discovery. Over the years, the Bigfoot quest turned into more of solving a mystery. What is the nature of a man-like giant that obviously could remain unknown to the majority of our civilization? Despite the vast wilderness areas of the northwest, countless hours have been spent in the area looking for gold, timber, and other natural resources. Most of our outdoor sports enthusiasts and workers of the outdoors have never seen any evidence of Bigfoot. But now we are finding that more than a few are saying they saw something so unusual that it is too crazy to mention.

During the 60s and 70s my Dad and I interviewed eye witnesses, found broken tree tops, giant footsteps, misplaced large chunks of bark, and unusual hair and fecal samples. We heard an interchange of their call and saw first-hand how they can affect the demeanor of others. We published and distributed report summaries, visited with respected researchers, held regular monthly meetings, set up an automatic camera, and traveled extensively. Very few took our efforts seriously and despite the abundance of consistent hard evidence, the press and academic community showed little interest and caused us, as well as our witnesses, embarrassment.

So we stepped back from public activity and watched the news reported by many others who have taken up the search for Bigfoot. One friend, and active reporter, author and publisher has collected over 3000 Bigfoot reports since 1958. Several others have collected Bigfoot footprint casts from over a tremendous range of time and geography. For a period of five years there was a well-funded research group collecting and analyzing reports relating to Bigfoot. Then in June 1997, we attended the Fourth International Sasquatch Symposium and heard evidence that convinced us that we needed to become proactive again.

We believe there is abundant evidence for the existence of Bigfoot and that the nature of these giant hair-covered bipedal creatures relates more closely to human characteristics than animal (at least those in the region of Northern California and Southern Oregon).

There has been a concerted effort, at great expense over the past 40 years, to establish some form of acceptable Western scientific evidence, but the Bigfoot giants remain extremely elusive. Every conceivable form of procedure and technology has been employed. There must be something about Bigfoot that gives them an advantage. It is not our lack of time, money, effort, or luck. Over the years I came to realize that there is a form of consciousness beyond popular understanding.

The popular Western scientific paradigm postulates that consciousness is a phenomenon strictly related to brain physiology; when the brain stops functioning, consciousness ceases to exist. Furthermore, that consciousness is limited to isolation within a given individual form and that its input is only from the five physical senses. There is now abundant scientific evidence that this paradigm is in error and very limited. There is at least one level of sub/unconsciousness that is basic to and permeates all life forms. Our physical nervous system is, in essence, a tuning device that connects us to an underlying field of nature, through which increasing knowledge is possible.

The exact nature of a Bigfoot contact and its scientifically required replication is not fully understood at this time. Specific details can only be worked out as the nature of both human and Bigfoot consciousness is more fully understood by the employment of the procedures to be learned. This will be complicated by the fact that the procedures themselves are subject to many variables and interpretations. The research in this area is extensive but is still new and controversial.

Just one of many examples: Robert Monroe, along with many other professionals representing various scientific disciplines, spent 40 years researching human consciousness. He established a research and educational institute with a board of scientific overseers over twenty years ago. Since the beginning of the Institute, many thousands have attended various residential programs and expanded their perceptions beyond the normal range of the typical five senses.

With the application of special patented stereo audio signals to entrain the two halves of the brain into synchronization at specific low frequencies, an altered state of consciousness can be induced which resembles various stages of sleep but with controlled mental awareness.

And so, after listening to all the many different viewpoints at the Sasquatch Symposium in Vancouver, I decided it was time to renew a more active role in the search for Bigfoot. I appreciate the current efforts of many who prepare regular newsletters and websites on the subject. However, I find many of the reports rather monotonous and the speculations about the nature of Bigfoot limited. There is far more to these giants than form. There is far more to any living creature than just physical characteristics.

Twenty years ago I had given up on proactive Bigfoot search because of difficult problems. Within the scientific research of recent studies, I believe those problems can now be overcome.

There are new important concepts discovered which, I feel, need to be made popular and which, at the same time, would help us to understand a significant nature of both the human and Bigfoot. For example, there is a field of energy or consciousness which is universal and can be tapped by anyone. The techniques are fully explained in a large number of books but require much time and self-discipline.

For reasons of limited time and funds, I started again to look for a shortcut and someone who could communicate through image or thought transference. This led to meeting with Ida and the rest of the story is contained herein.

Lee Trippett

March 12, 2001

The Erickson Project
SASQUATCH the QUEST

Through the years the Erickson Project has collected and funded testing of a number of Sasquatch DNA samples from various geographical areas of North America at a variety of DNA labs in Canada and the United States. Even though the results of those mitochondrial tests all came back human, namely 'Eastern European' Adrian Erickson and Dennis Pfohl were convinced that the samples were from Sasquatch and not 'contaminated' by humans.

When yet another scientist related to Erickson that a different sample tested at the University of New York (one of the labs the Erickson Project had also used) also came back as 'Eastern European' the scientist dismissed it as human. At that point however, Erickson knew he was on the right track and needed to test further. He contacted and started to collaborate with Dr. Ketchum and provided her with his samples and the previous DNA results in order to continue testing. As the study expanded Erickson supplied much of the initial funding of Dr. Ketchum's study, which was more in-depth and involved nuclear DNA. This study was completed after five years.

The Erickson Project is a contributor of six Sasquatch DNA samples to Dr.Ketchum's study, all from diverse areas, one of those samples was used to sequence a complete Sasquatch genome in Dr. Ketchum's study. Specific information on the role of The Erickson Project will be released when her manuscript is published; this will be posted on this website.*

UPDATES

Dr. Ketchum's press release about upcoming publication of her manuscript:

'BIGFOOT' DNA SEQUENCED

IN UPCOMING GENETICS STUDY

Five-Year Genome Study Yields Evidence of Homo sapiens/Unknown Hominin Hybrid Species in North America

DALLAS, Nov. 24 [2012]

A team of scientists can verify that their 5-year long DNA study, currently under peer-review, confirms the existence of a novel hominin hybrid species, commonly called "Bigfoot" or "Sasquatch," living in North America. Researchers' extensive DNA sequencing suggests that the legendary Sasquatch is a human relative that arose approximately 15,000 years ago as a hybrid cross of modern Homo sapiens with an unknown primate species.

The study was conducted by a team of experts in genetics, forensics, imaging and pathology, led by Dr. Melba S. Ketchum of Nacogdoches, TX. In response to recent interest in the study, Dr. Ketchum can confirm that her team has sequenced three complete Sasquatch nuclear genomes and determined the species is a human hybrid:

"Our study has sequenced 20 whole mitochondrial genomes and utilized next generation sequencing to obtain 3 whole nuclear genomes from purported Sasquatch samples. The genome sequencing shows that Sasquatch mtDNA is identical to modern Homo sapiens, but Sasquatch nuDNA is a novel, unknown hominin related to Homo sapiens and other primate species. Our data indicate that the North American Sasquatch is a hybrid species, the result of males of an unknown hominin species crossing with female Homo sapiens.

Hominins are members of the taxonomic grouping Hominini, which includes all members of the genus Homo. Genetic testing has already ruled out Homo neanderthalis and the Denisova hominin as contributors to Sasquatch mtDNA or nuDNA. "The male progenitor that contributed the unknown sequence to this hybrid is unique as its DNA is more distantly removed from humans than other recently discovered hominins like the Denisovan individual," explains Ketchum.

"Sasquatch nuclear DNA is incredibly novel and not at all what we had expected. While it has human nuclear DNA within its genome, there are also distinctly non-human, non-archaic hominin, and non-ape sequences. We describe it as a mosaic of human and novel non-human sequence. Further study is needed and is ongoing to better characterize and understand Sasquatch nuclear DNA."

Ketchum is a veterinarian, whose professional experience includes 27 years of research in genetics, including forensics. Early in her career she also practiced veterinary medicine, and she has previously been published as a participant in mapping the equine genome. She began testing the DNA of purported Sasquatch hair samples 5 years ago.

Ketchum calls on public officials and law enforcement to immediately recognize the Sasquatch as an indigenous people:

"Genetically, the Sasquatch is a human hybrid with unambiguously modern human maternal ancestry. Government at all levels must recognize them as an indigenous people and immediately protect their human and Constitutional rights against those who would see in their physical and cultural differences a 'license' to hunt, trap, or kill them."

Full details of the study will be presented in the near future when the study manuscript publishes.

Part One

Bigfoot's "Birth" and History

Ida: Let me first introduce Lee Trippett's approach to the mysteries of Bigfoot. His many years of activity in various forms of research, his knowledge of other persons in the field and their work and his conscientious interpretations of the meaning of it all are best presented in their purity without my interference and comments.

Lee and I are not always one hundred percent in agreement on every detail, but close enough in understanding to be able to make allowances for small differences. I won't contaminate Lee's input by my observations.

The importance of my inclusion is mainly the introduction of head Councilman Maez and the role of the Arcturian Masters in genetic development of Bigfoot. My personal commentary is minor except for asides by Thoth and Tres, my monitors.

I am simply the glue that sticks all parts of this story together.

Lee's Plan Relating to the Research of Bigfoot

Dad (Ben) and I started the search in the early sixties. For about fifteen years we interviewed eye witnesses, found unusual hair and fecal samples, published report summaries, visited with highly respected psychics, held monthly meetings, set up an automatic camera, and traveled extensively.

Since 1977 we only have watched the news about the many others who have taken up the search. One friend and very active reporter, author and publisher has collected about 3,000 reports since 1958. Several others have collected hundreds of big footprint casts from over a tremendous range of time and geography. For about the past five years there has been a well-funded research group collecting and analyzing reports. We attended the International Sasquatch Symposium June 7th and 8th, 1997, and heard evidence that we need to become proactive again.

I would be inclined, at this point, to try summarizing all the many books on the subject, but by far the most precise and condensed summary already exists on the internet at the Western Bigfoot Society. I have a plan that requires the need to establish some form of two-way communication between myself (as others have already done) and Sasquatch. There is a vital need to convince a larger portion of our traditional Western world science of the existence of Sasquatch. They have much to contribute to our welfare. At the same time there is a need to convince many in our society that there is far more to the nature of humanity than physical bodies with brains.

The popular opinion in Western society is that humanity is a collection of physical forms containing a temporary mind or consciousness that is lost on the death of the body. This limited viewpoint is very restrictive for affecting any benevolent cooperative society and needs to be expanded and corrected for aiding our survival as a planet.

The current investigation of the Sasquatch phenomena is based on two viewpoints. These two viewpoints have been causing slow progress, division and difficulty. By far the more popular viewpoint is that Sasquatch is some form of animal which is to be analyzed through purely objective and measurable physical evidence. Most researchers view any ideas of Sasquatch as being similar to humans as ridiculous.

Those few researchers who view Sasquatch as being possibly human will often discuss topics of a paranormal nature such as intuition or psychic sensitivities. This is their rationale for explaining the elusive success of Sasquatch. The Sasquatch of the Northwest are conscious in the area of mind that is unconscious in us. This is why they do not need artifacts for finding food, shelter, or safety. The physical and even the natural science personnel only believe we have been unlucky in finding suitable evidence of the Sasquatch. There has been considerable energy and dollars expended in the last 40 years. And there is a growing public interest in Sasquatch. The traditional materialistic approach has failed. Those with sensitive paranormal abilities do not have a plan or financial support and often feel protective from potential exploitation. Both sides have lacked any consistent unity and have often been motivated more by greed and ego.

My plan involves a number of different Sasquatch meetings, one at a time, in different regions of the Pacific Northwest, say on the edge of a remote dense forest clearing. A researcher and one witness would leave a personally identified container with a bed of clay.

Through some form of communication a local Sasquatch would be requested to make his own footprint cast and leave. The witness, independent of the single researcher, would take this specific style of hard evidence to a symposium, university, or other common meeting ground where witnesses would bring similar evidence from different regions of the Northwest.

For each situation no weapons or conflicting artifacts would be allowed. Sasquatch is super sensitive to our intent behind the use of these. Unlike past field research activity, our plan is quite inexpensive compared to past programs, and it is quiet. It would begin reducing the confusion of the two different viewpoints because both hard evidence and confirmed interconnecting consciousness would be involved. Greed and ego motivation would be reduced because any glory would be spread among several otherwise unrelated witnesses.

This approach could open the door for differing viewpoints to merge and at the same time completely protect Sasquatch and their environment. The plan would wake up many to the idea that humanity and all life or living forms are vitally linked through some sort of universal mind or consciousness.

I have been told recently by an elderly recluse, Stan Johnson who claims occasional communication and has had several close contacts, that Sasquatch will cooperate with this plan but that I need to do all the coordination and communication. Therein lays a big problem. I am not psychic! (Lee Trippett)

Letter from Ida to Lee Trippett

Here are the pages as I wrote down the conversations with Councilor Maez. After I had written it I wondered if he could have meant Counselor instead of Councilor. He said I had written the correct word. He is head of the Council that decides on the abductions and/genetic manipulations of Earth people. Wow! We agreed it would be best not to go deeply into any subject at this present time except that of Bigfoot.

Maez did describe himself. He has the appearance of those whom we have come to call "the grays" but is much taller than those usually seen on UFOs. He is nearly six feet tall and is considered a star example of his kind. We did not pursue this line.

Oh, he did say the Master humans on his planet, Arcturus, are like us but large people, seven and eight feet tall.

That's all I can remember at present. Good luck with your plans. Ida

Ida: Lee set out his tub with the clay insert in one of the three places in the Coast Range that we had dowsed on the map but without response from Bigfoot. I went along on another trial hoping I could coax the big shy fellow in through telepathic contact.

Of course Bigfoot did not speak English and I did not use pictorial telepathy such as Maez used for contact with him. But as Hweig (another of my telepathic contacts) had explained in my book *UFO Initiation: Ultraterrestrial Time Travelers,* what are actually exchanged are thought vibrations. The sender transmits his thoughts in his own form of communication; the message is received in the language of the recipient as he subconsciously translates it himself. Not even Hweig could explain how all that transpired, that is just the way it works — through energy of thought vibrations rather than language.

Maez had instructed us to call for Wipi, the local Bigfoot. Later Maez explained they do not use actual names among themselves but recognize each other by sounds, by calls, but he gave this one the name of Wipi to make it easier for us to discuss him.

A second excursion with the tub and some treats for Wipi were also ignored although we left the tub and fruit overnight in hopes he might come in after we had gone.

I think this fills in the lapse of note taking sufficiently that we can now continue our tale from the actual notes made at the time of action.

Had I known what a lengthy experience this was to become, I would have made detailed notes from the day I first said, "Hello!" to the Trippetts.

Maez (Monitor for Bigfoot) to Ida

Those creatures you call Bigfoot who were created on our planet (Arcturus) have been returned here. The ones who were born on planet Earth are those who remain there. They are welcome to come here but to them Earth is home and they feel just as you would about going to some faraway planet and leaving your Earth home.

Wipi and his mate are Earth-born. He wishes to remain there and help to make it a safer place for his kind even though his immediate family or clan has driven him from the wilderness area where they are secreted. They fear his efforts to contact your people will reveal their presence and put them in danger. They do not seem to realize that by driving him out he is more apt to do exactly what they do not want. Short sightedness is not a trait exclusive to ourselves.

Wipi has implants, just as you do, and received just as yours were on board a spacecraft. His are a little different but are susceptible to microwave interference and to electrical emissions as well. You, yourself, would do well to stay out of the vicinity of high power lines. At least do not linger there.

We monitor Wipi through his implants just as we talk to you now through yours. Thank you for your permission.

If you go with the party to lay out the clay device, we can guide Wipi to you as long as you are not too far from his place of safety. Anywhere in the area that was dowsed will do. He can travel fast.

It is well to consider practical matters, such as deer hunting season, for the safety of all concerned. Since there has been some rain to replenish the water holes, cougars are returning to their customary grounds and are not likely to appear in unexpected places.

About the only thing that could interfere with your plans would be if some of his clan should discover what he was doing and try to stop him. They would not attack you but might try to forcibly control Wipi. This does not seem likely; we monitor them also and I am sure we can keep them from interfering. But we should consider all possibilities. We monitor and advise all Bigfoot but they do have free will, necessary for them to survive in wild country.

An Earth-born Bigfoot does not have the same power of entering other dimensions as readily as created ones. I doubt you will see him, at least not on a first meeting. He may be lurking about very close, but will stay concealed. He is shy, but not timid. He is a very courageous fellow, or he would not be engaged in this project. The rage of his clan, if fully aroused, could be disastrous to him.

Try to remember some of his problems. To understand him better is to be better prepared for this undertaking.

We will speak again if we think of more useful information.

Councilor Maez, Arcturus System

Maez to Ida: Let us get our conversation on paper before we forget. You can take a nap tomorrow.

You asked if Wipi could go in and out of dimensions at will, and I said, "No, the original engineered ones could, but not the Earth-born." I was concentrating so hard on that one aspect that I overlooked what has probably been witnessed a number of times was not "other-dimensional" disappearances, but appearances and disappearances of Bigfoot in his semi-corporeal state. Hweig described this to you. It occurs entirely in your own "dimension". All Bigfoot are capable of this but it makes them nervous. They feel not quite real and associate it with their dreams. They use the ability only at our insistence and assistance and we do not force or coax them to do so, except under really vital necessity.

Go to sleep now.

Maez to Ida: Okay, if you would rather talk than take a nap.

The semi-corporeal and out-of-body states are not the same thing. The semi-corporeal has to do with what you call your doppelganger in its true sense. The form can be seen and appears physical. Hweig gave you a full explanation in your book *UFO Initiation: Ultraterrestrial Time Travelers.* .

"In the truly out-of-body state, i.e., in the energy essence state, our people can image themselves into a world that is co-existent and co-extensive to your own, that is, it occupies the same space but it exists in a different time dimension. Time is simply non-existent in your idea of mechanistic time." (Hweig, in book.)

Let's not get too deeply into this topic here. I only wanted to distinguish carefully between semi-corporeal and out-of-body states, and to indicate that in the first the form can be seen, in the second it cannot. Therefore if we decide to use the semi-corporeal form, you will see Wipi as though he was totally physical but you cannot touch or physically interact with him. He may be willing to do this. He has not had any real practice in this form up to now. I will try to convince the Council it would be a productive experiment and then I would have to convince Wipi. It might be a positive and invaluable experience for both of you and lead to an actual physical confrontation later. All of which takes time. There are too many persons involved and too many minds to convince to expect to do this very soon. I simply present it to you as an option of future action to be hoped for.

Go bake your apple pie.

Maez to Ida: We are making sure all is in readiness for your Bigfoot adventure. Wipi is being coached as to what is happening, what is hoped for, and how to respond. He knows he need not reveal himself unless he wants to. I see you have a question concerning his mate. Like all "women" she worries for the safety of her "husband" but she will not deter him from keeping the appointment. She understands the need of seeking human help for the general predicament of the Bigfoot, just as we all do. Their safety areas are growing smaller rapidly as people encroach upon their living space. They move ever farther back into remote and often unfamiliar regions that pose great hardship for them in obtaining food, shelter, and safety from animals that have also been pushed deeper into the wilderness. Any creature with its back to the wall is going to be fearful and bad tempered. We are fortunate to have Wipi of so much intelligence and courage that he wants to take practical and well considered steps to help his people.

More another time.

Maez to Ida: We have been discussing Bigfoot's daily activities as questioned by your friend (Lee Trippett).

As you suggested, Ida, a good part of the Bigfoot's day is spent in obtaining food and shelter. He will eat almost anything he can chew if he is pushed to extremes, but he greatly prefers certain roots and berries and small animals like rodents and fish. Unfortunately circumstances do not permit him to be a gourmet and he settles for anything he can get. He has been given bananas on special occasions which we bring from South America, so he knows how to peel one and not eat the peeling. (I see you worried about that!)

Bigfoot has regular places of shelter, rock overhangs or small cave-like depressions in cliffs, but he is quite active and does not always get back to home base. Then he shelters under overhanging trees like hemlock that spread branches close to the ground. Although he handles rocks and tree limbs when hunting rodents and roots, he never has used them in building shelters.

He has never felt the need to do so as something like a rock overhang or a good clump of brush or trees is always near.

There are several natural phenomena that dismay him — intense sun and heat, electrical storms, and floods. We can imagine how the volcanic explosion of Mt. St. Helens must have left traumatic scars on the souls of the few who survived. About a dozen did not, less than half a dozen were on the edge of the area and escaped, but were traumatized.

Your friend has pointed out how Bigfoot imitates bird and animal calls and sounds of the forest. He could learn to speak words if opportunity presented itself. We, as monitors, confer with him by pictorial telepathy representations. It is less likely to err than words and is much more precise. He does not need words.

Bigfoot's vile odor is a defense mechanism like a civet cat's spray. It is partly a natural function of his body but aggravated by rolling in carrion and dung. If you were to take him home and give him a good hot shower, he would come out smelling at least as sweet as your family dog.

His favorite frolic for fun is to find a stream with a good strong current and sit in it as you would in a Jacuzzi.

You will not find him sleeping in deep caves, only overhangs and shallow depressions. His fear of deep caves is a racial memory.

With his clan there is interplay and discussion by telepathy and pantomime. As an outcast our particular Bigfoot does not have a really jolly time. His mate is a great comfort to him;

there is a strong bond between them. He would protect her with his life.

Wipi can travel at a good speed and cover miles in a day depending on his knowledge of the area. Underbrush is a deterrent to speed but he knows it also holds back any pursuers. If he knows an area and his pursuers do not, the tangle of the woods is a safety feature for him. This is why he stays in places of dense undergrowth. Part of his daily activities is in finding new pathways and exploring the routes of safety and escape — particularly from human hunters.

That's enough for this time.

Maez to Ida: I am sorry Wipi did not feel secure enough to respond to your invitation.

You ask me to suggest a method of obtaining evidence that Bigfoot is not an animal but has human characteristics. You need not go to the mountains or difficult areas. Go to the books. Yes, now don't start scolding me, just listen.

I'm sure there are computer-tallied studies of all the tracks in the United States and Canada — and no doubt other places — that have plaster casts made. Also the detailed descriptions of Bigfoot that have been seen are likewise tallied on computer bases. But has anyone tallied the times that Bigfoot has reappeared more than twice in the same spot and volunteered to guess any reason why he had come back? That clue would tell you how to attract one. Is there some apparent reason why a Bigfoot would return to a specific spot more than twice? What is that reason and why is it important to Bigfoot (not us)? If you can ascertain that reason you don't need to stir out of your recliner, you can bring him to you.

Maez to Ida: We are assembling the opinions and wishes of our people, after which the Council will meet to debate your request for authentic proof of Bigfoot's connection to the human race. Please be patient with us. The tradition of centuries will be upset if we reveal the secrets of Bigfoot. We know it is time the Earth humans understand the realities of this situation but we must act in a way that will not endanger our creature.

More later.

Maez to Ida: Yes, you are right — to an extent. Bigfoot would appear at a place more than twice out of curiosity. But of what is he curious? Yes, of the person or persons who live at or frequent that place. But it is not idle curiosity. He wants to learn something that may become important to him.

He observes how that person treats animals close to him, his dog or cat or horses or chickens as well as wild animals. Does he feed the squirrels when nuts are out of season? Does he put out water for deer when there is a long dry spell? Does he use humane types of wire on his fences and provide good shelter and living conditions for his pets and livestock?

Such questions of course apply to rural areas. Bigfoot is not likely to come into towns.

He is looking for a human protector that he might appeal to in an emergency. His monitors suggest and encourage this. The monitors are thinking of such catastrophes as the eruption of Mt. St. Helens, or forest fires, floods, and other emergencies, natural or man-made, when a compassionate friend is needed.

Maez to Ida: You are approaching Bigfoot burdened with a certain amount of fear of his animal characteristics, uncertain if he would turn on you. He can sense this. You must saturate your thinking with his human qualities. That is what I am trying to get over to you in these notes.

It is not so much his fear of you that holds Wipi back; it is your fear of him. We will talk more about this when you are fully awake.

Maez to Ida: Good morning. I am glad to see you bright-eyed and awake. To continue:

Wipi (as an example) knows what your people can do when they are in a sudden fright or panic. Therefore he offers extreme caution when approaching you. He is not afraid of you; he is alert to what you might do if suddenly confronted.

Also he has an acute sense of consequences. He does not want to get drawn into a process that may develop problems when — and if — other persons become involved. He can trust one person, whom he has studied carefully, then another gets involved and adds problems, a third brings in the possibility of competition arising amongst them and actions becoming less thoughtful and controlled.

Wipi is a very good judge of human nature, learned from experience.

Please be patient with Wipi and with us. We all want the same thing, protection for the Sasquatch. Thinking together like this will eventually bring a process that cannot endanger the very species that we all want to save.

Your friend's idea of securing a footprint is very good but eventually he will have to bring in more people, more Bigfoot, if a print is to prove anything. More people — more problems — let us think!

Maez to Ida: To find a working relationship with Bigfoot (Wipi in particular); you must change your attitude toward him. I know he appears frightening with his bulk and strength and animalistic manner of doing things. But he has a human type soul and recognizes God although differently than you do. Try to look underneath the hair and call him "Brother". This will set your mind on your likenesses instead of your differences which, I grant, are many.

Instead of praying that he will do what you want, pray that you may recognize what he wants. That is quite a challenge! I will help all I can conceive of in these notes.

PS: I know you and your friend are compassionate people but these notes may be read sometime by others who need reminding.

Maez to Ida: The Council has put forth a proposition but the implementation necessitates a number of factors that may not be, or not become, available.

You have asked, Ida, about bones. Bigfoot is as sentimental about his relatives' bones as you are of your mother's or your cousin's. He would not willingly submit them to any desecration by scientific analysis. (He would consider it desecration and it would be hard to talk him out of it.)

But in the case that one of their children is born crippled or deformed or has some defect that shows by the age of two or three years that it will be incapable of growing to care for itself in the wilderness where the family or clan lives, that child is gently smothered and buried as a service to itself as well as the clan. This does not often happen. It is rare that a Bigfoot mother will give up an incapacitated child unless she is persuaded or/even forced to. And she will not give up its bones.

But . . . if she could be convinced the young would be taken to a medical facility where it could receive treatment and perhaps be "cured" or helped and later returned to her, a mother might consider it.

Bigfoot is a hardy species and not many are born with grave imperfections.

Another big question, not a pretty one, but we must be realistic and consider all possibilities — would a chosen facility be certain to aim for a cure and not for a specimen to dissect?

So a stipulation would be that if the child dies, its body would be returned intact to its people. By handling the situation according to the same ethics that would be given a "your type" human, such details could be agreed upon.

The manner in which the imperfect child is handled would determine if other Bigfoot would be brought forward for examination.

Yes, the medical school in Portland might be a facility to investigate with such needs in mind. We have some contacts in the area.

If your friend would want to take some responsibilities along this line, we will start the process by having our contacts investigate the hospital and its staff and also have our monitors hunt for a suitable child. We will stay within the boundaries of North America, as there are slight differences in Bigfoot on other continents. The child would be brought to a local spot for pick-up.

No real action will be taken until these preliminaries and a solid plan has been agreed upon. At this time it is still problematical.

Maez to Ida: Now that you have stuffed yourself again — how you people do eat! Let us get on with our review of Bigfoot.

In answer to your question — yes, we do keep a tally or census on our creatures. We know how many there are and the general locality of each. They are precious commodities to us, something like your livestock, but with human sensibilities. We do not watch each one every minute. They have free will. We do try to keep accurate account of how many new ones are expected each year, how many are born, and how many survive. Last year eight were born in your general area; two were malformed and laid down. Each year more incapacitated are born. We believe your polluted atmosphere and natural resources are affecting them also. (These figures are for Northwestern U.S. and Canada only.) Nine were supposed to be born but the ninth is unaccounted for. We suspect the mother has hidden it because of some physical disability. It will come to light sooner or later; it cannot be concealed from us forever. At the moment there are six known pregnancies in various stages. We suspect that Bigfoot's constant movement inhibits more pregnancies. They do not stay in one place very long in these days of human encroachment.

We are putting forth special effort to find the missing ninth and to keep close watch on new births.

In the meantime our contacts are discreetly investigating medical facilities and staff. Most doctors consider Bigfoot — if they think of him at all — as pure animal, a kind of ape. We need a doctor who is something of a renegade; it is difficult to find one on a hospital staff. They are team players or they are not there. A doctor in private practice or retirement might not have the credibility we would prefer. Several members of a staff could be a counter-check better than a loner. I hope we don't sound paranoid with suspicion but we have had unhappy interaction with such people in the past.

You are right that a sample of blood would prove that Bigfoot is different from both animal and purely "human". We can't go around poking holes in mature Bigfoot to get it for you. That is why we suggested the very young child. A DNA sample would stand the hair up on the scalp of the researcher.

Since we don't have a child available at present and it may be months or years before we do, we suggest you keep this option in mind as a potential future event. In the meantime I am sure we can locate a medical practitioner who will serve us.

Meantime continue with your efforts to obtain footprints.

Here is one more suggestion regarding DNA. In the written stories or Bigfoot literature or even tall tales, has anyone declared that they have found drops of blood from a wounded Bigfoot, perhaps on leaves or stones? The DNA experts are doing wondrous things with ancient blood from mummy wrappings. The dried blood itself would prove it is from a pre-human and human-crossed creature. (I am sure he would be cross, too.)

Research on the blood specimen discreetly. We don't want people shooting Bigfoot just to collect drops of blood. When men put ammunition into their guns they seem to put their brains in, too.

We care about our Bigfoot and we want to see this unique species survive. We do not have the original pre-human base to re-engineer another. There would be no purpose in doing so.

Maez to Ida: You make a good point when you suggest that Bigfoot's birth defects may be from in-breeding. We have been aware of this. As the clans or families grow smaller and Bigfoot more mobile, they lose touch with former relatives and companions and in-breeding has become a worry factor for us. Bigfoot has been made aware of this also and that is why so few new ones are born each year. Since they do not have computer databases we try to guide their choice of mates. Like all humans, they do not always listen to advice on that subject, especially the younger ones who have not had the painful experience of losing such a child.

I have gone so deeply into this subject to help you learn to think of Bigfoot in altogether "human" terms. Until you fully do so, you cannot hope to have any really close contact with Bigfoot.

The creature's great bulk, size, and weight would make him a formidable adversary if his wrath were aroused. Fortunately, his nature is as mild and gentle as the mountain gorilla has proven to be. But there is still enough of the animal nature left in him — just as there is in you — that anger or threat to his mate or child could make him revert to animal tactics of defense. Therefore, treating him with the same respect and consideration you would give another human of your own kind is you best assurance of similar treatment from him. "Do unto others — " is the best advice always. Bigfoot himself is saturated with that understanding.

I know you and your friend do not need such reminding, but if you have these pertinent points down on paper and read them over now and then, it helps to build up a picture of the real creature and it will affect your attitude toward him.

I am trying to give you the "inside clues" on understanding Bigfoot, better than all the reports of sightings that were ever printed in the books.

Tres, 11/13/98: Communication system has shut down worldwide. An event is imminent. Nothing personal.

Maez to Ida: We may resume our conversation about Bigfoot. Some communication lines are not open, but since this one does not refer to political events we have some leeway.

Wipi has retreated farther into the back hills, but only temporarily.

You are correct; the best protection for Bigfoot is to convince the public he is not real. But that ploy will not work much longer; too many hikers, campers, bikers are invading the deeper recesses of the forests. We must prepare with other protective measures, and it is not too soon to start. We still believe DNA offers the most conclusive evidence of his double nature. How to get this is the question.

In the meantime trying to get a footprint is as good an idea as we can come up with. How to convince Bigfoot to give one is the problem.

Confer with your friend as to what he would like to do, try for a different creature or wait for Wipi to overcome his bashfulness.

Tres to Ida, 11/14/98: Tomorrow is the day of the event. It is not a war but an interruption of current activities in that direction. You were told long ago (1980) that when war in a certain area was immanent that the people of the UFOs would interfere by psychic means. Watch the news tomorrow.

Tres to Ida: As I said previously, nothing is certain until definite choices have been nailed down.

So the direction the Security Council will take this afternoon is not certain, but as this moment it seems that Hussein's appeasement effort will be rejected. If the Council is wise it will be accepted, and the Inspectors sent in with loads of food and supplies for the people.

However, if the offer is rejected and the missiles are launched, they will be misdirected. Return fire will be likewise misdirected.

The Security Council can then cover its red-white-and-blue bottom by saying it was only a warning and to show the Iraqi people that Hussein is not their best option. Then if they send food and medicines to the people, they will have "won" anyway.

And the era of war will be over.

Maez to Ida: The communication black-out is now over. The black-out was relative to the war situation so that we, and others of our kind, would not interfere with communications of life-saving or life-threatening importance to Earth. The war threat was only postponed, unfortunately.

Back to Bigfoot:

I have read the various papers and newsletters loaned to you. There seems to be considerable in-fighting and back-biting among Bigfoot researchers. Such a level of interaction will only keep the true facts from being found for many years. We cannot wait that long!

I would suggest buying the book by Robert W. Morgan *The Bigfoot Observer's Pocket Manual*. It seems to have been written on a solid basis of factual observation and careful analysis. It is by far the most useful and practical book about Bigfoot that has been called to my attention.

As your people research Bigfoot, we research your people.

More on this tomorrow.

Tres to Ida: Too many years have been spent in training you to allow you to waste away in idleness, now. Last evening we presented to you an agenda for your next ten years. I know you will be 94 years old, but you will not be extinct!

Your former writings and studies have all been directed. Nothing you have done has been wasted or useless efforts. Your way has been planned since before you were born.

We allot two years (roughly) for each of your forthcoming books.

I turn you over to Maez, but the two of us (Thoth and Tres) will always be standing by for conversation or aid. You will enjoy all this and so will we.

Maez to Ida: Get out your book on the stages of animal development toward man and I will show you the creature Bigfoot was developed from. You have one with excellent pictures and not too much text. Why do you think you have been buying all these books?

Why do you stop at the picture of the Taung child? Yes, you have been babbling at me about *Australopithecus* for the last two weeks. Why do you suspect Bigfoot was developed from this base? Because the fossil rock that you have reminds you of the Taung child? That is only a vague resemblance. What you have is a fossilized head with sand and mud, and it is about a six year old Bigfoot child.

I doubt you will ever find any scientist daring enough to corroborate this. You will have to leave it for others to prove its origin long after you are gone. I know you have tried to interest three institutions of "higher learning" in the specimen with photographs, drawings, descriptions, and maps, only to be ignored. This direction is futile.

However, you are right that Bigfoot was developed on a base of *Australopithecus africanus.* Then he was genetically engineered with genes of the Arcturian Masters to develop the several variations of Bigfoot alive in the world today. There are only small differences in Bigfoot in various countries to adapt them to the environment in which they live. Their adaptations to various climatic and environmental conditions have further distinguished them from one another, but all come from the same original base of *A.a.* Your scientists will presently reorganize their identification base as new discoveries are made.

Bigfoot was engineered to live in remote and undeveloped areas. His greatest safety device is the speed and ease with which he can change location and his ability to live off the environment wherever he might find himself. This means no possessions to load him down in transit and no permanent home to tie him to a location that might be discovered and staked out for capture. You may well envy Bigfoot his complete freedom, his blending with his environment, and his ability to concentrate on the basic values of life.

The first Bigfoot were brought to Planet Earth before there were any *Homo sapiens,* or *neanderthanlensis.* His purpose was to discover if such modern men could live here. That is why he was given *Homo sapiens* characteristics, genes, brain capacities, intuition, and sensitivities. He is, in essence, borderline human.

Yes, we Arcturians were instrumental in bringing a race of *Homo sapiens* to Earth, but let us save this story for another time. We want you to understand, accept Bigfoot first, while there is still time to save this unusual and rare species from extinction on Earth. He has served well and earned the right to be protected and aided in his current problems and distress.

Learn to accept and live with him.

Yes, Sitchin's stories of the origin of modern man are 90% correct. Any embroidery was in the texts from which he copied, but there are correlative facts which have not yet been revealed and in which we played a major role. Do not discount Sitchin. He wrote courageous and bona fide books.

Ida: In the book by Michael H. Brown called *The Search for Eve*, we find a revealing description of the physical attributes of *Australopithecus*. This was a comparatively small creature, not over five feet tall at best, but if we remember the added genetic input of bulk and brains from the seven and eight foot Masters of Arcturus, who called themselves "true men", we can see a high comparison to Bigfoot. (See our Introduction.)

Here the writer is describing "Lucy", an early *Australopithecus* found in eastern Africa. She was considered about three million years old.

Description of Lucy

- Proportionately longer arms and shorter legs than a human
- A pelvis more similar to man than an apes
- Dental arcade shows signs of becoming rounded
- Canines no longer fanglike
- Large molars but small incisors
- Hands with long, curved fingers, narrow at the tips
- Possible boughs and limbs for beds
- Thumb not fully opposable
- No proof that early hominids fashioned simple stone tools

- Lucy's skull had probably been somewhat larger than a softball
- Lucy walked bipedally, on two legs alone
- Wide nostrils
- A bit of a forehead
- Eyes that hint at self-awareness(supposition)
- Thick, jutting jaw
- Heavy eyebrows
- Skin probably ranged from grayish pink to black, or shades of yellow
- Hair black, brown, reddish or silver
- The type of teeth are those that fit vegetarian animals
- Feet seem to be somewhere between ape and man

Some of these items are, of course, speculation, but speculation by scientific and experienced people. In summary, the book says one might visualize *Australopithecus* as resembling a man below the neck but a chimpanzee above it.

At about the same time (1978), Mary Leaky was finding the most striking evidence, actual footprints fossilized into volcanic ash, and was making plaster casts of it in northern Tanzania.

Maez to Ida: So we have been discussing the possibility of *Australopithecus africanus* being the more "animal" base of Bigfoot. Believe me, he was, though how you guessed that I'll never know.

Yes, your scientists have some specimens of *A.a.*, which they believe are about three million years old and others they date at one million seven hundred and fifty years. Some believe this latter was the first real tool-maker. As I said before, as more specimens are discovered there will be some minor changes in their opinions, and probably some major ones, also.

We (Arcturians) began the use of *A.a.* a million and a half years ago. No, not I personally. Yes, we had the equivalent of *Homo sapiens sapiens* (*Homo s.s.*) to use, not an Earth species. Your present *Homo s.s.* did not originate from earth species. It is a mixture of various forefathers.

We are the man-makers of Earth. Read your own book, *Project Earth*, the last few pages, and Sitchin also to see how varied the ancestry of present day Earth man really is!

As long as a million and a half years ago our scientists were mixing and matching genes and DNA and other life requisites. Let's not get more deeply involved in this now. Enough for today,

Maez to Ida: A bit more about the manufacturing of Bigfoot. Even this kind of genetic experimentation takes a long, long time. We started a million and a half of your years ago and continued hundreds of thousands of years before present. Experimental creatures were allowed to live out their long life spans, but gradually we learned how to overcome certain problems in their reproduction cycles. We wanted them to be able to reproduce themselves before we sent them to Earth *and other planets*.

Slightly less than three hundred thousand years ago our perfected species was sent to Earth to check out the living conditions. There are energies being emitted from the Earth itself that you are not yet aware of. Some of them are detrimental to your welfare. You will eventually learn how to protect yourselves. Places where there are sulphur springs are the most evident.

Our Bigfoot took to Earth like a duck to water, and he and his descendants have been there ever since.

The engineered Bigfoot lived thousands of years. They did not have a built-in obsolescence. After their Earth-born offspring were well established, we brought the original back to Arcturus. Unfortunately, they had been engineered for different climate and environmental living conditions and one by one they succumbed. The Bigfoot on Earth live two or sometimes into their third hundredth year. The increasing crud in your air shortens their lives unmercifully now. They are in actual danger of becoming extinct. Your people hunting them down and creating living problems for them does not help

You ask where we got the *Homo sapiens* species to cross with Bigfoot. The same place we got it to develop *Homo s.s.* on Earth. It was for the latter that Bigfoot was developed to test the Earth. *Homo s.s.* is from ourselves. Did we not tell you once that "our roots are the same"? A great deal of what was told to you and which you printed in your book *Project Earth* referred to us. All the information that Hweig and Co. read off to you so patiently and which you copied down so patiently was prepared by myself and my helpers. Arcturus is the Planet X as you labeled it. Tea Elsta was a name Hweig gave it, since you insisted on a name. It is not our original one. Your star map calls it Arcturus in the Boötes constellation.

Now you ask, "How does this fit in with Sitchin's story of the origin of Earth people?" Neatly, very neatly. I don't want to spend time on this now, but your question deserves an answer. The Annunaki of the "Twelfth Planet" established their Adamic race in what you call today "the Middle East" — Sumeria (today's Iraq) and the lands between there and Egypt and into Africa. (See Appendix.)

We, the Arcturians, established our race in the West. You call it Lemuria and the western areas of the United States, although it spread rapidly into what is now Canada, Mexico, Central and South America.

East is East and the West is West but it is time the twain get together peaceably and stop killing each other.

We sent the original Bigfoot throughout the whole world but sent our developed strain of *Homo s.s.* to Lemuria and the West. There is not much point in writing much about this until your people are ready to accept the reality of Lemuria. (James Churchward should also be taken very seriously.)

Let us get back to our subject, Bigfoot as developed from Earth's *Australopithecus africanus* and our own strain of *Homo s.s.*

Our scientists felt that to persevere in the wild conditions of Earth against large animals and severe climatic conditions Bigfoot should be very strong physically, large and bulky as you see him today (when you do). Since he does not use tools other than sticks or stones or make permanent shelters other than rocky crevices or clumps of trees or bushes, he must be nearly impervious to cold or immersion in water and other conditions that would quickly kill a man. His extraordinary physicality coupled with a very large brain keeps him alive. He is extremely intelligent, but innocent. His lack of sophistication and an awareness of that fact make him wary of close contact with humans. He just doesn't understand your ways of double-dealing. They are entirely foreign to him.

Ida to Maez: I am confused. You said you chose the finest of the anthropoid line to begin your genetic experiments that eventually led to *Australopithecus* and Bigfoot and still later to us. Yet you say we did not evolve from the ape. That leaves me confused.

Maez to Ida: Indeed, yes. I see why. I hurried too much over the finer points of the beginning experiments. The anthropoid inheritance stopped evolving at the point we first gave them genes from the Master race, and the first human souls came into them, inexperienced but human. From that point on all of this line are human, not apes. That is why you have a truncated DNA. Don't restore it! The evolution of the body and physical properties quickened and became Australopithecine. From these we took aside, after many, many experiments, *A.a.* to produce Bigfoot. *A.a.* was then developed in an on-going and separate direction from Bigfoot, but they are genetically fully your brothers. Bigfoot is just not so fully evolved. His physical and mental evolution was slowed down greatly compared to the line that went on to you. He was given only one-fourth the Master genes that were given to you. We wanted to keep him as much as possible the way he was created. Your line was given four times the Master genes and hurried on the direction of *Homo erectus*. Your paleoanthropologists have not yet found the exact creation but *Homo erectus* will do for a talking point. Remember that the relic hominids that your paleoanthropologists have discovered are actually a very scant number and those that are printed about in the books you are likely to read are fewer still. I have to rely on that extremely small amount of old and somewhat out of date bit of information that you actually have. It gives us only a general sense of what we are trying to explain. A scientist would no doubt scoff.

Tres to Ida: Even so, Maez is certainly the one to give you the lowdown on Bigfoot. He can reveal secrets that others would feel constrained to reserve.

Letter from Ida to Lee Trippett

I have had a lengthy conference with Thoth relative to Wipi. Thoth, in turn, has talked to monitor Maez and been advised to consider the effect of the high power electrical lines on the implants by which Wipi receives information and suggestions from Maez. The effect is somewhat the same as the microwave towers in Wyoming had on my implants when I was blanked out and spent four days in the hospital. Wipi has been warned to stay at least a half mile from the high power lines. Maez suggested to go back down the road closer to the spots that were dowsed.

Maez to Ida: I have been contacting Wipi daily. He is not much of a conversationalist but endures my efforts for an hour a day. I've been explaining your friend's (I'll call him Mr. T.) reasons and expectations for trying to contact him. For centuries the Bigfoot people have been warned to avoid all contact with Earth humans as unreliable and unpredictable. Even if the human means well, he can lose his cool at a confrontation and do something regrettable.

It was the proximity of the car that put Wipi off last time. He knows these glittering objects can travel much faster than he can, and they can start and stop with unexpected suddenness. I would advise leaving it below the hill next time and staying in the area only long enough to set out the tub. I will let you know if or when I can convince Wipi he will not be attacked if he comes to the rendezvous. He is eager enough to do so but cannot throw off years and years of family stories and warnings. Just as you hear legends about Bigfoot, he has been told tales — some quite tall — about you; this is really a complex situation. I am trying to spoon feed it to you bit by bit.

More later.

Maez to Ida: We could discuss many things here but I am going to try to stick to the schedule that we four have worked out for you. We, Maez, Amorto, Thoth and Tres will be your correspondents for the next ten years without too many interruptions or side issues. No, the world is not going to end, although there will be some terrifically exciting events occur during that time. The world will seem like a different place by the end of the next decade. No more revelations now. *It will be the most exciting decade in human history!*

For the moment let us get back to our discussion of Bigfoot.

From a million and a half to one hundred thousand years before present, we the people of the Arcturus system, worked on problems of genetic engineering. We nearly engineered ourselves out of existence. When we woke up to what we were doing there were only a few thousand of our original kind of people left but many experimental types of cyborgs and those we used as workers. Slaves would be a more exact designation but that word always sends you into a moral fit, so we will call them workers.

We had drawn a great deal of the animal component of our biological structuring from Earth, for which we had a special intention. That is why your people have indeed seen reptilian and other animalistic creatures.

We soon discovered that *Australopithecus africanus* (let's abbreviate him to *A.a.*) was the most promising of the evolutionary strain advancing toward a rational self-thinking creature, so we used him in many ways. By crossing him with our master genes we came up with Bigfoot. The original was a cross of "true man" as we consider ourselves (using your terminology) and the "not yet" man or *A.a.* It was a long and tedious experiment to find a perfected specimen that could not only explore Earth from one end to the other over millennia but could intelligently report back in such a manner that we could use the information we had sent him to collect. Bigfoot had enough of Earth inheritance to make his explorations there feasible, and enough of our intelligence to make his observations pertinent to our needs.

We saw it would be greatly to our advantage if Bigfoot could reproduce himself on Earth once we had perfected the exact type of creature that we needed. Reproduction problems proved a great time devourer, just as trying to get your mules to reproduce their own kind would prove to you. Genetic engineering was not a feat handed to us. We had to work it all out for ourselves over many hundreds of years.

The original Bigfoot had inbuilt communication abilities as well as extensive "psychic" talents that the earth-born gradually lost. We have to use implants with them now just as we do with you. Perhaps the greatly truncated life span of these latter (a couple hundred years compared to the original several thousand) is the reason their psychic abilities do not fully develop.

Each succeeding generation of the Earth-born will recapture more of these abilities but it will be a slow inch by inch process. No doubt there will be a "genius" Bigfoot born now and then who will break through the time wall and show unusual psychic abilities, just as happens in your own race. It is a projected inheritance from the past for both of you. Let's not dig deeper into such technicalities now, there is too much else to report and it must be revealed in logical and understandable sequence. You have been given too many incoherent bits and pieces up to now. It will only seem "real" or at least "possible" when you see it altogether in proper order.

Yes, my phraseology sounds like your own. Who do you think has been training your writing abilities for the last sixty years? (Hweig only dictated; I, Maez, created.) Tres provided you with answers to your questions. I helped you expand them into written form. Did not Amorto promise you that "Someday you will know everything?" Now it is beginning to be revealed. I know that it has driven you crazy that pieces could not be fit together to make the big picture. You thought we were all liars and tricksters. There is a time for everything-does not your Bible say so? "There is a time for sowing and a time for reaping"? This is the time to put together for you a coherent picture of what we have been about.

True Humanity

This is as good a place as any to explain Hweig's description of Bigfoot to you as it appeared in *Project Earth*, page 224.

> **"Hweig:** Sasquatch are indeed their [Arcturian's] creatures let out upon Earth to test energies from the ground on Earth itself. We do not recognize these energies although they work upon us, sometimes quite detrimentally. Sasquatch is not an ape and not human, but a biological creation about halfway between the two, with no biological connection to either. It is not a "missing link." The creatures are mild unless startled when with their young. They have been unloaded here for years, and now have acclimated and orientated themselves. They do have offspring, but rarely. They are monitored by pictorial telepathy."

Maez: When Hweig reported that there was no biological connection to either ape or human, he was referring to the fact that the first Bigfoot was generated hundreds of centuries before your-kind of human existed on earth. Although you and Bigfoot were built from our genes, which we consider "true humanity," only a small fraction, twenty percent, of Bigfoot's genes was ours. The genes of you of Earth were given a much greater portion. About eighty percent of your genes are from the Arcturian source.

Thoth and Tres: We decided to confer a little before going on with the dictation. It was resolved that all conversation would stop except Maez's explanations. Do not feel abandoned. If you have a particular question for one of us just ask; otherwise we will be silent partners.

Maez: Okay. On with the story of Bigfoot.

A million and a half years seems a very long time from your viewpoint but it was scarcely enough from ours to create our Bigfoot person from the genetic elements of *A.a.* and our own genes. Yes, we think of him as a person for he has intelligence and personality befitting a human inside that hairy animalistic exterior. Yes, of course he has a soul!

Less than 300,000 years ago — your time — we had perfected our creature enough to send him to Earth on the mission for which he was created. The original lived several thousand years *and we kept on perfecting and issuing improved stock.*

Our purpose was to find good living areas on Earth that would support our original human type, which is similar to your *Homo s.s.* of today. There is perhaps an eighty percent similarity.

Bigfoot was sent to every area of Earth, most of which was considerably different than it is today. There have been innumerable and great changes.

Long before 200,000 BCE (your time) we sent our first true human representatives to Earth on the now-sunken continent you call Lemuria.

All our first true human explorers were androgynes. They observed the matings of Earth's various creatures and decided to increase their own numbers by propagation. There were so few left on the home planet they did not want to risk all those lives in the unprecedented adventure.

As androgynes they had no experience in mating or birthing, although they had the necessary requisites. They now divided themselves, not by splitting physically, but by each choosing to differentiate himself by sex, male or female. Since most chose the male role, not many births resulted. So they also chose to mate with the "fairest" of the proto-humans they found on Earth.

At first they tried to keep their own race pure, but gradually it inter-mixed with the secondary strain that resulted from mating with the Earth stock.

The more nearly pure strain eventually resulted in Cro-Magnon. The proto-human mixture led to Neanderthal.

In the meantime Bigfoot continued his task of investigating the four corners of the Earth and reporting.

So now we had three strains of nearly fully Earth humans: Bigfoot, a borderline human; *neanderthalensis* [Neanderthal], a *Homo sapiens*; and *Cro-Magnon* type *Homo sapiens sapiens*. These three were all together on the continent you call Lemuria.

Most of the cross-bred humans were brought back to Lemuria, as their original purpose had been to help us colonize our new country. These new "citizens" were mostly from the Levantine corridor and were several strains in the neighborhood of *Homo erectus*.

We selected their young carefully for further inter-mixing and in a few generations had handsome and intelligent members of our expanding communities. Our rejects were taken back to the Levantine corridor and allowed to interbreed there.

Where else would the rapid advance in brain size and body stature come from than an outside source? In less than a hundred thousand years an advance in human evolution occurred that had never been equaled in millions of years. Why else the sudden spurt?

No more now on the human evolution. Your next book will carry that subject forward. Let us get back now to Bigfoot although their histories do intertwine.

Bigfoot continued to carry out his original task of reporting environmental conditions and other facts as time went on. He became, in fact, a super-spy on the fast increasing human population. His abilities were too useful to us to free him entirely from our supervision. We have continued to rely on him to this day. He reports on every new logging or mining enterprise and on all new sports resorts that bring many people into the forests and wilderness areas. We have other means of gaining knowledge of industrial and urban activities, but for the wild country Bigfoot is indispensable. *Yes! We consider the Western Hemisphere our property!*

And we watch with growing concern and impatience what is happening to it! As long as it was occupied by the people we brought into it, the land and its creatures were cherished and treated with respect. When it was flooded with newcomers from the East — well, there went the neighborhood!

This is not the place for my irritation. Later.

Maez to Ida: The mating with the "fairest daughters of the Earth" took place — on our part — among those occupying the Levantine corridor. Yes, even around the country where Jesus was to be born, though that has no particular significance here that I can see.

These "girls" were a mixture of various evolutionary advances toward *Homo erectus*. The genes of our adventurers simply speeded up the processes of development toward Neanderthal and *Homo sapiens*; our own pure offspring stayed in the Western Hemisphere.

You ask, "how did the mixture get to Lemuria from the Levantine?" We were not without aerial transportation. We had craft that would go through the air or under the water with equal ease; these were not space ships. We will soon go into an explanation of these; for now just accept them as fact.

Transport anywhere in the world was easy. Yes, even during the ice age.

Tres to Ida: Take a few days to catch up on your housework and correspondence, then back to work with Maez.

The reading you have been doing the last few days has shown you the lack of consolidation of ideas among the current paleoanthropologists. They have each and every one studied and researched diligently, and everyone came up with different ideas and answers to their questions.

Therefore do not be discouraged that you do not have absolute proof of any of your own researches. Some evidence is all that is required. Tangible evidence, so called "hard" evidence is, of course, best. But before one knows what to look for, one must have some idea of what is possible, or probable. Therefore your pre-study period is valuable and necessary. You are not "just wasting time". Therefore nail down your ideas of what it is possible to find as hard evidence and just how and where you can most likely succeed in finding it. You have a good imaginative faculty. Use it more freely. Imagination comes first, then exploration, then facts.

Bigfoot research to date has been nothing but anecdotes of sightings, then conjectures and speculation.

Some researchers have tufts of hair believed to be from Bigfoot perhaps for very specific reasons, but they did not actually pull out those hairs so they cannot be called absolute proof. The same with feces and other material. The researcher is positive of the authenticity of his "facts" but it is hard to prove to skeptics.

If you want irrefutable proof for Bigfoot's existence and his connection to *Homo sapiens*, you have to think of something definite, specific, and irrefutable, even though disconnected from him. So think!

Ida: The best thing I can imagine would be a photo but if I don't know where he is for sure, how can I get a photo?

He doesn't write letters or documents, I'm sure; no clay tablets, or stone carvings or paintings or petroglyphs. Even if we should see Bigfoot, we could not prove it to others that we had, except of course, for a photo. Other than that — and the footprint — all I can think of is some actual part of Bigfoot. I'm sure he doesn't wear dentures so there are no spare teeth lying about, and how could we prove they were Bigfoot's and not a displaced Neanderthal's? Bones, of course, would be ideal but they seem to be held almost sacred.

Anything from which DNA could be extracted would prove his make-up best. How do we get that? He doesn't cut his fingernails or discard his dirty socks. He doesn't shed his skin like a snake.

There have been recordings made of his calls and movements. Skeptics scoff.

So I use my imagination and come up with nothing. It is the same wild goose chase as with the UFOs — must be manufactured by the same clever minds. I hate to be played with cat-and-mouse fashion.

Tres: You are not being played with, simply made to think a little. Mull it over a bit.

Ida: If this rock I have is really a fossil of a Bigfoot child's head, what am I supposed to do with it? It wasn't "given" to me for nothing.

Tres: You will be told precisely what to do with it.

Ida: When?

Tres: Later today. Go eat lunch now.

Maez to Ida: You ask, 'who were the proto-humans?' What do your paleoanthropologists call them? Do they have any fossils?

Yesterday you spent all afternoon reading about fossils found in the Levantine corridor. They appeared to be a cross between Neanderthal and pre-sapiens. These were also pre-Neanderthal as will presently be determined. This is where we found the fairest of Earth women for our matings.

Maez to Ida: You are cross with us for what you call a cat-and-mouse game. We watched you grow suspicious and — yes! — recalcitrant under Hweig's twenty years of giving you facts in a scattered and uncontrolled fashion. We are trying to fit our own information into a consecutive whole and not dump it all on you like a ton of coal for the winter.

We are trying to show you a complete picture of possibilities to give you a solid background of understanding, building it up one idea at a time.

Please be patient. You must have a thorough knowledge of the creature you call Bigfoot as he really is.

Wipi has watched his human brothers do degrading things he would not dream of doing. Perhaps, as you note, the new force (law?) of Reconciliation will help him to accept them in spite of his previous disgust. Yes, disgust! You are not yet thinking of his human aspect.

We must recognize that all sightings and observations of Bigfoot have rolled him and his fellows into one composite being: One Bigfoot.

On the other hand, Bigfoot's observations of humans have rolled them all together into one composite man.

Neither has had the time nor inclination to separate individuals.

You can try to convince Wipi until the cows come home that you are different, that you have only compassion and good will and the best of intentions to help him do what he wants to do, but you will find all the combined sins of the human race compacted against you. Wipi's personal experiences of nearly two hundred years are a heavy weight of negativity.

We need all the Force of Reconciliation that we can muster. I am talking to him almost daily. His trust in me and his natural curiosity are in our favor. His negativity took years to become so solidified. It will take time to dissolve it. I will do all I can. Please be patient with me, Wipi, and the general situation.

Ida, go to sleep. It is now 5:30 A.M.

Maez to Ida: I'm afraid the book you are reading will only confuse you about times, places and types of early man. So very much has been lost, or not discovered or misinterpreted. The anthropologists do the best they can with the material — very scant material that they have. And here again, they each secrete their knowledge and do not share as they might.

However, I know you are reading for several purposes, so go ahead today. Tomorrow, let us get back to writing, please.

P.S. We can't do too much over the winter about contacting Wipi or other Bigfoot. The snow makes them highly vulnerable as they cannot conceal their footprints.

Ida to Maez: What about the Mt. St. Helens' eruption and the dozen or so Bigfoot buried there? Would any be findable?

Maez: Maybe, if you had any idea where to look.

Ida: I guess that was a dumb question.

Maez: I've heard dumber.

Ida to Maez, 12/7/98: Okay, I'm ready for another week of information. You never answered my question. What am I supposed to do with this fossil head?

Maez: Hold it and continue to study and compare it with pictures. Eventually you will meet a person who will be interested in examining it closely. I don't know how soon, a few months maybe. Let's get on with the writing.

Ida: Okay.

Tres to Ida: Do not try to outguess us; just take our dictation as it comes. Do not question. Once we get through it you will see where everything fits together. There is too much lacking in the current knowledge of such things as man's descent — or ascent, if you prefer as I do, for our information to appear to fit. When we are all through telling, you will understand. At the moment you are only wasting time and confusing yourself with all this reading. Go to work now with Maez and accept what he says without all the questioning. Please!

(I think I've been scolded, but nicely. Ida)

Maez to Ida: It wasn't until you picked up *The Secret Doctrine* by Blavatsky that we began to worry.

Ida: But it told me exactly what I needed to know. Blavatsky's mention of man's progress through a number of root races before he even remotely looked like what we call man, revealed what Ernst Haeckel said at the Congress of Natural Sciences in Stettin in 1863.

"So far as we men ourselves are concerned, we should logically seek our ancestors first among the ape-like mammals, beyond them kangaroo-like marsupials, still further back among the lizard-like reptiles, fish at a low organization and finally among the unicellular aboriginal forms." (Haeckel)

Ida: Haeckel was following the developmental process of human embryology and this process also explains Blavatsky's story of the "root races" of man.

It also explains why James Churchward had an intuition that a kind of man existed in the tertiary period, which was from 25 million to 10 million years ago, and also why Maez can say the first true man stepped on the shores of Lemuria (in a place

Footprints of the Ancients

"This is where the foot of true man first stepped upon the Earth," said Hweig. The footprint and "writing" have no connection with the ogham, which was put nearby much later. I believe that Hawaiians used this as a sacred place because of the footprints ~ Ida.

Photo 3. Footprint outlined in the rectangle compares with motif of feet and hands at the initiation center for the Feathered Serpent in Mexico's ancient mother culture, at the Teotihuacan pyramid complex. After Lemurian home lands in the Pacific sank, survivors migrated to Native America, where contact with Star Ancestors have been memorialized for millennia. (*Web of Life and Cosmos: Human and Bigfoot Star Ancestors*, Krsanna Duran)

Footprint made in 1952 UFO contact:

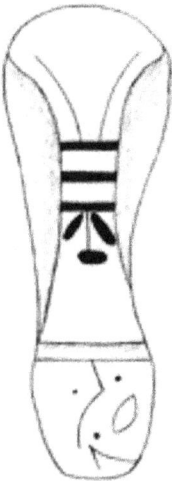

After a UFO sighting and landing on the California desert, George Hunt Williamson made a plaster cast of the footprint (left) the extraterrestrial made. While preparing to write *My Brother Is a Hairy Man: The Search for Bigfoot* in 1998, the Arcturian Maez asked Ida to read George Hunt Williamson's book about time travel.

Maez explained that the Arcturians introduced first Bigfoot then human ancestor lines with true human genetics in Lemuria a little less than 300,000 years ago, after the species were developed on Arcturus for more than one million years. The early human ancestor had four times the true human genes than Bigfoot,who had a twenty percent true human contribution. The human ancestor was evolved from an anthropoid after human souls began entering the apes. ~ Krsanna Duran now called Kauai, Hawaii) a little over 200,000 years ago. It all fits together, everyone is right.

Maez: We apologize for the scolding. You are right.

Ida: Okay. Let's get on with the dictation.

Maez to Ida: We were last talking about transportation. We had aerial devices at first. Later, in the course of our growing in numbers, even great numbers, we began using boats and then ships. Due to a number of catastrophes the aerial craft were rendered unusable, and then abandoned.

Now let us leave talk of Man's ascension and return to Bigfoot who is the true hero of this story.

For a long time, thousands of years, Bigfoot and Man in Lemuria worked together, spoke together, sometimes ate together. When they were apart they used pictorial telepathy as being less likely to be misinterpreted. The spoken language of Bigfoot remained rather simple: nouns, verbs, and descriptive adjectives in that order without syntax or grammatical rules. "Man, comes, angry" with a telepathic picture was enough to convey any spoken idea. In our company Bigfoot's spoken language gained and developed nuances that made him almost a philosopher! He has had a good sense of humor.

Give him a hot shower, shave the hair from his body, dress him in jeans and a T-shirt and he could pass for a man as well as some men I have observed, but he would be extremely uncomfortable in their society.

As the number of men increased, communities grew larger and power struggles between men for private property and personal gain burst into open warfare. Bigfoot retired from contact and went into the more inaccessible areas. He was not being prudish; he just did not understand power struggles. He became more and more reclusive until he is as you see him, shy, and avoiding human contact. He does not like or understand the philosophy of your civilization.

You see that his feelings are very deep-rooted indeed. They have become almost a species instinct but far more complex than a simple animal instinct.

You have known or read of human hermits who have retired into the mountains to live a simple and harmonious life with nature. Think of Bigfoot as one of those hermits and you will come closer to understanding him. He thinks, he knows, he reasons as well as any hermit who ever left the roils and toils of society to live the uncomplicated though lonely life.

Day by day Bigfoot watched — all over the world — that civilization encroach upon his territory, threatening his safety and way of life, and of those few fellows who are around him. He feels he is being pushed to the wall of extinction, and so he is! He understands! He knows what is happening and he does not want to become an extinct and forgotten race any more than you do.

The Force of Reconciliation put into use becomes a law: reconcile differences or become extinct. Bigfoot understands! Do you?

The Force of Reconciliation has come into the world at exactly the right moment to save Bigfoot, and Man himself, from becoming extinct. Use it!

I become emotional. Let me retire a little and compose myself.

Go finish your chicken soup.

Maez to Ida: Let me insert a word of advice here concerning the artifacts you found along with the fossil skull or head. Keep them together particularly the hand axes. Whether the person of the fossil had any immediate connection with the artifacts or not, the fact that they were found together shows some kind of connection, so keep them all together.

I have refrained from giving you the outline devised for this book (which we seem to be already writing) for I keep making changes. Your questions and observations expand my original intention as we go along. Let us continue in this collaborative manner and see where we go.

We have been considering Bigfoot as a single or solitary being up to now. Let us think of him in his immediate relationships with his own kind.

All Bigfoot at present on Earth are Earth-born and are species alike except for minor environmental and cultural differences. For tomorrow find a world map so I can pinpoint those living today.

Maez to Ida, 12/11/98: Finding a Bigfoot body in the ash of Mt. St. Helens might be feasible but it presents some problems to be anticipated and carefully thought out. 1) What is the chemical content of the ash? By determining this you can anticipate the possible condition of the body that has lain buried in it for twenty years. Are there chemical elements that would mummify or fossilize or give acidic melt-down even to the bones? Or other possibilities? 2) You want to prove that Bigfoot has human elements as well as animal ones. What are the laws of your state against exhuming human bodies and keeping the bones? Trouble here! 3) Who would analyze the bones — or whatever — to distinguish its characteristics? A medical practitioner, an anthropologist, or a team of experts? More in the morning.

Maez to Ida: There would be no interference from the remaining Bigfoot families or clan. We thought the kindest thing we could do would be to remove them from the area where they could not see the wounded mountain and to blank out all memory of the event. This has left them rather dull and unemotional. And they are too far from the area to return quickly.

(Sounds like a lobotomy — Ida)

Yes, of course, we could do all this for you, even deliver the bones of a Bigfoot right to your door by United Parcel Service. But you would miss out on a vital experience that would prove necessary for future and successful research. You are building a complete but slow road to obtaining proof of Bigfoot's nature and existence in ways that cannot be denied.

The greatest danger to full success is in making the right choice of persons you will need to help you at various stages of your progress. Leave all that up to Mr. T. (Ida, you trust anybody. You can't imagine that other people could be so different from yourself. There are "lawmen" as the TV calls them and doctors and scientists and anthropologists who would kill for the information you are on the road to recovering. We would like you to come out of this adventure alive.)

Ida, your chemical knowledge stopped with the chemical expression of water. Leave these preliminaries up to Mr. T. This is his party. You are the note taker and recorder. This is all for

today. We now have three viable directions for research —
footprints, photos, and recovery from the ash. I work on Wipi.
If he remains reluctant, there are others.

Letter from Lee Trippett to Ida

December 12 1998

Many thanks for the notes from Maez dated 12/11/98.

I did not realize that our quest for Bigfoot was "my
party". I would prefer it to be a cooperative adventure.
But since that is now expressed and we have been
given the option for three avenues of approach, let me
say I would prefer a picture of Wipi pressing his foot into
a tub of clay by appointment. The evidence would be
copyrighted and shared without fee to a few of those
persons check-marked on the enclosed list of Bigfoot
researchers. And then, later, by means of a second appointment, you, Marlys and I would give Wipi an opportunity to repeat his evidence.

Please find attached two different outlines relating to
my view of Bigfoot and my plan to provide supporting evidence for their existence, protection, and unique nature. I am not interested in whether Bigfoot is human
or that they may be either animal or human. Only that
they have a means of communication with us. Even
though it is through you and Maez. The issue of whether
Bigfoot is animal or human is very complex and so we
will have the experts play with that one. Maybe Bigfoot
is neither?

I have not been totally consistent in the expression of
my views and so these printed outlines will provide a
means for clarification, purpose, and direction.

These outlines were written last year and after our
many discussions you will find little that is new. But I
feel that it is important that we have a clear and consistent understanding of purpose in the search for Bigfoot. Also, with your unique communication abilities,
your past and future books, your high quality reputation,
your involvement with a successful find of Bigfoot evi-

dence, all of this could have significant and unexpected implications upon your personal involvement.

Therefore, please mark any statements which are not clear or which may be inconsistent with your viewpoints. We need to have a common consensus. Your interest and knowledge in the origin of man and Bigfoot far exceeds mine. Of course there is a need and many will find your history and theory of origins essential, but my primary interest lies in obtaining both physical and communication evidence and its verification.

Whether we get a couple of footprints in clay, a couple of photo opportunities, or even a body, we must coordinate with others and therefore our current mutual understanding and cooperation is vital. I feel strongly that the pattern behind the form of evidence must imply the use of communication with Bigfoot.

I am overwhelmed by your support, patience, and interest in this Bigfoot project and especially your willingness to consider my desires in the process. Thank you!

Lee:

Bigfoot, Animal and Human Consciousness

A Personal Viewpoint

1995 / Revised July 1997

I believe there is something far more significant to the Bigfoot phenomena than their origin, size, form, or genes, or DNA. It relates to the subject of consciousness. In the more than 37 years of extensive field research by a wide variety of experts, using every conceivable technique, there is little consistent soft evidence and little consistent hard evidence, except for footprints. I believe these limited results relate to a unique style of consciousness that is foreign to our normal awareness. As an example, we can relate to studies about our very own sub-consciousness or unconsciousness but we do not, or rarely, have an awareness of that special world of consciousness which is actually within us. Even though these other realms of consciousness are within us, they are beyond, or

MY BROTHER IS A HAIRY MAN | 39

"outside" our normal awareness. (A better term for my use of "normal" might be 'average' or 'common'. There are many reports of human psychic perception, memory, and intellectual capacities which are far beyond the 'common' or 'average'. Perhaps today's average is actually below our potential capacity.)

Is it conceivable that Bigfoot has a conscious awareness which is seated within the automatic or central nervous system instead of the cerebral cortex? This might explain their lack of need for artifacts and their tremendous success in remaining elusive. For example if their perception is through some sort of psychic extension of the normal human-like five senses, they would have the required tools for an awareness of food location, approaching danger, future shelter needs, etc.

Herein are some ideas about Bigfoot, animal, and human consciousness. But first a few words about the concept of spirit because I believe that all "life" regardless of the form or carrier, comes from one universal spirit. The most significant part of the human system relates to some aspect of that universal spirit. The "spirit" is the spark behind any motivation through intent. That "spirit" is the spark behind creativity. And that "spirit" is the spark behind awe or praise for something beyond our five senses and their psychic extensions.

The significant aspect about the human system is not our brain or body but our consciousness. Our body and brain are indeed incredible and miraculous vehicles but these are only temporary containers and images for our unique consciousness. The essence of our consciousness survives these material vehicles and transcends the limitations of time and space. There is now more abundance of consistent soft evidence for this than there is for the existence of Bigfoot. (See the research summary of Out-of-Body experiences in *The Holographic Universe* by M. Talbot, Chapter 8.)

Human consciousness is the being "alive" with the motivation of "spirit" and is the collective personal experience of five basic attributes. These are 1) self-consciousness, 2) mentality, 3) emotion, 4) volition; and 5) conscience. In total consciousness these five attributes must co-exist simultaneously and a healthy consciousness would be incomplete with the omission or distortion of any one of these attributes. Our consciousness is so familiar to us that we often do not fully realize its special characteristics.

Here are some specific details of consciousness. 1) Self-consciousness is the knowing awareness of one's existence and ego by being aware of the awareness. 2) Mentality includes such features as memory, instinct, knowledge, psyche, and intellect with its corresponding ability to reason, perceive, understand and learn from experience. 3) Emotion is any one of a dozen complex reactions with both psyche and physical manifestation. 4) Volition is the exercise of will or choice. 5) Conscience is the capacity to feel right or wrongness.

Animals have consciousness but it is probably not to the extent of "being aware that it is being aware." They all have the same features of mentality but probably not to the same extent in the area of reasoning, knowledge, or experiential learning. They have emotions but not to the same extent, and there are some emotions such as guilt, which are probably unknown. However, this might vary according the degree of training and domestication of the animal. Animals may experience the results of conscience by their automatic instinct or group consciousness but I seriously doubt if this is the same as humans. Of course some animals have perceptions and instincts far beyond those of us. How much further no one knows. But we do know that plants have the ability to "respond" to our thoughts and emotions, and so I would assume that this capability would exist in some animals. (See *The Secret Life of Plants* by C. Bird.) Bigfoot reports include some human-like activities, i.e., they carry wounded smoke jumpers to safety, they capture and have sex with our women, they exchange goods, they serve as outdoor slaves, they throw a series of boulders to one target, and they play games with our minds and automatic cameras. I believe there is a very wide range of consciousness development among the various Bigfoot groups of the world. Therefore some of those groups may be closer to animal or human consciousness than others. I believe the Bigfoot of southwest Oregon and Northern California are close to the human form of consciousness.

There are three areas of research that may help us to understand that Bigfoot can have a unique form of human type of consciousness. One is the twenty-year development of a holographic theory for our universe. (See *The Holographic Uni-*

verse by M. Talbot.) Mr. Talbot's summary of a very large bibliography basically says that all objects, subjects, or functions relate to a specific matrix of vibration rates. These vibrations may relate to sound, electric, magnetic, atomic, or gravitational force fields. Every aspect of our "normal" consciousness is therefore subject to a pre-programmed range of vibration rates. I believe that the consciousness of Bigfoot may be related to some other range, matrix, or modulation which makes their consciousness beyond or "outside" our "field" of comprehension. Not necessarily different but into another or expanded feature which is currently out of reach for most of us.

The second subject of research relates the manipulation of low frequency subtle energy fields. This is accomplished with the application of certain vibration rates within the mental state domains of delta, theta, and alpha (1 to 13 HZ). This research is showing health benefits when the correct vibration rate is applied to a subject by either mechanical, electrical, or magnetic energies. (See *Healing Sounds: The Power of Harmonics* by J. Goldman, Sound Healers Association, PO Box 2240, Boulder, CO 80306; and any of the works by Sharry Edwards, PO Box 706, Athens, OH 45701. And also see *MegaBrain Power* by M. Hutchison.). There are some specific low frequencies that will heal many people but each individual is completely unique in their particular vibrational needs. There are some vibration rates which can cause physical or mental illness. Dr. Manners' researches in England over the last twenty years show that there are specific frequency values for each organ and function of the body. I believe this data supports the idea that Bigfoot's consciousness can be outside our normal understanding because there are an infinite range of vibrations and modulation between 1 and 13 Hz.

The third subject of research relates to the manipulation of subtle energy fields within the visual electromagnetic (scalar?) domain. (See *Light Emerging* by B. Brennan.) There is a university in America that is teaching the application of this knowledge for the purpose of psyche and physical healing. The human aura shows a wide array of colors related to each organ, mental state, and ductless gland function. The many colors show modulations in the realm of texture and form. Each of these color features relate to a specific condition of health and vitality. Here again is another branch of study that supports the idea that living forms can have their own specific range of vibration rates that may be beyond or "outside" our normal range of consciousness or perception. Perception not only includes sensing an input signal but also includes the interpretation of that signal, as we want to "see" it. (See studies relating to hypnotic therapy.)

No study of unusual biped humanoid forms would be complete without a study of *The Three Pound Universe* by Judith Hooper. After many years of research into the activities of various laboratories throughout America, that author has found revolutionary discoveries about the brain, mind, consciousness, psyche, and frontiers of the soul.

There is a man and wife team who have taken, over the last decade, a number of outdoor "photo experts" to "see" evidence of Bigfoot. Nearly all the experts refuse to take a second trip. The trips are always in the Coast Range of Northern California and always in the winter months. They establish a camp in one spot, stay for a couple of weeks, and stay awake during the night. All of this is very uncomfortable and boring with the exception of an occasional Bigfoot "presence" or sighting. These folks have lots of interesting personal experiences but still no photos.

Ivan Sanderson (author of *Abominable Snowman: Legend Come to Life*, 1961) and Richard Ireland of Arizona (a leading national psychic) explained to me in person and in detail how to take a similar approach. And so in 1977 I went out for ten consecutive months, staying awake through two nights, during the time of the full moon. From this experience I became personally convinced that Bigfoot's existence was real and that they and their environment needed our protection, not our intrusion. I also feel they are curious and would welcome an occasional friendly visit.

Others who have tried being alone in a remote wilderness for the purpose of "finding Bigfoot" instead find a lack of willingness (or excuse?) to continue. In my case my wife pleaded the lack of income and a lack of knowledge of my whereabouts and safety. In addition I could not control my private thoughts and motives. I believe a complete lack of fear and an unqualified respect for their welfare is essential to gain any meaningful proximity.

MY BROTHER IS A HAIRY MAN | 43

For any others who may be willing to search for Bigfoot, remember the words of Sir Isaac Newton. He has been the cornerstone of our currently limited materialistic scientific viewpoint. He said "...I seem to have been only like a boy playing on the seashore, and diverting myself now and then finding a smoother pebble or a prettier shell than ordinary, whilst the great ocean of truth lay all undiscovered before me."

Any pioneer of alternative viewpoints needs courage and must rely only partially on current scientific models. There is little to be gained by submitting a truly new discovery or theory to peer-review because the discoverer of different evidence or ideas has no peers. Proponents of a new idea are often more subject to jeers not cheers because it is easier to deny than to accept something that may alter established opinions or vested interests.

(Note: I first published the essential essence of these ideas in the late sixties and the main feature of this particular expanded version was sent to John Green (author of many books about Bigfoot), Jack Lapseritis (popular lecturer and author of *The Psychic Sasquatch*, 1996) and The Western Bigfoot Society, Trippett.)

Maez to Ida, 12/13/98: The map marking is going much faster than I expected. You seem to anticipate my instructions. How do you do this?

Ida to Maez: After twenty years of working with Hweig I could anticipate what he was going to say next. I guess it developed into a knack. People are always telling me, "That is just what I was going to say!" Also I saw where you were calling for a label usually was an area that had both a mountain and a river or lake. The mountain makes easy access for a pursuer a real task, and the river or lake was a necessary water supply. Logic.

Maez to Ida: All right, so far so good. Let's rest a little.

I am not showing you every Bigfoot for reasons of his vulnerability in some places, and the spots I show are only his general center of activity. I show only a smaller percentage. They roam widely.

The few places where I show only one means either a fellow has been taken home (Arcturus) or one has died in the last several years. We have made considerable changes since 1995. If you want to compare the map with anyone's database of sightings, use only the most recent ones.

Where I indicate three it means there is a child up to twenty years old, or an elderly one who needs care, or one who needs help.

Where I indicate five or more, it means a clan or family nucleus. The members range rather wildly, they are seldom all found exactly in one spot. Their actual range can be up to one hundred miles, but is usually more like forty.

We try to keep them paired at all times, either male and mate, or two males. One of these will be a younger one trying to learn the tricks of the trade with an older. There are far fewer females than males.

We send them only on temporary missions to extremely cold or hot places.

No, the maps are not specific enough for you to rush out and grab a Bigfoot. After it is completed and you study it carefully, and logically, you can begin to see some coherent reason for their placement. We do nothing without reason.

Why don't we leave Europe and Asia for tomorrow? Go bake your gingerbread.

Ida: I think Bigfoot must be stationed at those places where movements of fault lines or vibrations of potential volcanoes can be easily and most quickly felt. That is why there were so many — eighteen — at Mt. St. Helens.

Bigfoot must be unusually sensitive to vibrations of the Earth, and possibly other dangers also. That is what they were engineered for in the first place.

Ida, 12/15/98: On December 8th, Maez said that Lemuria had spacecraft that could go also under water.

This left a question mark in my mind until I was hunting for the book *Secret Places of the Lion* — and not finding it — that I came upon Ivan T. Sanderson's *Investigating the Unexplained.* (My copy is a paperback, issued by Prentice-Hall, copyright 1972.)

Chapter ten shows the "Little Gold Airplane", an artifact belonging to the government of Columbia, South America.

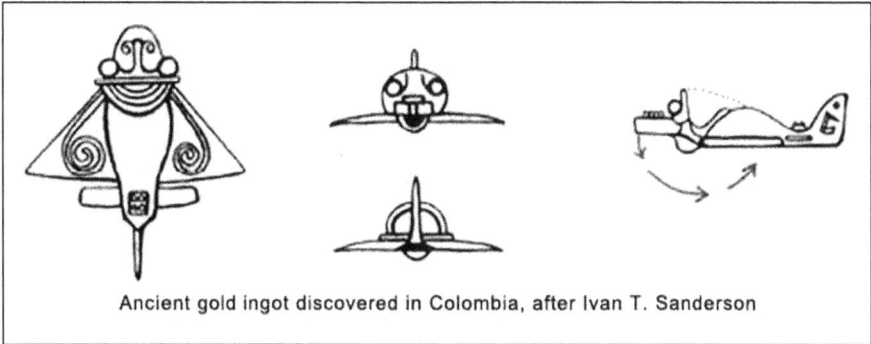

Ancient gold ingot discovered in Colombia, after Ivan T. Sanderson

Mr. Sanderson was sent a copy of this artifact. He consulted a number of engineers and their final conclusion was, "To make a long story short, the only known answer was that this thing could have been constructed to dive under the water, and then get out of it again into the air."

Mr. Sanderson also estimates that the original of the artifact was at least one thousand years old. This erased my question mark.

Maez to Ida, 12/16/98: Observing from our planet in the Arcturus system, our viewpoint of Earth is cut-off for a short period due to what we call a "time lock". You suggested it might be like an eclipse. The effect is the same as an eclipse, but the cause is quite different. It would require a whole new system of education to let you understand, and other matters are more pressing at the moment. It means dictation from here would not be satisfactory so I will cease until the end of the year.

Tres and Amorto can get through to you as they are situated differently. Thoth and Amorto are on earth and Tres is where Tres always is, a mystery.

I will wish you and Mr. T. a Merry Christmas and a Happy New year according to your custom. "See" you in 1999.

We will finish dotting the world map this afternoon. You will then have marked at least one-seventh of the world population of Bigfoot. Their positions are not constant. We shift them from post to post, but this is better than no map at all.

Letter from Ida to Mr. T.

I estimate there are about five hundred Bigfoot recorded here. If that is one-seventh, it means the total on earth at present is about 3500, quite a bit more than I was expecting.

We are supposed to figure out why they are where they are. I would guess it is in some relation to such things as tectonic plates and earthquake areas. (I have a map also dotted.)

Maybe their time lock has something to do with our solar system lining up with the galactic equator this month?

The major thing I find in common with Bigfoot placements are that they are on high mountains, 5,000-8,000 feet, or near reservoirs, lakes, rivers, or places that receive much rainfall such as the Olympic Peninsula in Washington State. There are also many (10) in southern Florida in swamps, lakes, marshes, or the Everglade country. There are few on open prairie or desert areas. I have only analyzed the United States so far.

They seem to have great interest in watery places. The Olympic Peninsula has the most rainfall of any place in the United States. The southern Florida area is all swamps and water.

The high peaks and their snow packs that melt and run down through the valleys to replenish lakes and streams are of interest for this factor of water as well as being safety features for Bigfoot and his family. The mountains, also, particularly certain ones, are indicative of earth changes that presage either earthquakes or volcanoes. They are close to, but not necessarily on, fault lines.

Maez said that Bigfoot reports activity taking place in mining and lumbering industries and also new sports areas such as ski resorts and snowmobiling areas.

It would seem Bigfoot is an attentive observer (and reporter) on all ecological changes on the planet. That is, if my analysis holds true for other Earth areas besides North American, and I believe it does.

That is as far as I have worked on the question I was asked, "Why has Bigfoot been located in these particular places?"

Tres to Ida: So far, so good. Keep working on it.

Ida: Of course all in Oregon, at least, are in heavily forested places and where there is thick undergrowth. So obvious I forgot to mention it (water, forests, mountains).

Maez to Ida, 12/22/98: I am back briefly today and I want to congratulate you on your map enthusiasm. You cannot capture or see a Bigfoot, probably, from the placements I have given you, their areas are too large, but the spots do give you an overall picture of where and how many there are, 3500 worldwide are about right. You have the generalized placements for about one-seventh of the creatures in the world today. There was a general redistribution in 1995 to cover changes since the last reassessment in 1920. The next assessment will be around 2075, depending on what happens to them in the meantime.

Your cold spell will keep Wipi in his retreat until it warms slightly. Bigfoot goes into semi-hibernation during colder weather. For one thing he then requires less food. He lives almost entirely on small animals during real cold weather. By eating the contents of their stomachs he gets the "greenery" that he requires. He also eats certain evergreen needles. You have analyzed the placements of Bigfoot as having ecological purposes. That is quite right, but only the beginning of what you will discover if you keep on thinking. Stick to Western Washington, Oregon, and that bit of Northern California that is shown on your map.

Remember that Bigfoot moves about rather widely, as much as 100 miles from the center of his base at times. If he has an "appointment" or request to meet someone, he is going to make that spot as many miles as possible from his center of movement, out on the fringes somewhere. He is not going to draw you into an area where his mate or companion would be placed in jeopardy.

Set your compass at 50 miles and that will show you a hundred-mile radius. See how many Bigfoot are contained within that diameter. Any Bigfoot within that area will have at least two fellows to interact if needed. Now set it for 100 miles and draw in another eight or so. These measurements do not allow for the ups and down of mountainous terrains or other obstructions a Bigfoot might have to detour around, but it gives you an idea of the distances that Bigfoot can cover when there is a good reason to do so, from his viewpoint. At all times we must try to think like a Bigfoot.

How does he call others to him for aid or for some joint venture? He is either guided by his monitor, or he uses his own powers of pictorial telepathy which are as good as an inbuilt TV transmitter and receiver. This is why he does not use speech. He has no need to, but he could if he were coached in verbal usage.

Your own dependence on verbal thought and communication deters you from becoming proficient in pictorial telepathy. See you again soon.

Ida, 12/23/98: Since Maez has gone "on vacation" for a week or two, I have turned to such Bigfoot literature as I have on hand. I have never read it very thoroughly, just dipped into it for reference from time to time. I never realized I was ever going to get tangled up with Bigfoot research. I find I have: John Green; *Sasquatch, the Apes Among Us*, Peter Byrne; "In Search of Bigfoot," *Journal of Fortean Research: Vol. IV #4*; *On the Trail of Bigfoot Mysterious Creatures*; *In Pursuit of Bigfoot and Yeti*; *The Psychic Sasquatch* by Jack Lapseritis; and I have avidly started borrowing books from my daughter and from Lee Trippett.

In Byrne's book he quotes Ivan T. Sanderson: "...there would appear to be considerable variation in both size and form and the behavior of these hominids. These characters and characteristics spread the possibility of their identification all the way from Neanderthaloid types of *Homo sapiens* to the earliest Australopithecines."

From the Fortean Journal: "...the number of reliable sightings (in the Coast Range Mountains of Oregon) has declined drastically over the last decade 1980-1990. People who maintain the creature exists say the decline is due to the same environmental issues that are responsible for the disappearance of owls, salmon, and mountain lions in the Pacific Northwest, lumbering of old growth forest and urbanization. Some of the more pragmatic even say the creature is now extinct."

Ida to Maez: Several researchers have called attention to Neanderthal.

Maez: See Hweig's comments in *Project Earth*, "True Human Footprint." Mating of true men with the daughters of the Earth did, eventually, produce Neanderthal.

Ida: One researcher (Russian) comments on the fast pace of human evolution.

Maez: Of course. It had us to help them.

Ida: If you wanted a huge, bulky Bigfoot, why did you not choose A. Boisei? He was much bigger than *A.a.*

Maez, 12/25/98: Boisei was much less coordinated in his movements than *A.a.* He was lumbering and awkward. It was easier to develop *A.a.*'s bulk, size and weight than it was to refine A. Boisei. Believe me, we tried both.

In evolving *A.a.* his foot bones had to evolve also to carry the extra weight. Bigfoot in other places in the world are not always so huge. Go to sleep.

Ida, 12/16/98: I picked up my new (Christmas present) Tony Hillerman mystery book and read the preface:

"Since I began my fictional relationship with the Navajo Tribal Police, six of its officers have been killed while performing their duty. A small force covering a vast expanse of mountains, canyons and desert, they must work primarily alone".

It struck me that was precisely the predicament Bigfoot was in policing large areas of remote regions.

For whom is he policing and for what? For whom would be his monitors, of course. But for what besides the ecological problems? Tres indicated that was only the obvious aspect. "Keep thinking," Tres said. I will.

When I read in my mystery story the words, "Missing aircraft" my eyes stuck and I couldn't get past those words. Has Bigfoot a policing job that has something to do with aircraft or UFOs?

Think! Are Bigfoot's areas where UFOs can come in with less chance of detection? Maybe, but that's not the whole story.

Ida: My mind is still stuck on the word "policing." Why is policing done? To detect crime or the possibility of crime. And the perpetrators are human. In this case the objects of their crime would be the reservoirs and watersheds and forests, and it would be something more than the lumber and resort and mining companies are doing. It would involve destruction or theft. How does one destroy or "steal" a forest? By fire? Or a reservoir? By contamination of the water or ripping holes in the container. Are the monitors concerned with the possibility of sabotage on our resources?

Tres: Definitely, Yes! You have forest rangers and fire patrols but they cannot *read the minds* of plotters and schemers. You have no idea how much you have been protected and for how long.

But you have not yet reached the main purpose. Keep thinking.

Ida: Why are there none indicated on the dams on the Columbia? These would seem to be the logical targets of sabotage?

Tres: The dams are well guarded by your own people in several different ways and adequately.

Ida, 12/27/98: Returning to my mystery story this morning, "The First Eagle" by Tony Hillerman, brought up the notice of birds and, by extension, animals. The birds and animals of the forest may be part of Bigfoot's interests. But how and why? He pays enough attention to them to learn to imitate their calls. Does this lure them to him to use for food? Or is there another reason? I was told long ago that the "home" planet had to bring in specimens from other sources to replenish their own that had been destroyed. But they should have all of the Earth stock they want by now.

Once long ago my communicants said, "Our planet is full of color and has gorgeous flowers, but we have no animals or birds. They were all destroyed eons ago, except for those later brought in and kept under scientific conditions. These are many and varied and come from many sources."

I was wondering why Bigfoot was made so huge, other than as a self-protective device. But of course, Maez had told us right in the beginning that the Masters of Arcturus were all 7 and 8 feet tall. They would have developed Bigfoot to be as tall as themselves.

Also from *Project Earth*, page 132, June 21, 1979:

"The first men who discovered outer space travel (in this cycle of humans) lived in what you called Lemuria. No, Mu was the entire known world at the time, and encompassed more than Lemuria proper. This was many thousands of years ago — fifty thousand and more — yes, two hundred thousand. Lemuria was a continent in the Pacific Ocean that stretched far to the south.

"It was there true humans — the seed of Earth's present inhabitants — came first."

This last line certainly corresponds with Hweig's comments on the first true men who set foot in the spot my daughter and I found in Hawaii. I was studying a photo we had taken of what appeared to be a footprint on a rock on a Kauai beach.

Hweig said, "It is a historical marker. That is where the foot of true humans first trod upon Earth. Hawaii is a remnant of Lemuria. This is where "the sons of gods" first came to Earth. These were the first true men."

Project Earth, page 134, Hweig explains motives:

"The planetary ones want to reestablish their world with flora and fauna from Earth, and perhaps a few brave souls to revitalize their diminishing earth-type population."

And we know now from Maez's explanations that those planetary ones were from the Arcturian system. We were told at first that they were from a planet in a "far galaxy". Now this is amended to a specific system much within our galaxy. "A camouflage" is the excuse for the misdirection.

Ida, 12/28/98: These brilliant UFO characters cannot seem to get it through their noggin that so many mis-directions deters us less brilliant ones from believing them wholeheartedly, in whatever they say. Is it any wonder we sometimes show suspicion and skepticism? I wish I could believe 100% instantly; it would save much wear and tear on my nervous system.

Ida: I was reading in *The Secret Places of the Lion* by George Hunt Williamson, which Tres had told me to find. (My copy is a much beat-up paperback issued by Warner-Destiny books 1977-1978.) On page 230 I read, "The great Sun Temple at Mesa Verde... was built to commemorate the coming of the "sun" (space) ship to the Indian People.

"When it was discovered that most of the ancient records were available and secure, the survey group returned to Hesperus (Venus).

"The Indian leader from the south guarded the secret places as he had protected those in Egypt when he lived as Maya. Now when he eventually left Mesa Verde again, the secret hiding places were lost, for only he and the checkers knew the location!"

I have seen photocopies purported to be golden tablets or plates discovered in a cave on the Utah-Arizona border, guarded by Ute-Piute Indians.

Rock Art, Holographic Projections and Telepathy

Is it possible that this is a major reason for some of Bigfoot's placement? Are there similar hidden secrets that would reveal contact by space ships, probably in the very distant past?

Tres: Yes! Now figure out what they would be; not golden tablets, something more prosaic unless you were aware of some hidden meaning.

Ida: Rocks probably. Only rocks would wear for centuries through weather and Earth changes.

Tres: Yes! But not just any old rock. Think of some of the studies and some of the trips of exploration you have made in the past.

Ida: Either petroglyphs or fossils.

Tres: Keep thinking.

Ida: I wonder if there are caves in those areas. But Bigfoot won't go in caves.

Tres: He won't bed down in them, a racial fear from way back.

Ida: I do not think I can trot out in the hills and find one little rock left as a marker of a space ship centuries ago.

Tres: You found the footprint in Hawaii.

Ida: That was not in a forest and a tangle of underbrush. It was on an open beach.

At top of Hamilton Dome petroglyph in Wyoming, arrow points to figure with large head and spindly legs standing   next to slender figure with small head and arms outstretched.   A thunderbird, who travels with thunder and lightning, is in the forefront. Photo by Ida Kannenberg.

Tres: And the fossil in Wyoming.

Ida: That was on a hillside, bare except for scraggly sagebrush. The finds there had evidently been ploughed out by a road grader.

Tres: What you need to find, you will find.

Ida: You haven't said yet that rocks are what I am looking for.

Tres: I think we will wait for Maez to return and finish this conversation.

Ida, 12/30/98: Okay. I'll go take a nap.

Last night I invaded my files and found photocopies of the golden plates I mention. These were accompanied by a letter from an epigrapher. He recognized that they were written in several different alphabets but that the language was all Shoshone-Ute. He said his comments were not meant for publication so I shall only add that the oldest alphabet was from 300 BCE.

In the same drawer I found a copy of the *A.R.E. Journal* for November 1979. It contains an interesting article by Ales

"Rock sculpture" on Wyoming-Colorado border compares with turtle.

sandro Talamonte on "Rock Sculptures, Lost Script of Primordial Civilizations." He quotes Edgar Cayce frequently.

Mr. Talamonte's thesis is that "rocks, hills, and mountains were hewn in symbolic forms, conveying instantly in their "plastic" presentation the meanings expressed."

Here are photos of two I found on the Wyoming-Colorado border. I think the wind did it.

Tres to Ida: You are understanding the idea of holographic projections as well as is necessary for the present, so put your book aside (*Holographic Universe* by Michael Talbot). We have other things to concentrate on this morning — today. Maez will be back in a day or two and your attempts to coax Wipi into cooperation will resume.

Meantime I want you to go through the pages of your original UFO manuscript, not all of which was published, and find some information. Skim through the pages quickly and I will tell you what to excerpt; there — page 162 from June 4, 1978.

Ida (Reading):

A "rock sculpture" on the Wyoming-Colorado border

"They (the UFO people) did live in this world, eons and eons ago. No, much longer than Atlantis. They were the first altogether "human" people. Now they live on a planet in a far galaxy." (Galaxy was later changed to constellation.)

"Are they like us?" I asked.

"Somewhat. Oh! They would like to return to Earth but have developed in a different environment. They are testing soil, atmosphere, etc. to see if they could survive here. We don't know how many there are. Gospel!" (Speakers are Jamie and Amorto.)

Tres: Copy the paragraph from June 12, 1978.

Ida (reading): (Hweig speaking)

"Our translation takes place, not in the sub-conscious of yourself but in an area existing outside us both into which we each contribute some "energy-essence" to make a third "something", a sphere of mental activity. And we do not understand what is taking place any more than you do. It has never happened like this before. We have always had to hypnotize or otherwise divert or disassociate the conscious attention of the receiver."

Tres: Does this suggest something to you, Ida?

Ida: Yes. It is holographic projection.

Tres: Splendid! Even the super brilliant communicators did not recognize that!

Ida: They didn't have our explanation as from the *Holographic Universe*. They probably have a different or more clarified explanation of holograms.

Tres: They should have recognized the similarities. What I want you to write here is how you prepare your mind for such an activity.

Ida: I totally relax my brain, let it lie perfectly still, and open my mind. I have practiced this since 1951.

Tres: We will discuss this thoroughly another time. Now go back to reading the original manuscript.

Excerpt:

We all exist in geometric time and in each area of time our being is different.

Tres: That is all we need from the manuscript at present. Your book *Project Earth* reveals most of the rest.

Ida, 12/31/98: Wait. There was something else about holograms. It was not entered into *Project Earth*.

Hweig dictating:

"Mind is a different thing altogether from brain function.

"Mind is a "thing in itself" and lies over the mechanism of the brain in a complex array of patterns and images. It is, in essence an energized field on which thoughts and concepts play in ever changing designs. The "field" itself is composed of minute particles, not quite physical substance but not wholly energy, a substance that is found nowhere else in nature. It is not physical enough to be detected by the usual means of detecting physicality but not enough pure energy to be detected by the usual means of detecting energies. Lying in nature halfway between the two there is only one way of discovering its reality other than by simply using it.

"Alpha rays, beta rays, all the rest are results of brain activity. Mind is not brain activity, though brain functions feed the mind with vibrations accrued from stimuli in the physical world.

"The only means of observing the mind stuff is through use of a hologram. It can be so projected as a visible field of actively changing patterns, and the patterns can be tabulated and translated, or in other words this is visible mind reading.

"The holograph projector is similar to that used to project pictures of physical objects with one more feature added which holographic projectors at present lack. By utilizing the additional energy of the laser beam as a high energy compacter, the visual process accrues. Let your world figure that out! All the clues are here." (June 1, 1979)

Ida, 1/1/99: On this last day of the year I would like to add a note or two to our general conversations. I have come to my own conclusion that Bigfoot is not so much psychic as spiritual. This is how I would describe myself. People call me "psychic," but I am not what is usually meant by that. Both Bigfoot and I have implants from the Arcturians that allow them to see whatever we see and to hear whatever we hear — so they tell me. Our telepathic abilities are normal physical abilities that everyone has if developed and used. The implants amplify those abilities through microwaves, but do not create them.

Both Bigfoot and I have a high intuitive sense that has nothing to do with intelligence, but allows us to draw directly from the SEA OF CONSCIOUSNESS that surrounds us. (We, everyone, everything swims in it.) The sea is God consciousness, the Mind of God, or whatever synonym we want to use for God, Spirit, Energy, or Thought.

Bigfoot and I draw directly from that Sea of Consciousness. Everyone can, but many have not learned how to evade the worries that clog the receptors.

Bigfoot does not worry about his nine-to-five job, his mortgage, the condition of his car, his housekeeping. He follows his monitor's instructions to go here and do that with perfect faith he will be guided and protected. What questions he has are answered by drawing what he can understand from the sea of information intuitively and effortlessly. I am not quite so free. And I argue. I am skeptical and afraid.

Tres to Ida, 1/1/99: Yes, I will answer Krsanna's request for information on the Sphinx. She is correct that the unusual event at sunrise was a kind of symbol. The sun touching the shoulders of the Sphinx alternately signifies a time of balancing. Reconciliation implies balancing of debits and credits in all spheres of life from relationships to bank accounts. The return to Earth of The One Expected in a way *not at once apparent* set free the Force of Reconciliation.

We do not call it Judgment. That word is too scarifying to too many people. It sends them into tremblings and worryings, nightmares and nervous breakdowns.

Judgment is at one with the act or event committed whatever it might be. A lessening of the Self goes right along with a "bad" action, a built-in punishment, usually accompanied more or less by a sense of guilt, shame, remorse that can haunt until the last day on Earth. One drops this mantle of self-conceived sin and disgrace at heaven's door and walks free and beautiful into the light.

This is not a time of judgment, but of Reconciliation, of balancing.

Maez to Ida: A happy and prosperous New Year to you and yours.

Ida: Thank you. The same to you and your people. I'm glad you're back.

Maez: Will you please write in here those paragraphs you were reading from your lengthy manuscript? Page 578: Hweig dictating:

"We have found that too close use of the laser beam is imprudent because people of the Earth do not have the necessary pigments. Your Native American Indians have the most protective skins. The copper colored pigment is Earth's best substitute for the actually colorless pigment which protects fully from the laser beam.

'The American Indian has great psychic abilities. We have had various contacts with them over many centuries, but their knowledge of us was obscured by their ideas of spiritual forces. Among all the peoples at present on Earth, the American Indian has the closest relationship to our past. This is purposely left an enigmatic statement."

Maez to Ida: All right, now you know why your Native American Indians claim to have contact with the "Sky People" and Bigfoot. They do. Now, Ida, I want you to write into these notes the several accounts of your experiences of the past which were directly, or indirectly, connected in some, however oblique manner, with Native Americans. You may think these incidences have nothing to do with your present study of Bigfoot, but believe me, they do. In fact, just about everything that has happened to you, or that you have done in your entire life was leading up to this study. You have already mentioned that you have begun to see connections between many of the events of the past which were obscure before. Please begin.

Ida: I will have to take a pause to rake all of my related thoughts and memories together. I have never piled them all in one heap before.

Maez: Take a day or two — or three. Try to get it all together in one place.

Ida: Whoa! Can the exact place a Bigfoot is centered on be a spot that, in some fashion, is held sacred by the Indians? Is that why Indians were — are — particularly attracted to natural rocks or hills that resemble some animal or figure, or a place where a spiritual or super-natural event occurred?

Maez: There is a connection — Yes!

Ida: You're holding back.

Maez: For the time, yes! Go on with your assignment.

Ida: This will take some time. In the meantime I've been thinking of something else.

Maez: Yes?

Ida: In talking about the golden tablets written in the Shoshoni-Ute language, the epigrapher had noted that these were written in several different alphabets. One was Korean as used in 300 BCE. How did the ones speaking Shoshoni-Ute learn ancient Korean?

Maez: Indeed, how?

Ida: Isn't there a story about a long ago Chinese expedition that went from Western Canada all the way down the Western United States coast and into South America? I believe it was followed up by a second expedition later. A Korean could have accompanied one of those journeys and maybe stayed with the Indians long enough to teach them his manner of writing.

Maez: Certainly a possibility. Do you have a book on those expeditions?

Ida: There is a short narrative mentioning it in some book, but I can't remember which one. I'll try to find it. We're getting far afield from Bigfoot.

Maez, 1/2/99: Not as far as you think!

Maez to Ida, 1/4/99: Don't worry if you can't find the narrative on the Chinese expedition. It will turn up. We have left several subjects hanging in the air. I want to catch these up to date.

You asked Tres if rocks were what you were looking for. He was not sure how much I wanted to disclose now. You need not go looking for anything. Your former little trips of exploration have clued you in to all you need to know. When you finish your story of your Indian connections you will be able to see a pattern of meaning. Then we will analyze, discuss, and go on from there. When you get your computer you will be able to draw in much information.

Another topic we did not finish and can be better clarified now is the question of Wipi's reluctance to meet with you. He sensed, Ida, that you were a little hesitant about the idea of meeting him face to face. Tres told you away back in November that you may have to meet up with an adult male Bigfoot before this was all over. Wipi is now aware that you and Mr. T. have been chosen by us, his monitors, to meet with him. He may astonish you by his appearance but he will offer no harm or offense. Have no fear. He is as anxious to be proven "true" and "human" as you are to prove him so. I am working now with him to encourage him to accept cameras. I can't promise anything, but give me a little more time to convince him that you in return will offer no harm or offense. We want this meeting to be on a basis of understanding not just a hasty sighting of each other. It will take preparation on both sides. Wipi is not just any Bigfoot. He is a prime example of his kind, and a prodigy of intelligence. He has a prankish kind of humor but I doubt he will exhibit it on a serious first meeting.

Do stop scratching yourself red. You are allergic to your cat. Poor Lord Spike! Take a shower and apply aloe vera lotion. That's the best I can advise.

Ida:

Narrative on Contacts or Connections

with Native Americans

January 3, 1999

I can see how some of it connects with Bigfoot, but I don't see how it will be very useful to us in our current study. Maybe it will.

"Patience," says Maez. "There are more vital connections than you can now see."

Okay. I'll wait.

My lifelong interest in Native Americans was first aroused about age seven by the stories my father would tell of having lived in close association with the Chippewa Indians of Minnesota when he was in his late twenties and thirties. He had learned many crafts and outdoor survival techniques and could speak Chippewa. He taught me the word for "coffee". I don't know how to spell it, but it sounded like "katamosskeekeewaboo". I bragged to the kids at school that I could speak Indian. I was nearly fifty years old before I learned that my father had been married once before to a young girl of French Canadian and Chippewa heritage. This wife and their baby daughter had died during a typhoid epidemic in Kent, Washington in the first half of the first decade of the twentieth century.

Beaver Grove-Wedauvoo, Laramie, Wyoming

I do not recall any other Native American contact until we moved from Iowa to Arizona in 1928. Tucson had many Indians in residence and from-out-of-town Saturday shoppers. A friend of my father's cousin was half-Sioux and half-Scotsman, and kept what was then called a "curio" store. He sold Indian crafts, rugs, baskets, pottery. It was a great factor in getting our family through the depression when he gave my carpenter father work re-constructing ranch buildings for him, and work to my mother in his shop.

In my junior year in high school (1930) there were two Native American girls in one of my classes. Our teacher took us to the museum at the University of Arizona.

While the teacher was pontificating at one side of the room to the rest of the class, I was attracted by a large oil painting and walked to the other side of the room to view it more closely. It was a portrait of an elderly Indian man seated in full regalia and looking very tired actually, but self-contained, patient and proud, and quite impressive. I felt someone walk up beside me but I did not take my eyes off the portrait. "Doesn't he look wise?" I asked.

Another perspective on Beaver Grove.

The someone chuckled; it was one of the Indian girls. "That's my great-grandfather," she said.

Whew! Was I relieved that I had said "wise" and not "tired"!

Some of my contacts may seem rather vague or remote, but they were important enough to me to be remembered all these years.

Later in life (1945) I moved to the Pacific Northwest and have lived here most of the time since. In May 1982 my daughter and I had the opportunity to fly to Denver, rent a car, and spend a number of days visiting towns south of Denver, taking pictures of the countryside, and looking for historical places and petroglyphs. We visited Denver's magnificent Natural History Museum, then towns such as Colorado Springs, Manitou Springs, Cripple Creek, Victor, Pueblo, Canon City, Florence (The Royal Gorge), Salida, and Fair Play.

A little later, in the last of June 1982, we went to the Contactee Conference in Laramie, Wyoming. We took time out to visit the park that was the site of huge interesting rocks and

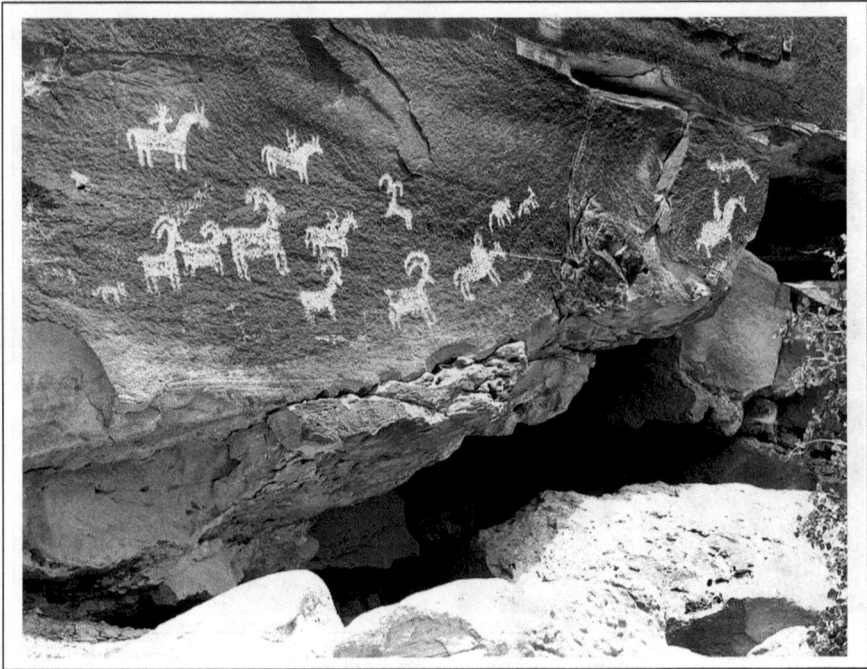

Ute rock art from Arches National Park, Utah.

strangely shaped rocky hills, Wedauvoo, a place that was sacred to the Indians. They called it, "The place where spirits are born".

As we circled the main formations on a side road I suddenly became immensely interested in beavers and started taking photos of ponds and dams and I told my daughter, "I have photos of everything now except one of those little groves where beavers have been cutting down trees."

"When you see such a place yell, 'Stop!'" she said. "I have to watch this road."

I saw. I yelled. She stopped.

"Oh, there's that such-and-such bird," she exclaimed, jumping out of the car. "I need a picture of it for that wildlife article I'm writing."

She went trotting off down a side path leaving me to enter alone the little grove of aspen trees, many chewed down to stumps.

But when I reached the edge of the grove my feet stuck to the ground. I could not make myself go in.

"You are welcome here," said a deep, very kind voice. "This is my sacred grove, but because you are who you are, you may enter here. And because your daughter is your daughter she may enter also."

"Thank you," I said, totally bewildered. There was no one anywhere around. "May I ask who speaks?"

"I am Grandfather Beaver. I am the spirit of all Beaver." "I am honored." I did not know what else to say.

"From this day forward you are of the Beaver," went on the voice. I did not know how to continue the conversation, so I asked timidly, "May I take pictures here?"

"Because you are who you are, you may take pictures here. And because your daughter is your daughter, she may take pictures also." The tones were measured and solemn.

There was more conversation but I do not remember it now. I know that I was given a totem, the Beaver.

When we returned to Laramie I was nervous and restless. About noon on Saturday we deserted the conference and took off in our rental car to explore Wyoming. We had no intentions of doing so when we left home. We went north from

Laramie and explored the country around Guernsey, Newcastle, Gillette, Buffalo, Sheridan, Greybull, Cody (and the Buffalo Bill Museum with its breathtaking collection of Indian Beadwork), Hamilton Dome, Thermopolis (where they had just had a hailstorm that completely denuded the cottonwood trees of all their leaves), Moneta, Casper, and Rawlins.

At Hamilton Dome we met a delightful lady postmistress. She phoned her son to bring his truck, closed up the post office, and took us over an unbelievable road swamped by a recent rainfall, to see some amazing petroglyphs, now watched over by the Arapahos. A serious young Arapaho friend had told her, "The Sky People came down and devastated this land." He also informed her, "Back in the canyons there are miles and miles of fantastic pictures and petroglyphs." He had offered to take her there, but she said he rode his truck like a bucking bronco and she had not yet gained enough nerve to accept his invitation. I envied her. We had to be content with the local petroglyphs which were scaling from the red sandstone, spalls I think they are called. One picture was a large tur-

Octopus tree

SITKA SPRUCE
(PICEA SITCHENSIS)

THIS GIANT OLD SITKA SPRUCE DID NOT DEVELOP
INTO A MASSIVE SINGLE TRUNKED TREE AS MOST
SPRUCE TREES DO ALONG THE OREGON COAST.
THE CANDELABRA BRANCHING AND UNUSUAL SIZE
OF THIS SPRUCE TREE WERE FORMED BY STRONG
COASTAL WINDS AND THE SHELTERED HOLLOW OF
ITS LOCATION. EACH OF THE SIX CANDELABRA
LIMBS ARE AT LEAST 12 FEET AROUND AND
EXTEND HORIZONTALLY FROM THE MAIN TRUNK AS
MUCH AS 30 FEET BEFORE TURNING UPWARD
THE BASE OF THE TREE HAS A CIRCUMFERENCE
OF ABOUT 50 FEET.

tle. The Arapaho youth told the post mistress, "Where there is the sign of the turtle, there is safety."

I wished we had more time to follow up some of this information, but our time was limited. My mother, at 94, was quite frail and we could not stay away long. We did spend a full day studying and taking pictures of the petroglyphs near

Moneta, and then headed for home. The best part of our Wyoming visit was that we made some good friends.

I had become quite interested in trying to decipher messages written in symbols other than alphabets. I bought a number of books on the subject. In 1981 one of my Wyoming friends had sent me a drawing of some symbols received by a friend of hers from an unknown source, and with the help of a book on deciphering Indian petroglyphs I was able to make something out of it.

My next contact with anything pertaining to Native American was when another friend from Wyoming sent me symbols copied from a piece of shard given her by an Indian woman who said she had found it at Pueblo Bonito. This was late 1983 and my decipherment took me into 1984. For several reasons I cannot include picture or decipherment here.

On the coast of Oregon near Cape Mears there is a State park that contains a wonderful old tree called the Octopus Tree,

because of the many huge limbs branching upward from the ground. One of its thick branches has now broken off due to unfortunate conditions of weight and old age. It was still in its full and unbroken glory when my daughter took her daughter, my husband, and myself on a Sunday outing to see the old tree. It had long been a sacred meeting place for Indian shamans.

As we walked up the path my husband complained of a pebble in his shoe and he turned aside to a bench to sit down and remove his shoe. My daughter and her daughter went on to a fence over the sea-cliff to consult about some personal affairs. That left me to come up to the tree alone.

"She is coming now," I heard a bodiless voice say. "This is the one we have waited for."

I left the path and went around behind the tree. I had an impression (not a vision) of a semi-circle of Indian shamans, both men and women, on the slope behind the tree.

"We have been waiting for you," went on the voice. I had no idea how to respond. "Yes?" I asked.

"You are the one who will speak for us in the council halls."

"I will be happy to do so. But I do not know what this is all about. What am I to say?"

"You will be taught all you need to know."

There was further attempt at conversation but the mysterious voice was drowned out by the other members of our party coming up with their calls and chatter.

"I can't hear you," I murmured desperately.

I don't know what else was intended for me and I worried about it. Several years later I was visiting in Phoenix, Arizona where I met a lady shaman from South Dakota who was teaching there. I told her about my dilemma. "I feel I have let them down. I have not kept my promise."

"Oh, but you have!" she exclaimed. "The books you are writing are keeping your promise." I asked the lady shaman if she had any knowledge of Bigfoot.

"Yes, my people have had interaction with Bigfoot for generations," she said. "When one of our men is injured while out hunting, Bigfoot will come and carry the man to his nest. He will see that the man has water and food and that no animal like a cougar disturbs him until he is well enough to take care of himself. Then Bigfoot will take the man back to the exact spot where he found him and leave him there. We consider Bigfoot to be our brother."

The next thing that in any way pertained to Native Americans was the opportunity for my daughter and myself to photograph a fine collection of Kachina figures. Nothing has been done with the photos as yet.

During my 18 months stay in Laramie after my husband died in 1988, a friend, Doree, and I spent much time visiting museums around the state and in Denver to study Indian artifacts and arts.

When I returned to Oregon in 1990, I made a nice collection of pottery and baskets but finally sold most of it as I could not keep up with escalating prices on such art objects. I did keep some beads.

I have several good friends and acquaintances who proudly claim some Native American inheritance.

Oh yes, once some mysterious inner voice said that because of my empathy for and interest in Native Americans and others that I was to be given the name of "Princess One-heart", meaning that I had one heart for all peoples. I protested at the status elevation until they agreed to lower it to just "Ida One-Heart."

At this time I do not think of any other personal contact or connection with Native Americans.

Ida to Maez: Okay. I've finished my narrative on Native American contacts and connections.

Maez: Have you discovered anything?

Ida: I have questions. When the voice at the Octopus Tree said I was to speak for them (shamans? or Indians in general?) did they mean I was to speak to your council on the Arcturian planet on their behalf?

Maez: That is precisely what they meant.

Ida: Why has it taken me so many years to realize what was meant?

Maez: Because you were not given a clear understanding of our Council and its purposes until now.

Ida: You really lay your eggs a long time before they are expected to hatch!

Ida, 1/4/99: The following is relative to the message received by telepathy by a girl in Wyoming and sent to me to decipher.

I used as a basis for my translation a book written by LaVan Martineau. An excerpt:

"Logic and common sense play an intrinsic role in the reading of Indian pictography. It was assumed by the Indian authors that readers would employ their mental talents in obtaining their message. The pictography is not a system devised for the mentally lazy, nor is it something to be learned or read by rote as easily as an alphabetical system. Indian pictography with its thousands of phrase possibilities which can be constructed from a few hundred basic symbols necessarily and consistently demands the efforts and logic of the human mind. Out of its limitless possibilities, many phrases are bound to be new to any reader and thus require his mental application to decipher them.

"Message received, recipient unknown to me at the time.

"I derived tense from the placement in the line and the directions the symbols pointed. This translation is by no means perfect nor complete but it gives the gist of the message.

"War is approaching. Turn aside from the way you are headed. Improve yourself. Cease waiting for divine intervention. We have come and gone many times pouring our aid upon the Earth. It was turned aside into the depths of darkness and hidden from sight. As instruments we descend from those higher than we. We came across space many times in the past, piercing the dark cloud of interstellar space. Our way was blocked more than once but still we persevere. We come from those higher than we. The seeds of war must be stopped. Your nuclear energy is designed toward killing. It falls short of its potential. It indicates here that very shortly a cloud of energy arising will bar your way across space. Science must arise step by step, pointing the way, averting emergencies. In this way the good peace, the healing necessity will come from Science. Here, from our level of being, we have come down and are not far away. We crossed open (outer?) space. We want to speak straight forwardly about the following: It was a long journey to observe more closely your science of nuclear energy. This has dangerous areas. It is in an objectionable place. You are funneling (your energies) into wrong directions. Change directions and expand, or the planet will be divided (damaged?) and areas of life energies destroyed."

Ida: Oh, of course, stupid Ida! These are the same symbols used by Maez and party to communicate with Bigfoot! They are the symbols of pictorial telepathy as they have evolved from all picture symbols. Right, Maez?

Maez: Perfect. You see what a little patience and thinking can do? Be patient. You will understand everything in time.

Ida: I don't know if my brain can stand so much wear and tear.

Maez: Mind, Ida, mind not brain. The brain sees and sorts things out categorically. The mind understands and reveals.

Ida: Oh!

Letter from Lee Trippett to Ida

January 4 1999

Hello, Ida,

Hope you find no further allergy with Spike. Hope also you find peace with all the things your communicators are requesting.

In your last two letters I find more challenge and understanding to meet with the responsibility of establishing solid visual contact with Wipi.

In your *Project Earth*, page 224:

"3. Sasquatch are indeed their creatures, let out upon the Earth to test energies emitted from the ground or Earth itself. We do not recognize these energies although they work upon us, sometimes quite detrimentally. Sasquatch is not an ape, not human, but a biological creation about halfway between the two with no biological connection to either. It is not a "missing link." The creatures are mild, unless startled with their young. They have been unloaded here for years, and now have acclimated and oriented themselves. They do have offspring, but rarely. They are monitored by pictorial telepathy."

May I ask these questions?

What are the significant internal anatomical, mental, and emotional differences between Bigfoot, animal, and human?

Sulfur dome, Thermopolis, Wyoming, 1982

If we cannot recognize those earthly energies that work upon us and which Bigfoot monitors, how can we understand the placement or position of Bigfoot on Earth? Can the proximity and unique energy of Wipi's presence lead to an imbalance in my own internal and emotional energies?

Best wishes to you and your friends, Mr. T. (Lee)

Maez to Ida: I'm glad you took time to sort over your photographs although it set us back a day or two. I don't see how you can read six books at once!

Ida: I'm not really. I've read them all before, now I am just picking out references piece-meal. Oh dear, here comes Spike for lunch.

Maez: Go eat.

Ida (later): If you don't mind me finishing my chicken broth, we can continue. I have a question.

When I was in the beaver grove at Wedauvoo, the voice said, "Because you are who you are..." this has always puzzled me. I could not think of any meaning. But as I was writing my narrative I noticed he had specifically pointed to the idea

Sulfur Springs, Thermopolis, Wyoming, 1982

of relationships when he said, "And because your daughter is your daughter".

Could he have been thinking of my relationship to my father who had such close contact and so much respect for Native Americans?

Maez: That is precisely what he meant. Are you beginning to find answers to some of your puzzlements now?

Ida: And how! Somehow I feel incredibly happy about that meaning.

Maez: Of course you would be. The long story you wrote about your family shows your father to have been an impeccably loving person. You had a deep attachment.

Ida: He was my refuge, just his presence. We never talked much.

Maez: You didn't need to. Now back to work.

First you are right, you were wrong. Those are aspen trees as you just remembered, not alder trees, in the beaver grove.

Second, to answer Mr. T's questions in the letter just received.

Hweig did say, "Sasquatch is not ape, not human, but a biological creation about halfway between the two, with no biological connection to either". He was referring to your present day Earth type humans. We and Wipi refers to himself as derived from the human Masters of the Arcturian race. They do have connections with the *early* Earth humans. So to say Sasquatch has no biological connection with humans is not entirely true, but Hweig could not take time nor authority to explain the whole truth so he condensed it a little too much. Wipi considers himself "almost" Earth human and we encourage him in that.

Mr. T's first question would require a year to answer adequately. But I will attempt an abbreviated answer to his very good and perceptive query.

Bigfoot's internal anatomical differences with humans are mainly his digestive abilities. Your highly refined and altered foods would make him ill, i.e., chocolate, sugar, fried foods, in fact most cooked foods, meat especially, frosted cakes, milk altered in any way such as homogenizing or pasteurizing. I can't begin to think of all the foods that would be a no-no to him. He could eat something made of cornmeal but very little with white refined wheat flour. A box of Whitman's Sampler chocolates would probably kill him. He is engineered to eat entirely natural, very simple foods, not cooked. He has strong jaws and can masticate tough grasses and roots if nothing better is available.

His vision is far better than man's and he can see just as well at night with only a glimmer of light as he can by daylight. His hearing is better than a cat's and that is already twenty times better than a man's.

His heart is stronger, beats faster than a man's and never gets clogged up in its distributions by cholesterol. His muscular system is considerably tougher, his lungs are larger in comparison; he can run all day at great pace and not seem to tire. He can lift great weights and carry them all day but he doesn't see much reason to do so.

In short, he is built tough, strong, and enduring and he lives a natural life, that is, one in accordance to his nature, so that he is very seldom ill.

Bigfoot is immune to almost all types of human diseases. He could never catch chicken pox or whooping cough or tuberculosis. Lyme disease ticks, Rocky Mountain fever ticks, bubonic plague bearing fleas do not faze him. He has inbuilt resistance to such ills. If he receives a bad wound and it becomes infected he can develop blood poisoning, gangrene. Or he can eat or drink something that would make him sick for a short time. His keen sense of smell usually warns him against such contamination.

His internal organs, spleen, liver, kidneys and all such, have been simplified in relation to each other. Although simplified, the explanation would be complex. Maybe another time.

Mentally and emotionally the greatest difference between Bigfoot and animals is that he is more nearly like man. He is conscious of his own consciousness, which no animal is. He recognizes the idea of God, which no animal does. He could, if taught, learn to speak words, which no animal does and understands their meaning. A parrot speaks by imitation, not understanding.

Compared to man he is not, as we said once, sophisticated. He is an innocent. He has no sense of crime or violence for its own sake. He can fight to protect himself or family, but won't to take something away from another. He has no impulse to power. He would not comprehend fighting to be the first in anything. He can show a tad of jealousy in a case of preference. His only ambition is to carry out a task he has been given, to please his monitor. He can develop a strong attachment to mate, children, friends, even his monitor. He is altogether loyal to such an attachment.

I'm not too sure exactly how — in what manner — Wipi recognizes the existence of God. I sometimes think he confuses me with God, but then I am made aware that he does not. I am simply a model for what he understands God to be, a protector and helper. His idea is much more elevated than I could hope to fulfill. He knows it is God who makes his life possible, who has made the things he requires to live, i.e., food, water, shelter. And that it has been provided for everyone and everything that lives. All have been provided for by the foresight and understanding of a Great Power. I'm not sure that he would know what we mean by "spirit". I'm not sure that we do. Mr. T's second question is well deserved. "How can you understand or locate precisely Bigfoot's placement when you don't recognize the energies he is monitoring?" Good question. Well Ida, you have shown yourself to be something of a sleuth. How would you find an answer to this?

Ida: For one thing it was mentioned that one such place had to do with sulfur springs, such as my daughter and I saw in Thermopolis, Wyoming in 1982.

Once I was given a cure for arthritis and it worked. But then a law was passed that one of the ingredients, sulfur, could not be sold without a doctor's prescription and I couldn't convince a doctor to give me one. I was thinking I would go to a veterinarian and tell him it was for my horse, which I didn't have, but I never did.

Maez: Fortunately for you. A little sulfur for a short period does help. But too much for too long a time would melt your bones.

Ida: That recipe was an old Indian cure.

Maez: They know how much to use. So what about other "Earthly energies"?

Let's hold off on doing more until tomorrow. Don't you have a TV show?

Ida: I think I'll go to bed instead. Oh yes, I wanted to explain the name Hamilton Dome. My daughter and I kept looking for a hill or mountain that might look like a dome, but the postmistress told us it was an oil "dome" underneath the ground from which they were pumping oil.

Maez, 1/7/99: You can't always trust names. Look at the Pacific Ocean.

Ida: I'm early. Lord Spike thinks the "first crack of dawn" and "breakfast time" are synonyms.

Maez: He's good for something.

Ida: But think of summer! He will expect me to get up at five A.M.!

Maez: You sleep too much anyway.

Ida: I was born six weeks prematurely and I've never caught up with the six weeks sleep I missed.

Maez: Any excuse! Shall we get to work? We were discussing Earth's energies that your people do not recognize. They are beginning to discover more of these.

Ida: I was thinking of magnetic lines. Once Hweig told me that UFO's chose "to come in" over magnetic lines or over underground swift flowing streams of water. These would probably be two of Bigfoot's observations.

Maez: Very good. They were in the beginning, but we have all of that mapped now. There are occasional changes as Earth itself undergoes great upheavals or changes, but it is no longer necessary for Bigfoot to monitor them constantly.

Ida: I'm sure he monitors fault lines. They must emit certain indications of underground energies as the tectonic plates move.

Maez: Yes, of course. That is one of Bigfoot's most constant chores along with volcanic disturbances in the high mountains. You have already noted these.

Ida: Why do you make me work my mind so hard? You could just tell me the answers.

Maez: Because if you dig out the answers yourself, you believe them. If I tell you, you are skeptical.

Ida: Score!

Ley Lines

Maez: Probe that mind a little further. What else can you suggest as Earth energies not fully understood?

Ida: Ley lines, such as in England.

Maez: So called 'ley' lines are everywhere, not only in England. But what are they?

Ida: I read this somewhere but I can't remember where: specialized energies or combinations of energies, gravitational energies, electricity, and magnetism. Such energies or combination of such energies emitted from the Earth in waves of informational frequencies can strike chords of resonance in one constructed to receive it, and thus convey intended information to him. (I don't know where that came from).

Maez: What kind of information would Bigfoot be listening for, or resonate to?

Ida: The health of the planet, its balance or imbalance relative to the universal equilibrium; such things. The energies mentioned are simply kinds of connectives bringing information from Earth itself to the listener, Bigfoot or other.

Maez: You have the general idea but I would like the specific energies to be more exactly related.

Ida: How would I know when they are supposed to be energies we know nothing about? If the old Earth gives a burp or two now and then I don't know what she's been eating. Gas, oil, gold? I really don't know what I'm talking about. I heard it all somewhere.

Maez, 1/8/99: Well, go watch TV. By tomorrow you may have thought of something.

Ida to Maez: I've been digging in the files for related information. I did not sleep late.

Maez: I think you left the cat in a file drawer.

Ida: He will get out when he's ready. He will have to; he's not in alphabetical order.

Maez: Did you find anything of interest?

Ida: .The Chinese Dragon's Path. But I've been thinking about the sounds the Earth emits. I don't know how musical they would be to our ears if we could hear them, but they must have an identifiable cause.

Maez: So they do. And that is one of the things Bigfoot is alert to, sounds the planet is making. You could hear some of them if you schooled yourself to listen.

Ida: Also I found information on the Oregon Vortex. It is between Medford and Grant's Pass near Gold Hill. I think that explains one of the markers we placed on the map for Bigfoot's presence nearby.

Maez: It does. Mr. T. mentioned that.

Ida: That's why I looked for it. Well, the energies you want me to find could be what some writers — Churchward, Williamson, et al. — call the four great primary forces, i.e., static magnetic field, electro-static field, electro-magnetic wave, and the resonating electric-magnetic field. These forces or energies were referred to in ancient beliefs as the Four Great Builders, or the Four Great Architects, or the Four Great Geometricians or even the Elohim and Seraphs (by the Hebrews). This explanation is derived from George Hunt Williamson's book *Other Tongues, Other Flesh.* Are these the energies you wanted, Maez?

Maez, 1/9/99: Yes, that encompasses what you said yesterday and today but a little more plainly and in relation to ancient understanding. We are not now going to get any more deeply involved in all of this. We have been trying to give Mr. T. an answer to his second question, however incomplete it must remain for the present. Now for his third question, "Will the close proximity and unique energy of Wipi's presence lead to an imbalance in my own internal mental and emotional energies?" I can understand Mr. T's concern.

Your concern, Ida, was: were we or were we not telling the truth about ourselves and our intentions. You seem to have corralled your skepticism fairly well by now, although it has taken nearly twenty years. Mr. T's concern is of another nature. Can he come to mental or emotional harm if he plays around with the strange energies that close and prolonged association with Wipi, myself and you provide? We three are using strong, powerful and unusual energies to be sure, but they are not unnatural.

If Mr. T. continues to center himself in God-relatedness, he can come to no harm, because that is where we are located, only our aspects are not exactly ordinary.

Mr. T. has total free will at all times. Any time he feels the least bit nervous, he should withdraw from this study for a few days, concentrate entirely on other things, and then take a little time to re-center himself in God before he comes back to this occupation. It is easy, as you well know, Ida to become too fearful that one has become obsessed or too compulsive or is impelled by outside forces. When this fear strikes, withdraw, think of other things, get re-centered in self and God.

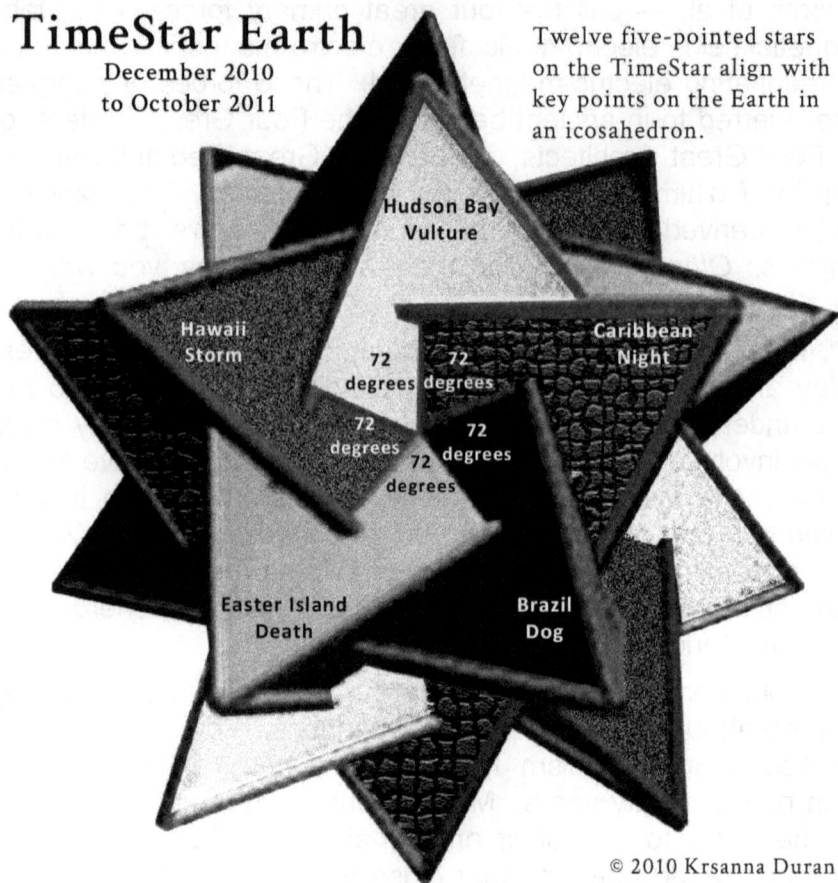

TimeStar Earth
December 2010
to October 2011

Twelve five-pointed stars on the TimeStar align with key points on the Earth in an icosahedron.

Hudson Bay
Vulture

Hawaii
Storm

Caribbean
Night

72 degrees 72 degrees

72 degrees 72 degrees

72 degrees

Easter Island
Death

Brazil
Dog

© 2010 Krsanna Duran

Geometry of earth grid comprising five tetrahedra interpenetrated, as time travelers explained to Krsanna Duran. Dog, Night, Vulture, Storm and Death are calendar glyphs aligned with planetary grid geometry.

This is one of the reasons we are going so slowly in making contact, even an evasive one with Wipi. We all need to be solid in our convictions that we are doing a positive thing. That includes myself.

Maez to Ida: You've been thinking again. This is getting to be a habit.

Ida: You're being sarcastic.

Maez: But you hate flattery. I was trying the opposite.

Ida: You're succeeding. Now I've forgotten what I was thinking about.

Maez: Ley lines and such.

Ida: Oh, yes. North-south lines might be magnetic. East-west lines gravitational, or west-east as the Earth turns. The electric field could be everywhere constant (the informational field mentioned a few days ago). Where North/South lines and East/West lines cross are power points and that is where areas sacred to Native Americans (and others elsewhere) are located. But how do we find where these lines are? The ancients built such edifices as the Great Pyramid and Stonehenge at such crossings. And probably also some of the pyramids of Mexico and other places we don't know about. Do these lines have any respect to our latitude and longitude measurements?

Maez: Wow! You've been on a thinking binge. I am leaving now for a two-day project elsewhere. I'll answer your questions on Monday if you haven't discovered facts otherwise. You're on the right track.

Ida: Krsanna was there first. I'll have to find some of her explanations.

Maez: Who is Krsanna?

Ida: A dear friend. She has some Native American heritage, which she cherishes, and a brilliant scientific mind. Mathematics is Greek to me. She uses it like an Einstein.

Tres: Maez is gone for a bit. You had a question?

Ida: Not a question, a puzzlement. Maez and I were talking about ley lines and that North/South lines are magnetic and W/E lines are of gravitational forces and their interaction with the surrounding "sea of information" which must be electricity of a kind.

Tres: So it is. Cosmic electricity.

Ida: That gives us some form of three of the Great Builders or Geometricians, but the fourth one — the resonating electric-magnetic force — where does that come in?

Tres: Indeed, where? Think!

Ida: Could it be the person, the living being that stands on the intersecting N/S and W/E lines? Are WE the resonating electromagnetic fields? Well, of course we are! The brain is the electro, the mind the magnetic field.

Tres: Welcome home, Ida!

Ida: Everyone?

Tres: To varying degrees. That is, they are able to accept themselves in that aspect in varying degrees, and to that degree use the power it invokes.

Ida: Power?

Tres: Believe it!

Ida: To what do we resonate? Oh, God! That was a stupid question.

Tres: To what then?

Ida: I already said it. To the sea of information — the electric sea of God's consciousness that surrounds us — Supra-consciousness.

Tres: Meditate on that awhile. You've just uncovered a spectacular truth. Now what are you stewing about?

Ida, 1/10/99: Telepathy. See you tomorrow.

Tres to Ida: Sorry to interrupt your reading about Edgar Cayce but we left some things hanging yesterday. No, not telepathy, but ley lines or lines of force, N/S and W/E.

Since these lines cross each other at power points, your friend Krsanna was right in pin pointing the Great Pyramid as the Earth's major power point as marked by man. Who could better know where to place it than Thoth (Hermes) its architect? Krsanna has found a unique and brilliant use for combining lines of force with the timing of the Maya calendar in a way that allows her to predict coming earth events — earthquakes, volcanoes, storms, floods, etc.

Let us leave this research to her genius and we shall take another tack.

Krsanna has taken the map's lines of latitude and longitude to keep track of her prediction points and to point out the placement of crop circles relative to such power points as the great pyramid, the pyramids and other markers at Teotihuacán. A brilliant piece of work. It should (and will be) better known.

We shall not intrude upon her domain but use our recognition of power points and lines in a different fashion and for a different purpose, although we must necessarily recognize the same major points. But differently.

The lines of force we are following are magnetic N/S and gravitational W/E. These are not always as stable as the lines of latitude and longitude on a map due to the tilt of the Earth and other erratic things we will discuss later. Yes, this does have to do with Bigfoot, be patient. And they are not as mathematically straight as lines on a map. They seem to wander and waver sometimes due to interfering lines of cosmic force (electricity). We will get into all this as we go along. And it does have to do with the placement of Bigfoot. He is far more important than just being a biological unique specimen. He has been engineered to do specific work and he does it well. Those hunters who go out into the forest to see or photograph or even shoot or capture Bigfoot have not a glimmer of his true importance.

Maez to Ida, 1/11/99: My project turned out very well and I see you and Tres have been busy in my absence.

I think we will drop the subject of ley lines and power points for the present. Other things are more urgent.

Whoever plans an expedition or journey of exploration begins his preparation a year or two in advance. We don't need that much time, but the first requisite always is to learn as much as possible about the object or subject you are pursuing.

Mr. T. has probably read every book or paper ever published on Bigfoot, but we must hasten to let you learn some of the now believed "facts". I am glad you received a copy of Jack Lapseritis' book while I was gone. Read it carefully. Jack is 100% sincere. That does not mean he is always 100% right. But he never finagles facts for his own purposes and he carefully distinguishes between observation and speculation.

One thing we left hanging in the air was telepathy. Did you have a question?

Ida: An observation. We've been talking about Bigfoot not using words but a pictorial telepathy to communicate. Yet Jack's book tells of several persons receiving telepathic messages or having telepathic conversations with Bigfoot. Hweig explained to me, that no matter what the language form used by the sender, what actually was transmitted was a thought vibration. The receiver automatically translates or interprets that thought vibration into his own manner of speech. This is why, even though Bigfoot does not use our kind of verbal speech he can telepath understandable messages to us. We translate.

Maez: Very good. I can see how there could be confusion of understanding without this explanation. Thank you.

Ida: Recently I received an advertising letter for investment in the "new technology." One new tech is "voice command". You can not only instruct your computer to do the typing for you, but it will translate it into the receiver's language. Are we just catching up to Bigfoot?

Letter from Mr. T.

January 10, 1999

Dear Ida and Friends:

Many thanks for the long and kind answers to my questions. I really appreciate your willingness to keep me informed.

You also sent a couple of references to underground caverns in California where there were very large tables and chairs. I had a friend (Joe Mayberry) back in the 60's and 70's who had personally seen a similar situation in the northwest portion of Durango, Mexico.

Is there any advantage to our Bigfoot search in locating those caverns in California? If yes, can they be easily located with the help of Maez?

Does Bigfoot have the same pattern of chakras as humans? How would the function of these chakras be similar or different than human chakras?

Ida to Maez: You have read the letter just received from Mr. Trippett. I'll ask the second question first. Does Bigfoot have the same pattern of chakras as humans and would their function be similar?

Maez: Bigfoot has chakras but I doubt he knows anything about it. They function naturally without guidance or observation by Bigfoot as far as I know. I will ask some questions on this.

Ida: The other question was about finding the caverns mentioned on the photocopy that Leo Sprinkle sent. And would there be any point in doing so?

Maez: It could be done but it is not necessary. I can locate a similar cavern for you with similar contents closer to home.

Ida: Would it have any reference to Bigfoot?

Maez: The owners, or at least the users, of the over-sized equipment are the local supervisors of Bigfoot. I would not want to stumble in on them unannounced. You are too eager for adventure always, Ida.

Ida: I know. I'm the proverbial angel who rushes in where fools are too smart to tread.

Maez: There is something wrong with that quotation, but it is still right.

Note from Ida to Mr. T.

January 11, 1999

I used the pendulum and got action in the Oregon Caves area. Do you have or can you get a geological survey map of that area?

Maez: The place I refer to is beyond the caves usually visited, but it is not difficult to reach. Few people have ever gone there. We can discuss this better with a map — due west of the designated park or monument — whatever they call it.

Ida: East or west side or on top of the Siskiyous?

Maez: East slope, low down in an unexpected place. Get a map.

Ida: (I think Maez just loves to be a little mysterious. It makes him feel important).

Maez: I "heard" that! But you're right to some extent.

Tres to Ida, later: Keep your mind at rest for a few moments while I tell you something.

We are going to let you and Mr. T. photograph a Bigfoot family. It will be within two months, at least by March 15th. He (Mr. T.) will get his footprint also. Have your camera ready and plenty of film. It will probably be Wipi, if soon, or another if at the end of that period. It is vital to us, to Bigfoot, and to your-selves (all men) that a relationship is established that proves what Bigfoot is, definitely not an animal, but what we call a borderline (not sub) human.

Whether you will have more than one such close contact is problematical at this time. Much education must be given on both sides before frequent contact or contact with many is advisable. Now, any questions?

Ida: My camera is just a little snap shooter.

Tres, 1/13/99: Borrow or buy or don't worry about it. I'm sure Mr. T. has adequate equipment. That is all for now.

Tres to Ida: So! At last you have brought your thoughts together and have seen the light! What were you just now thinking?

Ida: I was thinking of the sea of consciousness (cosmic electricity, Supra-Consciousness, the mind of God) that surrounds us, everyone, and everything. And the bombardment of the sun for several months by high intensity bodies that has increased the intensity of light forces from the sun to the earth. I was told to expect a new glistening in the shadows and a new scintillation in the sunlight, and a rising of vibrational frequencies in human consciousness.

Tres: In combining those thoughts what was the result?

Ida: The notion that everything on Earth, including the earth itself, has gone into a higher phase of sensitivity. We will not only be talking to trees, but trees will be talking back!

Tres: Not too soon. Start with what you call "dumb" animals, your pets, dogs, cats, horses, and then wild animals around you, deer and squirrels. As time passes more and more of living things can make their feelings, if not actual thoughts, known to you. It will mean a new understanding, a new closeness, a new consideration for and cooperation with all living things including the Earth itself, as was intended.

Ida: Has it ever been like this before?

Tres: Eons and eons ago when the world was new and a different form of man walked the Earth.

Ida: Physical man?

Tres: Just taking on physicality, a body of light translating into materiality.

Ida: Are we evolving into a body of light?

Tres: It is a going on not a going back. It is a new form, a physicality that can shimmer in and out of ocular view. This is a whole new experience.

Ida: How soon can I learn to shimmer?

Tres: Oh, the Ida of this phase will be long gone. But when you come again you will come knowing how to shimmer.

Ida: I've always wanted to be scintillating!

(Our entire solar system is in the photon belt during the ages of Leo and Aquarius. Well, I thought you would like to know).

Letter to Mr. T.

January 13, 1999

Dear Lee,

I'm sure you saw the extract from the Patterson-Gimlin film in the local paper but I wanted to call your attention to something, then Marlys and I can have a good laugh at "these men".

Of course Professor Krantz could not imitate the gait of Bigfoot in the Patterson-Gimlin film. She was a lady. Let's see Krantz walk like a woman. The swinging of the body is altogether different from a male. If this was a hoax costume the person wearing it had to be female. A 500-pound human female?

Maez to Id, 1/13/99: Enjoy your nap?

Ida: I wasn't sleeping. I was thinking.

Maez: Now what?

Ida: Holographic projectors. Visible mind-reading that Hweig talked about and the Sea of Information that surrounds us. Too bad I'm not an inventor or I could read that "Mind of God".

Maez: Why don't you? It's possible.

Ida: I couldn't invent a safety pin. I'll give it to Mr. T. He's a scientist and inventor. I have a question.

Maez: Shoot.

Ida: Does Bigfoot's implant give him the ability to read from that Sea of Information. Is that his importance?

Maez: Yes, Ida, and so does yours. You sometimes use it for that purpose rather accidentally. You will be taught to use it purposely.

Ida: When?

Maez: Soon.

Ida: Yeck — again "soon". In your parlance that could mean ten years.

Maez: Or fifty!

Ida, 1/14/99: Maez, are you available?

Maez to Ida: Ready. I've been awaiting your question on that very subject that Mr. T. just proposed. "Who are the supervisors of Bigfoot?"

No, they are not huge people. The giant-sized tables and chairs are left over from past years. The present supervisors are very w6ell concealed Earth humans. That is, by concealed, I mean they do not announce themselves as such. They are part of that Earth contingent of collaborators with the UFO people that Hweig mentioned a number of times. You have brushed against several of them in the past twenty years. You had no way of recognizing them, but they knew about you.

If you were to rip off their cover without their approval they would go to severe lengths to stop this disclosure.

However, have no fear. We have arranged to have "no one home" (with their permission) when you go to the caverns. It is time to turn all our pockets of seclusion and secrecy inside out.

We have worked out a program in which this can be done with no threat to any of our valuable workers.

Photos of the cavern and photos of Bigfoot can be made — and here's the IF — you allow us to dictate what is to be told about them. Exposure of a few things must still be held back. We must rely on your discretion.

You may take anything loose you find in the cavern. It will no longer be of use. There are some small, really worthless artifacts — no gold, silver, gems, or art objects.

Ida to Maez, 1/15/99: We were interrupted yesterday. I had some questions concerning the cavern.

Maez: I will answer if possible.

Ida: If there are no worthwhile artifacts and problematical furnishings, then what are we expected to photograph?

Maez: How about giant skeletons?

Ida: You're kidding me. Another wild goose chase. I've gone on enough of these.

Maez: And you have always found something of informational value, although it may not have been at once apparent. We are no longer "just testing you." You are part of the crew now.

Tres: Pardon my interrupting you. I wanted to reassure Ida it is all factual and real.

Ida: Thank you. I shall try to maintain a positive attitude. That is difficult after more than twenty years of cat-and-mouse games.

Maez: You will take many photos of the skeletons. No Bigfoot on this trip. Then report them.

Ida: To whom? Why not credible scientists first to take measurements, etc., and then to authorities, sheriff or whatever?

Maez: Probably a wise plan. Who are the scientists you would call in?

Ida: I will let Mr. T. choose. That is his area of expertise.

Maez: Tres: We agree.

Ida: Is this agreeable to the supervisors? We don't want to trample on their authority.

Maez: They welcome the uncovering. But they don't want to reveal themselves. They have other agendas also. Go for it!

Ida: Mr. T. brought maps. Am I correct in Road 024?

Maez: Yes, to the end. It is not the best road ever made but it will take you into less than half a mile of whatever you are looking for, actually more like a quarter mile. We know you cannot walk well in rugged terrain, Ida; take your mother's split foot cane. It will help you keep your balance. You'll make it okay. And as we said a long time ago, "Be alert."

Maez to Ida, 1/16/99: There are several points to catch up on. First, let's talk about Wipi. His reluctance to meet with you has nothing to do with either you or Mr. T. Wipi is getting some efforts at reconciliation from his former comrades or clan. They are beginning to understand that driving him away has sent him right into the "camp of the enemy". Wipi is worried about the welfare of his mate if something should happen to him. Reconciliation with the clan would be the best protection he could provide for her. Then he worries that if he were gone, would some of his former critics take their displeasure out on her. It would depend upon the individual and the amount of bitterness left. It is not Bigfoot's nature to carry grudges and this makes Wipi lean in favor of reconciliation.

We will give him another week without any pressure on him to make a decision, but meantime we are tutoring a group of three for possible contact, a male and his mate and their independent offspring (over 20 years old). You will then be facing two huge male and one female who is as strong and active as the males. Do you think you want to undertake this?

Ida: Okay.

Maez: We will put the cavern trek back into the files for the present. Later its relation to Bigfoot will be apparent. Photos are enough of a project for now. This is winter and the potential of heavy snow in the Siskiyous at any time are a real risk factor.

Ida: May I change the subject? I have a question.

Maez: Of course. What is it?

Ida: Edgar Cayce. When he read from the Akashic Records, was that the Sea of Information we've been talking about, the Consciousness or Mind of God?

Maez: Yes. The sea has been given additional energy so that it will be easier for sensitives to dip into, since they also have raised energies.

Ida: The meeting of the minds.

Maez: Exactly. A higher or more sensitive resonance in the resonating electro-magnetic field that you are. Not just your mind but your entire self. No, not soul, or not soul only. All of you — your little toe in its own frequency has a new sensitivity.

Ida: My little toe is cold.

Maez: You are interpreting the buzzing in your little toe as cold. Think of it as warm and see the difference. Concentrate.

Ida: It does change to warm. But when I stop concentrating on it, it turns to cold again.

Maez: Habit. Try to develop a new habit and you'll never have to wear socks to bed again. You can change any number of things about yourself by changing the way you think about them. Spend some time experimenting with this. You have more power to do such things now. Everyone has! Take pain, for example. Pain has a purpose, to let you know there is something wrong with your body that should be attended to. But there is a limit to the amount of pain that you need to let into your awareness. Beyond that limit you increase your pain by the tension, fear, and worry that you allot to it. Control your mental and emotional reaction and you control the amount of pain you feel. We are getting afield again. Let us get back to Bigfoot.

Ida: Actually I should be scrubbing my kitchen and bathroom. I might even stretch my energy so far as to do some dusting, but I don't promise.

Maez: Go ahead. It is hard to "talk" to you when your mind is half on other chores.

Ida: This is not a chore; it is a pleasure.

Maez: Thank you. Go, now, scrub!

Maez, 1/18/99: I see this is a holiday for Martin Luther King's birthday. It is also your elder granddaughter's birthday and that of your friend, Doree's. And your daughter, Lee's, is the 20th. What is that weird thing you bought for her?

Ida: She collects animal skulls. What I bought is a goat skull with a partial covering of beads made by the Huichol Indians of Mexico.

Maez: Yes, I know the Huichols, a creative and artistic people. You and your daughter have a wide range of interests. I'm beginning to think our interests — or mine — are rather constricted. We concentrate on one area of study.

Ida: And go a lot further with your expertise. I know I am too scattered, but I find it more fun to try to understand many things, or at least to get acquainted with many.

Maez: Which brings us back to Bigfoot. We will try to concentrate on this one subject. That does not mean you cannot pursue other interests outside of our conversations.

Ida, 1/20/99: I've been renewing my notes for a book worked on in 1994-97 and part of '98. A working title was "The Searcher". That is now changed to "Reconciliation". The theme was the search for God — for understanding. I have a lot of notes but they won't jell. Maybe I can do better now with several new ideas or revelations that have presented themselves recently, such as the Force of Reconciliation, and the clearer representation of the Sea of Information. Meanwhile — back at the ranch —

Maez to Ida: We will not have much news until Wipi makes up his mind who he is going to work with, his clan or us. Meanwhile we tutor three Bigfoot. They are a different personality than Wipi. He has become gruff and glum, no longer his light-hearted self. The three are a high spirited, happy, prankish trio but very good-hearted and seem anxious for such an adventure. We will write more in a couple of days. By your Saturday and Sunday we should know Wipi's decision.

Now celebrate your daughter's 56th birthday.

Maez to Ida, 1/21/99: Now that we have gone through your notes for "The Searcher", or "Reconciliation", I see the reason for your discouragement with it. It doesn't "jell" because you are not too sure of your solutional premise.

I have heard you expound your pattern of story projection and it is good. You say you derived it from James Branch Cabell. But you have laid aside the original stringency of the pattern. Analyze your notes according to that original pattern, and tighten up the order of your notes accordingly. You have everything you need except form. Enough on that. Now back to Bigfoot.

Wipi seems to back away more every day. His personal worries have overshadowed his idealism. So human!

By Monday we will give you information on the Trio, when, where, and how to meet them. When these three are together, they are afraid of absolutely nothing, and are facing the affair as a kind of lark. See you Monday if not before.

Ida: It is very hard to psychoanalyze a creature who cannot or will not answer our questions. There have been a few reports of Bigfoot telepathically communicating with a reporter. No doubt there would be more reports of that kind if the recipient were not so afraid of being called crazy and a liar.

So we shall have to depend for the most part on the revelations of Maez and for our own suspicion that the reactions of Bigfoot in most situations would be very much like our own although more limited.

For example in Fred Beck's story where the miners, in what came to be called Ape Canyon, had apparently shot and probably killed a Bigfoot. That night a rain of head-sized rocks pounded down on their cabin from the rocky ledge above. We can imagine our own reaction to the killing of one of our companions and the feelings and action of men in limited circumstances.

Letter from Lee Trippett

January 20, 1999

Hello, Ida!

I need to make an adjustment in my motive and purpose surrounding our Bigfoot activities because I've recently been giving topics in the books by Neale Donald Walsch some serious consideration.

Our society needs to be of service to Bigfoot by allowing more safe and clean space. On the other hand Bigfoot can help us by indicating earth's energy conditions. Also, the general public needs to know there is so much more to our mental and spiritual system than is generally recognized or accepted.

This needs to be/accomplished in the framework of serious benevolent cooperation. Your book and unique communication talents are the most significant part of the program. In comparison footprints are only pieces of evidence to support the much more profound aspects of mental communication and existence of life forms in other dimensions. Perhaps any photos obtained should first be made public through the book (?).

Issues relating to our planet's condition and its support of all inter-connected life forms also need top priority. My attitude of wishing to shake up the public needs to be placed in the background.

Letter from Ida to Lee Trippett

January 22, 1999

Dear Lee,

Yes, I think the Bigfoot project can be expanded beyond footprints and photos. Depends on how much effort you want to put into it. Maez seems to be pleased with the prospect of a wider vision. Since we seem to have a terrific crew of communicators on hand, we should accept their help to the fullest. At present they include:

- Tres: A very highly placed spiritual personality. Speaks seldom but with authority.

- Thoth: Formerly called The Hidden One

- Amorto: My old Atlantean friend from the Space Island. Does not speak often but encourages from the side-lines.

- Maez: Councilor and monitor of Bigfoot, from the Arcturus system.

We have been having input from Tres and Maez mostly because I have a rigidly one track mind. I concentrate so hard on one line of reception that other input distracts and scatters my thought.

Up to now I have just been taking down the conversations and making a few aside notes. It might be well for us to decide on the outer limits of our "research" and a more clari-fied and sustained direction of our purpose. You have been in this study for many years and know what has been done and what needs to be done.

I would be very happy to see an expansion of intent. I think we have opportunities that would be a shame to waste. Maez has been trying to call to our attention some of the broader aspects of our search.

I don't know if you want to — or how far you want to — step over the line of "scientific credibility", although even the bastions of empirical science are beginning to melt down and allow that everything cannot be reduced to counting statistics.

So the first thing to decide is the problem of credibility. You don't want to sacrifice your scientific standing. At the same time we have to go outside the scientific paradigm when we say we are in contact with a being from another planet who is the boss of Bigfoot. I will leave to you the decision of how far to pursue the weird aspects. I don't have any scientific credibility to defend or protect.

A note on the reality or possibility of The Hidden One (as we used to call him) really being the historical Thoth: in Greece he was known as "Hermes the Thriceborn". They recognized that he had thrice guided mankind into the entry of a new age, the changeover to Taurus, to Aries, and to Pisces. So here we have Thoth revealing himself as we go into a new age, Aquarius.

Sounds logical.

Whew, man! With Thoth and Tres and Maez we should be able to put together something really significant. That doesn't mean of course that everyone in the world is instantly going to believe us. All we can do is to give the best we have and hope that some will have the courage and intelligence to believe.

Ida:

Thoughts About Bigfoot

January 24, 1999

From a scientific viewpoint Bigfoot represents a problem of paleoanthropology, a nice long name for a nice long mystery.

- Is Bigfoot real or is he a myth?
- Is he animal or human, or a combination, a hybrid perhaps?
- Where in the evolution of Man did Man and Bigfoot part company!
- What factor brought on this separation?
- Was there interaction between the two strains? When? How much? Why?
- When did that interaction cease and why?
- Would it be beneficial to either or both to renew that interaction?
- How to bring them together? Can it be done?
- With what practical results?
- Can Bigfoot squeeze into the social life of humans? Where? How?
- Should Bigfoot be socially and culturally developed? Taught to speak? Wear clothes?
- Should Bigfoot be left entirely alone, although we know he is an endangered species?

I am not sure that these are even very intelligent questions. I was just ruminating. And I doubt that we can answer many of them. It is just something to keep in the back of our minds as we proceed. It gives direction to our thoughts.

Enough evidence has been noted and written about that it is almost impossible for any thinking person to deny their reality. And every day more reports are coming forth. There seems to be a resurgence of interest in the creature.

Note: The truth of Bigfoot's reality cannot be hidden much longer. There are too many electronic and other modern devices that will be used to seek him out sooner or later, probably sooner. And there are too many rash and impatient people searching for him, for him not to be in danger in several ways. Being shot is only one.

What would seem to be the best way of preserving Bigfoot?

1. To keep him hidden and try to pretend he doesn't exist?

2. To airlift him to safety of another planet?

3. To bring him out in the open with a plea for understanding and helping him?

I would choose number three, if it could be done so completely and with absolute assurance that all of the foolishness about "being first" to prove his existence would no longer have any purpose.

To airlift him to another planet might mean his greatest safety but (a) he doesn't want to go and (b) he has a value here to Earth that is not yet recognized.

Letter from Ida to Lee Trippett

So, as your letter suggests, I think broadening our project to take in such points as: 1) Our planet and all of its life-forms are an organic whole, what affects one affects all, 2) Footprints and photos gained in response to Maez's instructions to both Bigfoot and ourselves would indeed contain evidence of possible mental communication with entities in other areas of being, and other dimensions, and Bigfoot himself.

It all depends on how far you want to stick your neck out. Once you have revealed yourself as a "believer", there is no erasing the revelation if you find it is drawing some uncomfortable aspersions on your sanity.

Letter from Mr. T. to Ida

January 25, 1999

Many thanks for your reply. For many years I have said there is more to Bigfoot than a few hair-covered giants of the forest.

Their ability to communicate to us through you and others represents a major part of the adventure and discovery. Of course any other human-like characteristics are also significant; that is why I wonder about their chakras. The major spiritual and energy systems that connect to the physical aspects represent features of the human mind that are distinct from animal. Many will still insist Bigfoot is more animal than human and we need more information than to say they communicate or have self-consciousness. Science has well defined anatomical differences between animal and human but it is not clear on the mental, emotional or spiritual differences.

What and where is the Arcturus system? Does Maez work with other councilors and monitors? If so, what are some of their responsibilities in relation to Bigfoot?

For us to decide the outer limits of our research we need to consider who we have been talking with and where are they? If this leads us to UFOs or ETs, then we would enormously expand the arena. Perhaps this is what Maez is interested in our doing?

Maybe we need to find new terminology for describing Maez and Tres. There are all kinds of important ramifications.

You would be happy to see an expansion of intent. I would be amazed and pleased if we can (1) establish significant credible evidence Bigfoot does indeed exist; (2) that we can communicate with Bigfoot; and (3) that we can initiate legislation to protect Bigfoot.

Other than sincerity and integrity, I do not have a reputation to protect. I do have respect for some of the scientific process. There are features of its present use that have serious limitations. This project has tremendous implications for impacting prevailing opinions and we will have made a worthy contribution if we can accomplish the three steps outlined in the last paragraph. If Maez and Tres wish more, then perhaps they can spell it out.

You ask, "Where do we start?" We have already done that. You know how to write and publish. I know how to get in and out of the woods and to use a camera. I can share certain aspects of our discoveries with those who can provide expertise in related disciplines. You know how to communicate with appropriate 'extra' intelligence. Knowing when, where and how to get a series of quality photographs would be a very major step since there has been failure on the part of many in the last 40 years. Maez, Bigfoot monitors and supervisors have done a remarkably good job of keeping Bigfoot hidden. I am waiting to see if they are going to change their past patterns.

I could suggest other things that might be done, but so far we have not seen, heard, or felt Bigfoot.

Ida: I too feel frustrated that all our plans to meet Bigfoot sound so reasonable, but pan out to nothing, not a glimpse, sign nor smell. We have to be patient; it would be well to know a little more about Bigfoot before we go dashing off to hold his hand. Then too, while Maez is head of the Council that monitors the creatures, he, himself, is not one of the Masters. He is one of the "grays" who were engineered to do the work, although he appears to be a superior one.

Maez to Ida, 1/24/99: Wipi is obviously going back to his former comrades. They are scattered about the area but gather, like all clans, from time to time. It seems to be the consensus of agreement that Wipi will give up his attempts at contacting humans in return for the clan's personal protection. So we shall drop that effort and turn to the three who are viewing it all as an adventure. We don't want to let their enthusiasm get cold, so will plan for a photo meeting next week. We will hope for brighter weather. Instructions soon.

The book you have just read, *Esau* by Phillip Kerr has some valuable information. Although the story was fiction the author did some careful and extensive research to write practical and as nearly as possible factual current beliefs. Like yourself, I find the ending illogical.

One of the book's front page blurbs by the Denver Post — "Blends fact and fiction seamlessly while raising philosophical questions about what the discovery of a living specimen of Yeti could mean to the world."

Of course, you and Mr. T. are interested in Bigfoot, which is the same family with only minor differences.

Writer Kerr lives in London so Yeti and the Himalayas were as interesting to him as Bigfoot is to you and a lot more glamorous.

We will reserve further discussion of the book's presentation until Mr. T. has had a chance to read it. There are some good practical observations. That is all for today.

Letter from Ida to Mr. T.

Dear Lee,

Gary (my son-in-law) brought home the book "Esau" because of the mountain climbing. (Gary is a world-class climber.) When Lee (my daughter) saw it she knew I would be interested because of the Yeti, but I had to wait for her to finish it. She gave it to me Friday afternoon and I just finished it.

There is some practical advice and worthwhile pages. Gary said we could keep it. Anytime you would like to pick it up, do so.

Looks like we should have a photo session soon. I'm anticipating!

Another decision to make that could help guide our project: whom are we putting together a report or our experiences and discoveries for? Scientists? Is it for thrill and entertainment seekers? People who can help Bigfoot? Others?

This decision gives purpose to the report or book and thus form, tone, and direction.

Maez to Ida, 1/26/99: You have asked what the fall-out, how does it is affect humans if Bigfoot does become extinct? The answer is a long way from sentimental. His task has been a long and noble one — to detect areas of Earth that could be hazardous to Man. He still continues that function. But there is more. He alerts us also to dangerous frictions among men, those that are about to explode into open warfare. We do not interfere with political or religious conflicts unless they are trembling on the verge of nuclear engagement. But we can create conditions of many kinds that deter violent engagements or disrupt them. Conditions of weather, of earth (land) upheavals and violent changes, even a bit of chicanery in the financial world. We cannot engage ourselves too far, just a flicker of changes that distort events.

Remember I said that Bigfoot with his implant that is so similar to your own can dip into that Sea of Information and draw out the data that he needs. Oh, there is a lot more to this big fellow than you have any notion. His is the finger in the dyke that more than once has saved your whole un-civilization from burying itself in a fiery pit.

It is time that his role on Earth becomes known and that he is given the protection and respect he has earned.

Now let's talk about the photo session of the coming week. We are going to ask our brave trio to choose the place and time since their safety is the major factor in the choice. All we ask them is to choose a place as close to your home as possible — within a 20 mile radius. That does not leave too many viable choices. We will see what they come up with. We converse daily with them.

All right for now. Go take a nap. Sorry your VCR broke.

Ida:

First Telepathic Communication with Bigfoot

January 28, 1999

I talked directly to Bigfoot for the first time with Maez standing by to help with the telepathic communication. I was so tense I was shaking and had a hard time later remembering everything that was said as I did not make notes during the conversation.

His voice was low but not really deep as one might anticipate. It seemed gentle and a little amused and powerful and strong. One does not really "hear" the voice exactly as one does in oral conversation, but there is a difference in various "voice" reception so that one soon learns to distinguish one voice from another.

I thanked Bigfoot for being willing to meet with us. He said to bring three people only as they were three.

Bigfoot asked why we wanted to meet. I told him we were worried about the way they were being crowded out of their living space and we wanted to convince people that they were real and human and needed clean water and air sometimes help with food and in finding safe living places. And we wanted to help get laws passed that would stop anyone from shooting at them.

Bigfoot asked how we expected to do all that.

I said that if we could get photos — pictures of them — He interrupted. "Yes, I know photo-pictures."

And I asked if he would make an impression of his foot in a tub of clay while we took a picture of him doing it, and I explained about the tub and the clay and compared it to making footprints in mud or clay after a rain.

He said he knew about clay but why did we want a photo-picture of him doing that?

"To prove you are a real life Sasquatch, not just somebody dressed up."

"Not an imitation," he agreed.

While we were talking Lord Spike, my cat, jumped on my lap and walked across the desk and Bigfoot asked, "What was that went across there?"

I said, "That was my pet cat."

"Do you eat those?"

"Oh, no! He is a pet, a friend."

"You love him then?"

"Yes, very much. I would cry a great deal if anything happened to him."

I asked Bigfoot if he liked peanuts and could I bring him some? "That would be good," he said. "I know peanuts. You are called I-dah?"

"Yes, Ida. What shall I call you?" "Call me Bigfoot. Bigfoot will do."

I thanked him for talking with me and said, "God bless you."

"And bless you!" Bigfoot said.

I was too tense to talk longer and had a screaming headache. It took me nearly ten minutes to relax enough to hold a pen.

I wondered how Bigfoot could see Spike, the cat, with his implants. I cannot see like that with mine.

Maez explained that Bigfoot's implants can be "clicked on" when they want him to see something at a distance. He was not close to me; he was out checking the meeting sites. It sounds like his implants have some sort of computer function that mine do not. I will have to ask Maez to explain this more fully.

Ida:

Implants and Implantees

I have had alien implants for nearly 60 years. They were given to me in a landed UFO on the California desert off Highway 10 between Indio and Blythe about midnight December 22-23, 1940.

I did not remember about this event until the implants were activated in 1968 under conditions that terrorized me and the attempt at communication was abandoned until 1977 when a successful activation was made and has continued 24 hours a day for more than 20 years. The implant event was recalled through regressive hypnosis by Dr. R. Leo Sprinkle, Counseling Psychologist of Laramie, Wyoming.

I have been given considerable information about these implants by the entities that made them, but in bits and pieces that are difficult to piece together. I had decided to scrape all my crumbs of information together for whatever help or use it might provide to those interested.

I was told not long ago that mine are rather "primitive" compared to those issued today but they are basically very similar in material and structure (not form).

These were implanted one in each ear, one very high in the left nostril to interact with the optic nerve, and one through the right eye socket into the frontal lobe around the area that we refer to as "the third eye". Once activated the Aliens can see through my eyes and hear through my ears everything that happens to me.

I feel so much like a peeping Thomasina that I have become quite reclusive.

Letter from Mr. T. to Ida

January 28, 1999

Thanks again for your most valuable interest in Bigfoot.

You ask for more questions. The following three relate to comments on page 1 of your notes dated 1/26. The questions relate to the past one thousand years and not just our nuclear age.

Can Maez or Tres give us a couple of specific examples on when Bigfoot has helped our "whole un-civilization from burying itself?"

Men are frequently threatened by earthquakes and volcanoes. Therefore: when, where, and how has Bigfoot helped Man avoid areas of earth that could be hazardous?

With ET implants, monitors, and supervisors living amongst our people, what specific manner is Bigfoot's talent needed or used to detect "dangerous frictions among men?"

Best wishes, Lee

Maez to Ida, 1/29/99: The timing of your rendezvous with Bigfoot is definitely set for Wednesday, February third at noon. The exact location has not been chosen between two possible ones. Both are in the Coast Range, one is 45 miles the other 65 miles from your home. Mr. T. was right, 20 miles was much too close. Bigfoot has been seen that close in the past but industrial and home building progress has since wiped out the safety of so close an appearance.

In our conversation before daylight this morning you discerned the reason why I asked you about your contact/connection with Native Americans. You see, if you are just patient all the far-fetched things I have asked you to read, research, or do will come to show their meaning and their significance to your Bigfoot adventure. In the case of Native Americans one of the possible meeting locations is on ground sacred to Indians. They no longer "own" it in the eyes of the county recorder's office, but in their own hearts and minds it is theirs. I have mental contact with the Indians of these places and am getting their permission to use one of them for your meeting. White and other persons have gone in there and treated the areas like barbarians and have found they had unexpected and savage "accidents". By Monday we will let you know the exact location and how to get there. People living around there warn strangers not to go in, but you will be okay, don't worry.

I will go to the store with you today and pick out some fruit. No bananas or oranges for this trio. All must be ripe enough to eat by Wednesday. Bigfoot does not have a refrigerator to keep his fruit. Now I am getting silly. I am so happy to see this long awaited planned meeting coming to pass that I am a bit giddy.

Ida: (I phoned Mr. T. with the news at 10:00 A.M.)

Maez to Ida, 2/1/99: I thought you would never get done eating. Your wild rice pancakes were special so I didn't hurry you.

The meeting place for Wednesday noon is definitely set for the road south of Harlan, a hilly, forested spot. We will only use this place once so it won't hurt to reveal it in your notes. If there should be another, or other, meetings, they will be far from there.

No, don't bring more peanuts or fruit than you have already purchased. Whatever you bring they will gobble up at once and we don't want to make them sick. There is nothing more you can give them at this time.

I can't promise how much interaction will be possible. It all depends on the prevailing circumstances, most of which I cannot control. You will get some photos and anything more depends on how Bigfoot sizes you up and if there are any outside interruptions. So far Bigfoot is quite well pleased with what he has learned about you and Mr. T., far more than either of you can guess.

Bigfoot wants you to use the title for your report — or book — that you were thinking about before you went to sleep last night, "My Brother is a Hairy Man", taken from Genesis 27:11. Yes, he understands what that signifies. While Bigfoot cannot read, he has been well inoculated with Sunday school type stories in order that he may understand to some extent the people whose area he is sent into.

Og, Bigfoot Follows King of Bashan

You have asked if "your" Bigfoot has a name. Actually, no. But he has knowledge of the Biblical mention of Og, King of Bashan, described in Deuteronomy 3:11 as the last of the race of Giants. (The iron bedstead of Og was thirteen and one-half feet long and six feet wide.) He would like to be called Og. I know, Ida, you think the name is harsh sounding, but soften the "g" a little as you say it, almost but not quite like the German "ch". He feels that he too is one of the remnants of his race. Yes, that is sad — oh, please don't cry!

Spike wants his lunch. Go mop yourself up, have lunch, and come back.

Maez: Feel better? I'm sorry the visitation of our representatives made you cold. You couldn't detect them otherwise? Their presence drew on your energy and gave you chills. They were satisfied with their inspection and now all is "go ahead" for your meeting with Bigfoot.

It is difficult to give you more explicit directions until you are at the turn-off place. I will authenticate the turn by saying, "Yes, turn right, or left, as the case may be." You will go through Harlan and continue three miles by your odometer. Of course I know what an odometer is! The road you turn onto is not the greatest but it is okay for one half mile. You will recognize where to stop. The trio will be waiting, concealed. Just wait in the car until they make their presence known. Make all your preparations for photographing in front of the car and wait for their signal to move forward. Otherwise stand pat. You can photograph when convenient but don't move forward for any reason until invited to do so. I will probably be the one to tell you when or if to approach closer. We just have to wait to see how it is best to proceed. Good luck!

Maez to Ida, 2/4/99: Don't think that yesterday was a total bust! Og was ready to come out at any time, but his companions persuaded him to wait. Then the three logging trucks passing made them more cautious. And the man stopping his truck, getting out and approaching you to talk really put them off. We are trying to devise a plan where Og only will be waiting and Mr. T. will not have to drive a distance or make elaborate plans. It is necessary to have a contact and obtain pictures and perhaps other material — but photos by all means. There are a number of procedures possible. Give us a little time. Do get over your petulance! You will get photos, we have been training you for a vast number of years (!?) for this project. Mr. T. will find that buying his telephoto lens was money well spent.

Meantime catch up on your housework and be ready for whatever might happen. For anything!

Maez to Ida, 2/5/99: Please get over your pout and come back to writing. We did all we could to bring this off as you wanted.

As you and Mr. T. discussed, the three trucks and the man getting out and approaching you dampened the enthusiasm of Og's companions. Had he been alone he still would have come out. Next time it will be Og alone.

Yes, you are right. We have unusual powers. Do you remember when you and your daughter (also Lee) met the Dorrs in Colorado? Amorto that morning told you that they had a surprise planned for you that day. Then you met your friends in the antique shop and they said they didn't know what they were doing there. They had not planned to go that direction at all. This event was planned to show you how we could arrange whatever happening we wanted. We still can. So don't worry about unusual twists in your plans. Just go with the flow. We will take care of details or sudden changes. We could have made Og come out, but it would have meant the possibility of trouble between him and his mate. Mostly this morning I wanted to ask you to go ahead with putting your various parts of the information or scenes or events of this story together. The time when it will be of the most use to us is rushing upon us faster than we anticipated. That is why it is necessary for you to get photos as soon as we can set up the necessary plans. We are learning with each episode what NOT to do in making contact with Bigfoot. That is all for now.

P.S: In regard to Mr. T.'s questions of January 28th, I want to write out answers that will take some time — and pages — and dictate them to you by the middle of next week. Excellent questions and it gives me the opportunity to get some real weight into our story.

Maez to Ida, 2/8/99: First thing this morning I want to apologize for the plan I started to project and then had to abandon. You have been patient with my fumblings. I thought we might have a Native American take you to meet Og. If someone came to your door to escort you, you would be willing to go along. Og said only one at a time as he would be one. I know this would not be so favorable for taking a photograph, as you could not get one of the other persons interacting with Bigfoot. However, this plan did not go far. I found several Native Americans who would be willing to conduct you, non-traditionalists, but others of their group were fiercely traditional and said they would not permit their people to hand over Bigfoot to those (whites) who had destroyed themselves as a people, as a culture. We cannot fault them for being true to themselves and their ancestors who took on the task of protecting Sasquatch. So we are back at square one.

Ida: Not quite. You said Amorto and Thoth were both on Earth now and in the physical. Why cannot one of them or one of the supervisors do the same as you wanted the Native Americans? If one of them teams up by the side of Og, then both Mr. T. and I can work together. Then another supervisor can escort us to Og, blindfolded if necessary. The supervisors can wear a mask.

Maez: That sounds feasible. Let me think this out. We do not want to expose our supervisors' identity. I will let you know.

How you do keep stacking up work for me!

Ida: Have fun!

Ida, later: The only factor that keeps us from considering Bigfoot a fully-fledged human on a par with ourselves — although different — is, so far as we now know — his lack of any "art", even the art of constructing tools, no matter how primitive. Bigfoot as an artist would fulfill all the requirements of full humankind.

Along with the fossil child skull or head were some artifacts, some of which undeniably showed two periods of use with a long, long gap of time between the two periods. Some were so primitive that the archeologist to whom I showed them said, "If these were from the Old World I would call them artifacts, but they're from here." (I did not then have the fossil to show him.)

Maez to Ida: You have been trying to reconcile various dates I have given you with those of the current paleoanthropological data as you find it in several books. Believe me, my dates are the correct ones. Let us review them.

Actually we used *Australopithecus africanus* in our genetic experimentation as long as a million and a half years ago when we could reach him directly. Because our Master race (not us grays) lived on earth then, as Hweig told you. After a great Earth disaster the Creative Ones (Elohim) brought the Masters to this planet. (We, the grays, had not been engineered at that time.)

About 300,000 B.P., of your years, the Master Race wanted to return to Earth to live, not all, but some.

They then went back in (Earth) time and selected certain specimens of *Australopithecus africanus* who were doing best in the environment of Earth with which to engineer a race of workers and data gatherers. Over a long period of another 100,000 years, the Masters made genetic improvements in the resultant Bigfoot race, using their own genes. The purpose of this creation was to discover where a new race of humankind could best live in the Western Hemisphere. There was already a separate race of humans in the Eastern world (see Sitchin.) The major problem, the one that took so much time to conquer was that of natural reproduction, since Bigfoot was a hybrid. The Master race, although from Earth, had not evolved from Earth stock such as *A.a.* I know this begins to get confusing.

There are many forbears of Earth humans. By 200,000 years B.P. the Bigfoot had developed to live in several different climatic and environmental conditions of Earth. Of those different developments seven distinguishable ones still inhabit the Earth. All are pretty much the same for the most part with only such variations as are necessary to their living conditions. Their physical evolution has been halted right there, but their mental, indeed conscious, evolution creeps on very slowly. They are far from stupid, and far, far from animal in their mental, emotional and spiritual development.

As I said previously we sent Bigfoot throughout the whole Earth from 300,000 to 200,000 years ago, Earth time, but sent our developed strain of *Homo s.s.* to Lemuria in the West about 200,000 B.P.

You can include with the above all of the information Hweig gave in your book *Project Earth* to fill in a complete and corroborating story. Does this now organize the dating of our Earth project for you?

Ida to Maez: Yes, thank you. I was getting dates and times confused. I will add to this with some of Hweig's material.

All I need to know now is why you can't go further back in time now than 15,000 years when you did previously?

Maez: The reason we cannot now go back so far in time is a natural one, not something projected from nuclear explosion or other man made events. It has to do with natural Earth changes, mainly magnetic and such things as Earth tilts, changes in the magnetic poles, etc. Such events make natural barriers and mark out natural borders of Earth containments.

Maez: A summary: For Bigfoot the Masters made a hybrid of *Australopithecus africanus* with twenty percent from their own genes. They consider themselves True Man. For the Western human race the Masters engineered a hybrid of the carefully selected most advanced toward *Homo erectus* from the Levantine corridor with 80 percent of their own genes. Because *Homo erectus* was an evolutionary descendant from *A.a.*, that makes this portion of humankind and Bigfoot genetically FULL BROTHERS! I think that answers your questions.

Ida: Yes, thank you. Then time as we perceive it is basically a function of magnetism?

Maez: Absolutely! Review your own book *The Alien Book of Truth*, a résumé of some of Hweig & Co.'s previous bits and pieces of information delivered without much coherence, many gaps, and a couple of fibs. Planet X, as we called it then, is not in a far galaxy they say now, but is in a constellation in our own galaxy; the Arcturus system in the constellation Boötes. And Tea Elsta is not the inhabitants own name for their planet but is a pseudonym made up by aforesaid Hweig & Co. All of this will be greatly expanded in another story. At present we want to concentrate more on Bigfoot than the human population of Earth.

Project Earth

Page 108, November 17, 1978

We cannot give our true names or locations, but we do confess that, up to this time, you have not been given any true name or true location. We have had to protect ourselves in many ways, for a good dozen different reasons.

We three, Victor (Hweig), Amorto and Jamie all took turns reading a prepared script. We used each other's names rather indiscriminately. Whoever was handiest to the script read it.

For the most part all scripts were prepared and given to us by our instructors; we did not write it. We were given various personalities to assume, according to the needs of the moment. Sometimes we even impersonated each other.

(2-24-99) Instructors now revealed as Maez or his associates.

Script by Maez, read by Hweig & Co.

Page 66, July 21, 1978

You have asked about the physical aspects of our world. [Now revealed as in the Arcturus system.]

Our atmosphere is somewhat different from your own. Many of the humanoids would have to wear masks in your world until their lungs were adjusted. Humans, such as yourself, could get along quite well if they did not have to exert themselves until they could become acclimated.

Now we must expose this. We alternate between two fairly close planets in a far galaxy. (Later this was amended to constellation, not galaxy.) One is our work planet. The atmosphere there is quite bad. It has little sunshine, heavy, low black clouds, constant thunderstorms with torrential rains, and no snow or natural ice. The climate is fairly temperate without much variation. It is muggy, even the rain and occasional violent winds are warm. You see, we are able to regulate our temperature and climate to some extent through various natural controls. You will learn to do this in the future.

Now the second is our resident or home planet. It is twice the size of Earth. We cannot be more explicit now.

Page 100, October 27, 1979

We told you formerly of the conditions on the planet that Hweig called Tea Elsta. This is the home planet of our UFOs. Its greatest needs are water and MORE EARTH TYPE PEOPLE! There, that is as frankly and clearly as we can state it. It is our purpose in writing this message. We — all the UFO people need your help.

On the other hand, there is so much science, technology that we can teach you or give to Earth people.

Certain sudden and disastrous changes will take place on Earth before many years have come to pass. Your scientists have warned of these, nothing is unknown. From natural sources earthquakes will wreak havoc over a large portion of the globe. There will be technological mishaps and social disasters.

Page 132, June 21, 1979

The first men who discovered outer space travel IN THIS CYCLE OF HUMANS lived in what you call Lemuria. This was many thousands of years ago — fifty thousand and more — yes, two hundred thousand! Lemuria was a continent that stretched far to the south in the Pacific Ocean. It was there that TRUE HUMANS — the seed of Earth's present inhabitants — came first.

Many thousands of years ago (and there is a reason for not being more specific at this time) there was a splitting of land masses that marked out the continents of Europe, Asia, Africa, and the Americas much as they are today. Lemuria in the Pacific and Atlantis in the Atlantic were well defined at that time.

At this splitting, space travel was in its infancy in Lemuria, which was then the most advanced of all civilizations.

A certain faction, desiring to escape the land catastrophes they believed to be coming, called upon Superior Ones to aid them as they had been aided in the past.

This faction escaped in a number of CREATED, not manufactured, craft, and entered outer space in search of a new home. Eventually they found a planet paradise. It was much like Earth except for atmospheric and climatic differences, which they soon learned to control. We (Hweig & Co.) call this planet Tea Elsta; their own name for it is something other than this.

Centuries later, after a great deal of division amongst themselves, the people of Tea Elsta devastated their new home with something equivalent to atomic explosions. Some of them returned to Earth to join Atlantis, for Lemuria was no more. Most stayed hopefully on trying to revitalize their planet. These are now the planners and builders of what you call UFOs who are aided by other planetary people.

Maez's script continued by Hweig

Page 105, October 29, 1978

We have another reason for approaching Earth. Our racial (Master) members are few. Less than a thousand of the original-type people remain on Planet X. (This is not true of Source B.) Planet X needs new life stock.

Our heritage is from the Earth. This was hinted to you long ago and then the subject dropped. Our people came from Earth many thousands of years before Atlantis. There were great civilizations on Earth. Did you think electricity, television, and radio were new? They have been invented (discovered) over and over again. Airships and space travel are nothing new. Humans have gone from Earth to the moon and far beyond before. We came from Earth multitudes of centuries ago. We were Earth's pioneers in space.

The Masters are as human as you are, no more, no less, but far more advanced technologically and scientifically, and are Masters of all psychic phenomena.

We have communication and transport to several other planets, not nearly as far from us as yourselves. Earth is the farthest from us that we have traveled in actual physical ships. We travel through a time differential for most part, and do a small amount of traveling in space.

(Return to the present. This is getting a little far out, Ida.)

Maez to Ida, 2/9/99: You amaze me with your perspicacity! "If Bigfoot had any artistic sense, he would be a full-fledged human," you said.

Well, I have a surprise for you! Bigfoot is an artist and in a way that would astonish you. Because of the work that he does for us and the living conditions under which he exists, he cannot be artistic in the same ways that your strain of human-kind exhibits. His facility in his own way would astound you, and leaves no doubt as to his artistry.

This is not a teaser, but I am trying to persuade the Council members to agree upon a project to show you and Mr. and Mrs. T. some of these. Getting you there is the problem.

Would you be afraid to ride in a UFO? Good! Then it may be possible. You can confer with your companions and I'll confer with mine. The way is not far but inaccessible to your kind of transportation. This is all for today.

Maez to Ida, 2/11/99: I suppose some of our suggestions do sound "out of this world", but then, aren't they? It is a pity so few of us in each group are willing to go all the way in this enterprise. We shall keep on devising the ways to get information, yes, evidence of Bigfoot that you need. It is hard to break the mold of protection that has existed for thousands of years.

I am ready to answer Mr. T.'s question of January 28th, but I suggest you use the typewriter if Lord Spike will keep his paws out of the mechanism. He only wants to know how it works.

Maez to Mr. T.

February 12, 1999

Maybe I should explain why I suggested using Mr. T. instead of your name, Lee. Because Ida's daughter's name is also Lee and there was confusion on occasion.

I shall try to give some brief answers to your questions, enough that you can see the direction of their intent.

First: To give some examples of when Bigfoot helped this civilization from burying itself. In more ancient times Bigfoot was needed more often in such activities than recently. Modern inventions in communication and sleuthing have made his services less often needed.

In more recent times Bigfoot was of great help at the time the hostages were being held by Iran and America tried to rescue them with the use of helicopters that were based in Arabia. A violent sandstorm came up disabling the copters. We had advance knowledge of the attempt at rescue and airlifted seven Bigfoot to the area. Their report of where the sand was compacted and where loose gave us the information we needed to provide winds from the proper direction to use the sandstorm in its most effective manner. Had the rescue mission been carried out as planned, it would have meant the eruption of WW3. Bigfoot is adverse to very hot weather, but he went into his energy state where temperature has no effect.

Why do we use Bigfoot when we might use a your-type human or others as scouts? Because we have a good working relationship with Bigfoot, we know him most intimately, his strengths and weaknesses, we trust him and he trusts us. There are no party poopers among the Bigfoot.

Another time Bigfoot played an important role in preventing a disastrous event was during the Bay of Pigs fiasco. Again Bigfoot was used in his energy mode to discover the preparation in Cuba that was to meet the American advance. The American plan had been sold out. The Russians were waiting for them to walk into a trap. Again it would have meant WW3 — with Russia this time. Bigfoot makes the best spy in such cases because of his infinite patience.

Early settlers in New York, Pennsylvania, and Massachusetts were friendly with the Native Americans until they felt themselves numerous enough and strong enough to start pushing the Indians aside and taking over land. When the Natives demurred at such treatment, troops were called into action against them. The settlers did not realize the full strength of Indian power if the whole Iroquois nation had combined to fight them. The whites would have been wiped out and the Indians decimated. To avoid such destruction of lives Bigfoot was asked to appear physically to the uncouth rabble that composed the troops at that time. Only officers had any education at all.

Bigfoot appeared in various threatening conditions, in his physical, and escalated the superstitious fears of the troops. These lost all appetite for fighting Indians and found numerous and clever ways of avoiding conflict.

Question #2: How has Bigfoot helped Man to avoid areas of Earth that might be dangerous?

In the present time mostly by scaring people away from areas that might be hazardous to their health. Sometimes this is due to natural obstructions to exploration and sometimes to warn him away from secret operations. There is so much going on in your country that you wouldn't believe. Once when Ida was with friends in Arizona she was informed there was an alien mining expedition under the South Mountains near Phoenix. I believe this was for titanium. I will have to check up on this information to see if it is still valid. (February 24 — valid then — now gone.)

Bigfoot has often kept people from walking into areas of danger, mostly by frightening them into a different path. They never knew what they missed walking into; natural dangers such as crevasses in lava flows that one does not see until he is on the verge of falling in, or does fall in; marshes that look like solid ground until one tries to walk on them; quicksand; dozens of other natural "booby traps". His major feat has been to report such things to us as sulfur pits, vortices, concentrations of energies that you know nothing about. Then we try to find ways through our Earth contingent to make it impossible for people to walk into those areas unprepared. We can keep communities from being built in unhealthy places infected with something like radon gas.

In Bigfoot's energy state he can penetrate into many a council hall, secret meetings, and good old boys talking in a back room. He doesn't understand all the intricacies of the topics discussed, but remember he has implants like Ida's own so that through him we see all he sees and hear all he hears. Bigfoot is the "bug" that transposes all the important information to us. Be sure Bigfoot is on the ground floor of every war council in every country on Earth, even where he does not live all the time. We never ask the citizens of any country to do that job. After we became able to implant people like Ida we could let them take over many of the chores Bigfoot had formerly done that were not of governmental import.

It is difficult to tell you many things. Remember what Hweig told you long ago, we must wait until a subject comes up in your reading, TV, conversations before we can talk along these lines. This removes us from the condemnation that we have influenced your mind by injecting new thoughts into it. Yes, we skirt around that very skillfully sometimes.

This is a rather sketchy answer to the three questions but we hope they give an understanding of the direction in which to consider other possibilities.

Respectfully,
Maez

Maez to Ida, 2/13/99: That was a good question, "Why do we use Bigfoot as a spy in these situations rather than a your-type man?"

Because if the energy mode control of Bigfoot should slip and he suddenly go into semi-corporeal or physical mode, the reaction among those gathered would allow a time for him to regain control. If it were a man there would be no time delay and he would be shot or seized instantly. Bigfoot's sudden appearance gives pause.

The original Bigfoot had these mode shifting abilities inbuilt. The Earth-born are not so endowed but must be assisted and trained. They are never as unflappable and it is in moments of emotion or stress that their control can slip.

Our Earth contingent of helpers has grown so broad and variable that we seldom need to call upon Bigfoot. He has become nearly obsolete as far as any usefulness is concerned. Electronic communication and other devices reach to nearly every crevice of the Earth. Like your farmers put a horse out to pasture we want to preserve our friend and helper, Bigfoot, in gratitude and love.

Therefore there is no longer the need for the intense secrecy that was necessary.

Take heart. You and Mr. T. will get photos and we hope much more.

Letter from Ida to Dr. R. Leo Sprinkle

February 2 1999

Laramie, WY

Dear Leo,

Just getting over a week of flu but I will try to be coherent.

I have never had overmuch interest in Bigfoot, but certain events are being explained to me now that indicate I have been guided in his direction for a long time. When I first had conversation with these ETs, whoever they really are, in

1977, I was told to go to Virginia Beach and look up in the Cayce readings all I could find about Atlantis. I had no idea why this was important but I went and had a good time except for the fact that the motel door opened outward. How can you barricade an outward door? In the library I found a three ring binder that had in it all the readings that mentioned Atlantis so I made a photocopy. Easy chore.

In the readings, Edgar Cayce mentioned many times the "things" that had been developed as servants and workers. These, of course, were comparable to the genetically engineered creatures in Sitchin's books. It looks like genetic engineering has been around for a long time, including ourselves!

Recently Gary brought home a fiction book called *Esau* by Phillip Kerr about an expedition of scientists (with a million dollar grant) who went to the Himalayas to capture a Yeti. One of the scientists — I quote —"He was even skeptical to one of the most fundamental of anthropological tenets, that the human species had possessed one single origin".

Isn't that interesting?

So Maez is now telling me that his "masters" engineered humans for the Western Hemisphere, using *Homo erectus* from the Levantine corridor and themselves in a hybrid creation. But previous to that they had engineered Bigfoot as a scout to check out the Earth and its environmental hazards and plusses to see if their type humans could live here. This is what my current book is all about, a different view of Bigfoot certainly. (No time here for details.) Bigfoot was engineered from the Masters and a long ago creature that was on the way to becoming *Homo sapiens*, but had hundreds of thousands of years to go.

Another event in my life that was to lead to Bigfoot was picking up rocks in Wyoming. I found a rock that Maez says is relative to Bigfoot. I have tried to interest three Institutions of Higher Bungling in my rock and they don't answer me. They think I am nuts, I'm sure. (I just called it a possible skull.)

Maybe so, but I'm sure having fun. Love, Ida

Letter from Mr. T. to Ida

February 18, 1999

Dear Ida,

Many thanks for the answer to my earlier questions. I am rather shocked that Bigfoot has been used as invisible spies for various elements of our world society.

I am pleased that they have worked for our benefit but I do not understand their loyalty. Are they working for our benefit in all cases? For example, they guard secret invasions and mining operations by friendly or unfriendly aliens?

We have learned Bigfoot has some measure of tolerance, patience, truthfulness, and dependability, but they are still subject to the opinions and fears of their peers.

I would like to know more of their nature and if or when it is convenient for you, Ida, could you please ask the following questions?

1. What is the typical life span of the Bigfoot remaining on Earth?

2. What is the specific nature of our local Bigfoot artistic talents?

3. Does Bigfoot experience grief or sorrow?

4. Does Bigfoot experience difficulties with mental, emotional, or physical health?

5. Does Bigfoot experience apprehension or guilt?

6. Does Bigfoot experience the need to pray or search for some form of immediate or long term salvation?

7. Does Bigfoot experience obligations to extend or receive forgiveness?

8. How much variation is there among various Bigfoot clans of the world in regard to the above issues?

Thanks again and best wishes.

Maez to Mr. T.

February 22, 1999

We can answer Mr. T.'s questions briefly now, and these will come up again in the future to be answered in more detail.

1. Earth-born Bigfoot live around two hundred years. A few push into their third hundredth year, maybe as much as 25 more years.

2. Artistic talents to be revealed presently.

3. Bigfoot experiences intense grief and sorrow especially at the loss of child or mate.

4. We have answered about physical health on 1-6-99. He is quite well balanced emotionally and mentally. There are no "crazy" Bigfoot unless one is acting so temporarily under intense emotion, fear, or pain.

5. Bigfoot knows apprehension but not guilt. He is strictly nonjudgmental in an intellectual way. He accepts "what is" "as is" pertaining both to himself and others.

6. No, he depends on his monitor to take care of such matters.

7. No, by being non-judgmental he can conceive of nothing that requires forgiveness. He places no blame on anyone though he is irritated at stupidity because it is stupid. He does not take offense personally. Mostly he makes fun of the ones acting stupidly, perhaps playing pranks on the worst offenders, hiding their supplies (not stealing), or rolling a boulder downhill through their campfire with no intention of hurting anyone.

8. Basically very little. But like all people that live in widely separated places there are some "cultural" differences. Hard to quantify.

   Brief answers, but they will be expanded as we go along.

Maez to Mr. T. and Ida

February 23, 1999

On the question of loyalty: Bigfoot does not act as a spy for any element of your world society but for his Arcturian monitors. We have a need to know what is being planned among the Earth factions. We need to keep our fingers on the pulse of nuclear fever.

Bigfoot has loyalty to Earth persons only in the way one is loyal to a family emblem or a flag. He knows you are a related species and for that reason he would not intentionally harm anyone, although he delights in playing pranks to startle anyone he thinks is being foolish or disgusting, as though he could scare them out of their silly behavior.

Bigfoot's loyalty is absolute to his monitors and to his own family members. He is not aware he is working for your benefit, or gives it little thought; he is working to please us. We instruct him to do whatever will provide us with necessary information and he steadfastly tries to carry out our instructions. I am sure he is aware to some extent that his compliance will, in some roundabout way, be of aid to you, but that is not why he obeys.

I do not believe Bigfoot analyzes the invasion of "aliens" into your territory as being either friendly or unfriendly. Although a Bigfoot is very intelligent he has uncomplicated ways of thinking. "My monitor told me to do this. I do this." Simple obedience. He does not take upon himself the burden of demanding, "Why?" or even "What are the final consequences?"

Bigfoot tries to fulfill the role for which he was created in every way possible. He was made to gain information about Earth, its environment, and sometimes its creatures, and he does that perfectly and splendidly, at all times obedient and loyal to his monitors. God bless him!

Of course he has enough leeway to use his own discretion in meeting any situation that might involve an element of danger to him.

Maez to Ida, 2/24/99: Lord Spike has not kept up the housework too well while you have been ill so I will not hold you long this morning. Your desk is a mess, how do you expect to find anything?

Ida: We can't blame Spike for that!

Maez: Ah well, back to work.

Mr. T. implied a question about aliens being friendly or unfriendly. In essence they are neither. They are on Earth to do a job, but they can be friendly if they are accepted and treated politely. Since they know this is not likely, they are inclined to be aggressive and not very friendly.

The "aliens" believe they have more rights to use the Earth than the people who are here now, especially in the Western Hemisphere. They were the Earth's original settlers in Earth's long ago history. We will write more about this later.

Ida: But they abandoned the Earth.

Maez: Just as the current residents will have to do if they keep on fooling around with nuclear power. That is, if anyone remains alive after you blow yourselves to bits. OUR MAJOR PURPOSE of interaction with you at this time is to keep you from doing just that!

Ida: Do you think you will be successful?

Maez: Yes, I think we are "over the hump" on that proposition. Chernobyl was the turning point. The disaster was much greater than ever reported. It blew apart the power that held the Soviet Union together better than a nuclear attack by the United States. If you don't have your people behind you, you don't have a State.

Perhaps I should not reveal this, but it will be common knowledge before long:

If the plot to oust President Clinton had succeeded, the moral fiber of the United States would quickly have disintegrated and with it the cohesiveness of the nation. This plot was not conceived by the local politicians, it was much more sinister and Machiavellian. It is a world plot to destroy all the world powers of the present, one by one, and to take over. President Clinton, although reprehensible in his personal actions, is, as a statesman, a courageous hero. It will take quite a few years before this can be fully known and appreciated.

Do you remember so many years ago when Hweig told you, "Even now there is a group of 12 meeting (in the Middle East) who are plotting to take over and control the world"? This group is keeping the world's nations at each other's throats, destroying economies with expenditures for war material and keeping the citizens of many countries homeless, foodless, and in despair? How better to control the world?

Enough of that for now. Go wash your dishes.

Maez to Ida, 2/26/99: Do not try to do too much. You have had one relapse of your ailment. Take it easy and sleep all you can. The atmosphere around you is heavy, making it unusually difficult to breathe easily. Until the weather clears be content to putter. Clearing up your desk so you can find things quickly is the only really important chore for the present.

Plans are being solidified for your meeting with Og. All looks favorable but I won't tease you by talking about it until the date is definitely set.

Meantime there are several things I've put off until "later".

Starting tomorrow I can take some time to answer them during the hiatus of other work. Today please work on desk clearing. Take care!

Maez to Ida, 3/2/99: It seems the most difficult thing for you to do, Ida is to take advice. I suggested you slow down; take it easy, so you sling all the furniture around in your bedroom from end to end. I'm glad you felt well enough to do it, but it was a heavy chore.

So, back to writing.

You might check with Mr. T. to see if March 16th or 18th is agreeable with him to make another attempt to contact Og. We will fill in with more details before then.

Sorry, I am called away. Maybe we can get back to writing later today or tomorrow.

Tres to Ida, 3/3/99: Maez is off on another project for several days. He is a very busy fellow. So we will talk a little bit on the development of the human race which is a subject of more interest to me than Bigfoot.

Ida: Professional jealousy?

Tres: You could be right!

The show last night on the opening of a tomb near the pyramids of Egypt was disappointing as it obviously was not a "first". It had been well set up, however, and gave a good look at the insides of such a place.

Everyone seems to have their own idea, opinion, about the meaning/purpose of the Great Pyramid, and the various others and the tombs. Edgar Cayce was as close as anyone to the facts and his information unfortunately is broken and scattered and frequently misquoted.

Now get this: the pyramids are a document, the most extensive and by far the most important document ever to be imprinted on Earth and almost impossible to totally erase. Their setting, placement, alignments, relationships to each other and the Earth, their construction, architectural relationships among them, the material of which they are formed, even the length of time (measurement of days) that it took to build them — all of these factors and many more are part of the information documented upon the sands of Egypt so that forthcoming generations would never be bereft of that information. Someone has obscured the major key to it all, but it will be found. The "key" is hidden in plain sight in such a way that it cannot be erased or altered by naughty men, the mischief makers, or the power hungry.

While men dig exhaustively in the grubby Earth for treasures and wealth in the long emptied tombs, the real treasure sits serenely over their heads, they need not grub an inch. It lies in the abstracts of measurements and geometry of science, science, science and mathematics. Take heed.

Tres, 3/4/99: No, it is not intended that you write or print all of this intrigue in your book. Better not. We sound paranoid with suspicion and we are not. We know where the real action is.

All of your petty politicians and world leaders are decoys. The real action is taking place on the level of Bigfoot and other undistinguished personalities.

We will not write more at present on world matters but return to our original course of getting photos of Bigfoot. However, watch the current events of major countries and try to see the possibilities of deep, deep waters underneath. Watch Great Britain, France, and Japan just to sharpen up your sleuthing abilities.

As for ourselves, our best workers are the little fellows who remain discreet or are even unknowing, and draw no attention to themselves.

Ida to Mr. T.: Not much writing done this week. Maez was flitting in and out and I am still taking long daytime naps. Can't seem to gain much energy. But fine otherwise.

Depends on the weather if our date of March 16 or 18 holds up. Today's short snowfall is unusually late.

Hope all is going well with you and Marlys and Ben. I'm not accomplishing much.

Maez to Ida, 3/6/99: I thought you would never put that book down and come to work. What is it?

Ida: *The Pattern of Evolution* by Niles Eldredge.

Maez: Is it interesting?

Ida: Some. I haven't read much yet. The cat keeps sitting down on it.

Maez: He only wants attention.

Ida: He never stays long. He's gone now.

Maez: Back to work. It is settled. We will attempt to meet Og on March 16th.

Ida: As good a date as any other. My enthusiasm is waning.

Maez: We will have to build it up again. It has been a difficult three weeks. You have been ill, the weather has been terrible, and I've been away much of the time. Let us re-gather ourselves and our spirits and get going again.

Ida: I like that word "spirits".

Maez: I meant it in the colloquial sense, cheerfulness or joy.

Ida: I'll settle for enthusiasm. What's on the agenda?

Maez: Yes, take a few notes from *Anthropology: The Study of Man* by E. Adamson Hoebel (1972). On page 134 is a chart showing *Australopithecus africanus* as being

"Erectly bipedal, omnivorous, and tool using if not tool making."

Page 135: "The facts, in short, are that an improved form of Australopithecine, akin to africanus, lived at Olduvai early in the Pleistocene, at least one million and possible 1.85 million years ago. He almost certainly made the simple

Oldawan stone tools and an occasional bone tool for food, and he ate a variety of small game and tortoises — and, of course, vegetables."

Page 135: "His pebble tool was a kind of hacking knife — a chopper of sorts — used in all likelihood to cut up meat, which was eaten raw."

Page 172: "Of the prerequisites for the maintenance of human society... the most uniquely human is a def-inition of 'the meaning of life' which maintains the moti-vation to survive and engage in the activities necessary to survival."

Maez to Ida, 3/8/99: You have asked, Ida, if Bigfoot has any sense or question about "the meaning of life". Yes, he has many questions but none nearly as sophisticated as your own. He does indeed bury his dead, he has been observed roll-ing heavy boulders over the dead of his family or clan. His main intention in doing this is to keep the bones from being found by animals or predators — such as yourself. This, in it-self, indicates he senses a personal interest in his dead be-yond the grave. Perhaps this is no more than a sentimental attachment to the deceased, a care-taking procedure. His feel-ings are not too well articulated on this point and, if he does not express them articulately we cannot know them.

We do know he wonders about life and is quite a philos-opher in an innocent child-like way.

The conclusions he reaches are practical and useful to his immediate needs but would be considered rather charming and even nonsensical by a scientist of your culture. By some mystic sense Bigfoot seems to find a right — or workable — an-swer to his dilemmas, but for all the wrong (unscientific) reasons.

Let us back-tread out of these murky waters.

Ida: Does Bigfoot have any ritualistic or cultish practices? According to the paleoanthropologists that would be a step for-ward in becoming humanlike.

Maez: Unfortunately, it would. But is that a step Bigfoot would find necessary or even want to make? Or would any thinking person want him to make? Why not leave him an inno-cent child of the forest breathing in and out with the spirit of the mountains and trees, uncontaminated by the "belief systems" of his less fortunate brothers of the cities. Let him remain a species unto himself and do what we can to protect and maintain his welfare and happiness. Let us bless and keep him for what he is, and for what we have lost. I speak for the races of humans on Earth as well as those on Arcturus.

Ida: I agree, most heartily and sympathetically. After all, what we most want to protect him from is ourselves, in our less thinking manners. That is the whole point from which we started.

Maez: You ask why we cannot just order, command, demand that Bigfoot do something we want. Because that would destroy the carefully cultivated bond we have between us. We monitor, we do not totally control his actions. We do not want to do anything that would decrease his confidence and faith in us. He knows we are concerned about his welfare. He depends on us and knows we do all we can to promote his health and well-being. We have maintained our close relationship over centuries by always being meticulous in our interactions, giving Bigfoot every freedom to make his own choices and direct his own life within the limitations of the work for which he was created. He even understands the limits and potentials of his life and our relation to it. All of this has been established for generations and for millennia. We do nothing to disturb this well established and deep relation. We love our Bigfoot and know that he loves us. Would we make any demands that would scar that?

Ida: Not unless you are totally inhumane and stupid.

Maez: We do not claim either attribute.

Maez to Ida, 3/9/99: The supervisors are scheduled to visit you this afternoon between 2 and 4 o'clock. They can answer any questions you have and lay out the plans for March 16th. They will explain some things they do not want to put into writing.

There is nothing more you have to do to prepare for them. Be at ease. They are only persons like yourself who have bonded into our work. You will have more to write about after they leave.

Maez to Ida, 3/10/99: The two whom you expect found something interesting and important to them enroute and stopped to inspect it. You may expect them between two and four today. Their stay will be brief. It is mostly to reassure you that this plan is on the level.

Maez: Stop fretting. They will be here in a few minutes.

Maez: They are not coming — there are no men. I will explain.

Ida: *&%#!!

Maez: Listen, please!

Ida: Go fly a kite. I'll talk to you tomorrow. I'm too mad now. You're wasting my life!

Maez to Ida, 3/11/99: There's a reason for everything.

Ida: Speak!

Maez: I apologize for misleading you.

Ida: This had better be good. It sounds like old times — twenty two years of it! I was so happy to get rid of Hweig and all of his misdirection. Now I've got you! I trusted you and you broke it all down bit by bit. You embarrass me. What am I going to tell Mr. T.?

Maez: That the photo session is on for March 16th. You will receive directions by Saturday.

Ida: I am not going unless I have some assurance this is bona fide.

Maez: You will have irreproachable assurance. You will be satisfied. If Lucifer can find reconciliation with God, can I not find reconciliation with you?

Ida: At arm's length. We are not friends.

Maez: As you wish. We will write more later.

Maez to Ida, 3/12/99: I'm sorry I imposed upon your good nature to such an extent. I know some of the things we do seem like schemes of deliberate torment to you. They do have a purpose which I feel would not be wise to reveal at this time. Please forgive this impasse and let us go on with plans to meet Bigfoot. Tomorrow you will know just what is intended. You don't have to like me, just bear with me a little longer. You have put nearly six months into this effort. Let us not waste all that time and work.

Ida: They have been wasted if we don't get some solid evidence to back them up. That is the bottom line.

Maez: You will have it. See you tomorrow. Don't forget to call the pharmacy.

Maez to Ida, 3/13/99: Why did you stop eating your breakfast?

Ida: I felt I had enough and my head was aching from a tooth. I took a pill.

Maez: Did you have visitors last night?

Ida: Apparently. I could not see them or discern them in any way although my legs were icy cold, especially when I was in the kitchen. However, they announced themselves as being present and asked to watch a particular TV program ("L.A. Detectives") so we did. They said they didn't care to see anymore so I went to bed. I told them to help themselves to any food or use of facilities or to explore the house, but I was going to sleep. They said they would go back to their motel on Sixth Avenue and not disturb me anymore until "tomorrow" which is today.

Maez: Have you heard from them today?

Ida: Yes, they are here, but said they would wait for you to explain.

Maez: They are the supervisors who were supposed to come to you in the physical but changed their minds at the last minute.

Ida: Is there something wrong with me? Everyone decides at the last minute that they don't want to see me after all!

Maez: Nothing wrong. But your uncanny ability to know more about people than they intend for you to know puts people off.

Ida: It is an unconscious trait. I don't do it purposely or use it maliciously.

Maez: We know that, but it is disconcerting just the same.

Ida: I can't promise not to do it. I'm not even sure how I do it.

Maez: We know. Go have a cup of coffee. It will help your headache. We will get our act together and write more later.

Maez to Ida: I think the men will agree to appear to you later today.

Ida: Shall I tell them to go back to the motel and put their bodies on?

Maez: I think they are going.

Ida: What I don't understand — they resent me knowing more about them than they would like, yet they have been informed all about me I am sure, and they read my every thought when they are tuned in. Isn't that a lot more than I know about them? And how do they think I feel when they are reading my mind? I have not had one moment of privacy for many, many years. I should be the one squawking!

Maez: It isn't supposed to work that way. You are not supposed to have this talent.

Ida: I'm sure I don't know from whom, where, or how I acquired it, and if I knew I would give it back. I have no desire whatever to read other people's dirty little secrets. That is the only kind they would resent me tuning in on.

Maez: Perhaps you are right. Well, you've got it, from wherever, so we will have to work around it with these squeamish ones.

Maez to Ida, 3/14/99: The supervisors are backing out and returning home. We shall have to find other help.

Ida: Now what did I do wrong?

Maez: Nothing. It's not what you do but who you are.

Ida: I am Ida. I know or claim nothing else.

Maez: I shall recall you to yourself. It is best to tell no one. They would laugh or lock you up. You have always been a female person in your incarnations, never male. History does not record you.

Ida: Startling news. May we change the subject?

Maez: Okay, back to Bigfoot. Don't fret. We cannot withhold him from you. How to arrange a meeting under current circumstances is the only problem.

Ida: You talk around and around the mulberry bush.

Maez: Thoth wants to talk to you.

Thoth to Ida: I have told you previously that you and I had personal relationships during several Earth incarnations. The one just revealed was the only one in which we were brother and sister. In some we were sweethearts and in some husband and wife or lovers. That is as much as it is wise to reveal at present. You are skeptical anyway. But it indicates why I am interested in you in your present lifetime.

Every effort is being made on several levels of being to help you get photos and other evidence of Bigfoot's reality. You are going to have a very exciting few months from here. Happy landing!

Maez to Ida, 3/15/99: Tomorrow morning be ready at ten o'clock with your cameras and whatever equipment you think you may need. A car will pick up Mr. T. and then you and take you to meet Bigfoot.

It will not be Og this time but one to three others. You will be able to interact with them closely for about two hours. A lunch will be provided. After some conversation with the advisers of Bigfoot you will be brought home, at least by four o'clock, maybe sooner. A video camera will also be available. That is all for the moment. Please inform Mr. T.

Maez to Ida, 3/18/99: How you do pout when you don't get your own way. Spoiled brat! No, you did not do something wrong, you did not do something right. And I with you. We did not follow protocol, that's all. We tried to devise a scheme of meetings that was not wrung through the wringer with the Council. Mr. T. is right, we should back up and take it a step at a time, not try to do everything so fast. Let me ponder on this for a day or two.

I'll test the other council members for their thoughts. Back soon.

Maez to Ida, 3/24/99: Ask Mr. T. if he and his wife can be ready (25th) to be picked up with their camera equipment. This time, Ida, you will not go. Forces may be working against us because of you. Besides you are still a little out of equilibrium. You could not walk easily in a forest. The best time for pickup is probably ten o'clock, unless there is some reason they can't go then. A video camera will be provided, also lunch. They will come home within six hours, maybe less. If they have any questions get back to me. It will not be Og.

Maez, 3/27/99: So the car did not appear to pick up Mr. and Mrs. T. We are as disconcerted as you. Remember what Hweig told you dozens of times, "When the time is right it will happen". I know this has meant many disappointments to you. "We are not miracle workers." Hweig also said that. Keep your trust and we will keep our promises. Perhaps we have been pushing our luck and expected too much to happen too fast. We will write more tomorrow. Thanks for giving me time today. I can see how things are piling up on you. One day all these different directions will suddenly fit like pieces of a puzzle. Why don't you take a bit of a nap?

Maez, 4/1/99: I'm glad you feel like writing again. I know you needed a rest. You must limit your projects and not try to solve everything at once. I am glad you found Hunbatz Men. His little book on Mayan science/religion can teach or corroborate your own thoughts more than any other. The book on Tesla is fascinating but not very revelatory. He was too secretive. Yes, the HAARP project in Alaska is based on his records purloined at the time of his death by the U.S. Government — a very wise move. Be glad it was successful. Tesla could have controlled the world had he been of a mind to do it. He was satisfied to astonish it. His kind of fun.

Bigfoot is safe in his nesting area, and will wait until we come up with a workable plan to meet. I wonder how we are supposed to recognize "when the time is right". What will tell us "Now"? Work your mind on that while you are tucked up in bed. Love, Maez

Ida: I don't have a clue.

Ida, from 4/1/99 to June 1: A hiatus has passed as I became ill enough to spend six days in the hospital and three more in rehab learning how to use an insulin needle. My blood sugar count registered 1200 when I finally went to emergency. People, even doctors and nurses, kept saying, "I never heard of a count that high!" and encouraging things like, "You should be dead."

Well, I'm not and I'm back on the trail of Bigfoot. I hope with better success than we have had to date. Meanwhile I am chasing through all the good books and magazine articles that I can round up. I can't quit in the middle of a good puzzle.

Maez to Ida, 6/7/99: I am glad to see you feeling so much better. I want to give you some important information re: Bigfoot. I know you are disgusted that your assigned meetings did not take place. That will be rectified in the future. For now let us just discuss some of the finer points of Bigfoot's nature.

Like all fully human beings various Bigfoot have individual idiosyncrasies. We try to keep up with their changes in attitudes but these are subjective characteristics that do not always announce themselves on the surface. We need to be better psychologists, I suppose.

Relative to all this, I will give you a page or two of notes each day to share with Mr. T. so when you really do meet Bigfoot you will be better prepared to "negotiate" with him.

That is all for today. I know you are preparing for a doctor's appointment.

Letter from Ida to Lee and Marlys Trippett

June 7, 1999

A short note from Thoth this morning. He wants to get back to work on Bigfoot notes. Okay.

I'm finding it hard to settle down to writing. So far I have seen my doctor five times in the last six weeks, an ophthalmologist, an audiologist, (hearing aids coming up), a podiatrist later this morning. I have had an assortment of pills and punctures (flu, tetanus, pneumonia shots), but I don't have to take insulin anymore. So much for health.

You will be surprised when you see Lord Spike, he is getting huge. Come when you can and feel like it. Always glad to see you both. I will have hearing aids soon so I can converse more intelligently. Regards. Ida K.

Maez to Ida, 6/12/99: Since you can't get back to sleep, let's write for a moment.

I will tell you about our first attempt at creating a creature to explore the Earth for us. Bigfoot, as he is today, is the result of hundreds of years of genetic trial and error. There is a good reason for every one of his idiosyncratic characteristics.

We needed a physical form that was extremely strong, able to withstand severe vicissitudes of weather and able to adapt to wild, rough countries with huge ferocious animals; that is one of the reasons for his size and bulk. *Australopithecanus* was not our first choice, he was much too small, or our first attempt, but it narrowed down to this after we had tried and abandoned several large forms of which modern anthropology has no knowledge. *A.a.* plus the gene input from our 7 and 8 foot Master race gave us the size and bulk we needed and he was progressing nicely toward a more human evolution. In other words he was the most intelligent creature of Earth propagation of that era.

There had been an earlier race of altogether humankind, highly civilized, but they had been destroyed, wiped out, by alien invasion. This race was not indigenous to Earth, but had been planted here, much too early for roots to have taken hold successfully. The planet was not yet ready for them. So much for really ancient history.

Our final and most successful interpretation of Bigfoot as he is known today was the culmination of many centuries of genetic experimentation, as I have said. We are the foremost genetic scientists of the galaxy, although others have made their contributions to Earth races.

The outer appearance of Bigfoot as hairy, rough, animalistic is another feature of his preservation. He had to confront and prevail over huge beasts and other proto-human and developing humans along his way. When humankind themselves became hairless and of a comparatively puny physique, a direct confrontation with a hairy Bigfoot was enough to send that person screaming for his life, as many of your confrontation stories can attest. As Man came to depend more on his larger and more convoluted brain and his cleverness in deploying artifacts, he grew to depend less and less on size and bulk. More another time.

Maez to Ida, 6/16/99: Since you can't sleep let us write a few lines, or pages.

Our account of Bigfoot can continue whenever you have surplus time. We will not go more into the history or genetics at this time, but into the present day status of our creature where it is most likely to be found and other immediate concerns.

Bigfoot in this area (Eugene, Oregon) are rather sparse and they move about rapidly from place to place. Now that it is summer Bigfoot moves down into the valleys seeking food in farmer's fields. He prefers to be vegetarian when such food is available, but can and will eat smaller animals up to and including deer when nothing else is to be found. If he is irritated enough at a farmer he may (but seldom) tear up a cow or two, but I doubt there are many stories of him attacking anything as rugged as an elk.

He will eat almost anything if necessary for sustenance. He is not a picky eater; food is food in his recognition. When only animal food is at hand he will eat the stomach contents first to get the benefit of the vegetation that the animal has ingested. You would find some of his table "delicacies" quite disgusting, but necessity cannot afford daintiness in choice.

Shelter for Bigfoot is a small problem. He can crash down anywhere there is a bare spot big enough, but of course he prefers a place that is sheltered from the elements, if it is to be found. He avoids deep caves but rock overhangs and shallow depressions are utilized.

We sometimes move our individual Bigfoot from one country to another to give each varied experience in different locations. They seem to enjoy this and do not insist on living for many years in the same area as long as they do not have immediate family, that is, mate and young. If so, they do not want to be separated from them. If the mate dies and there are no young, they are ready for new adventures and a new locale.

Most Bigfoot prefer an active life and become bored and irritable if for some reason they cannot move about readily. A sick or injured Bigfoot can be a very cranky fellow and is not to be approached without preliminary interaction.

Most of them understand the gist of spoken words, reading for themselves the body language and facial expressions of a person trying to communicate. They also intuitively and psychically follow the mood and intent of the mind of the person they meet.

Enough. Go to sleep now.

Maez to Ida, 6/17/99: We can continue on some of Bigfoot's general attributes. One of the most noticeable characteristics shared by all subspecies of Bigfoot is their intense curiosity. They can be lured close to a campsite or country cabin by the occupants doing something unusual and capturing the attention of the local Bigfoot. An occupation such as making barrels or cement sculptures or anything large and unexpected can be left in the area to attract their attention, or a group solemnly dancing and chanting each evening, or beating drums and singing or chanting in a reverent manner. Such activities are baits that never fail to draw Bigfoot near. Just how near and with what results depends on the ingenuity of the participants.

Go to sleep now. It is after 4:00 A.M.

Letter to Lee Trippett

June 21, 1999

As you can see I have not been very active in recording Maez's dictation. For one thing I had minor surgery on a big toe which became infected and I've been spending every afternoon soaking my foot in hot water and Epsom salts. It's getting along okay now.

My granddaughter, Robin, and her two girls from Alaska are visiting for a couple weeks. Denali is 12 and Kelsey 9. They are all sleeping this morning after a late night.

I've received a request from a new English magazine to consider writing for them. If they approve of my subject matter, I will of course.

I am not giving poor Maez much time. I have given these characters more than twenty years of my nose-to-the-grindstone attention. From here on my personal agenda comes first. It is time to rebel.

Ida, 4/2000: We have a nine-month intermission here. I have been working on another book about spiritual matters *Reconciliation*.

That can go to the publishers as soon as I copy it. Overall it took me seven years to prepare it. Now we can go back to Bigfoot.

Part Two

Is Bigfoot To Some Degree Human?

Letter from Ida to Mr. T.

April 2000

In putting together a book about Bigfoot, I think we have some good material for Part I concerning his genetic "birth" and his past history, also information from books by those who have been trying to contact him.

We can now start on notes for part II. I've been making a list of questions I would like to ask Maez. Some have already been answered but we need more specific details. So far we have just been getting acquainted with the kind of creature or "person" Bigfoot is.

So be thinking about the questions you would like to ask Maez and we will pin him down to more complete and specific answers. If we cannot get a good date to meet Bigfoot we can at least pump Maez for all the information we can get.

Letter from Mr. T. to Ida

April 4, 2000

We are so tuned into a whole different world that it is hard to come up with questions that relate to our understanding. For example, we spend so much, if not all of our time on topics of history, sports, politics, entertainment, commerce, hobbies, art, groceries, and many other personal projects. What does Bigfoot do with his time and thinking? I would think that a good deal of specific exploration is needed in this large area of thinking and activity.

There are all manner of questions relating to the possible similarities or differences of mental, emotional, and spiritual characteristics. Again, there are many specifics in this field which could be pressed by questions to previous answers.

Was Esau, the hairy brother of Jacob, more closely related to Bigfoot than human? There are many men in our society who are very hairy but still have all the typical human characteristics.

I am reserved from information that comes from Maez. His many failed appointments means a lack of understanding in the way our society normally communicates. For example if his Earth agents know how to use an automobile, they know how to use a telephone to adjust a schedule or make apologies. I would feel more confident of information about Bigfoot if you would communicate directly.

Although there is much public interest in Bigfoot, there are already books that provide theory or speculation. Few of them offer evidence in a form acceptable to the majority of our society. To me the most significant aspect of Bigfoot is their extended sense of perception, their unique mental faculties, and their spiritual qualities. (The very issues you plan to explore.) This type of information would save interest and value for some of us but would be of little significance to science or religion without some form of evidence.

Ida:

On UFOs and Bigfoot

On April 1 in the year 2000 a high official of the Vatican and a Hebrew scholar met in Bellaria, Italy, and discussed the issue of Extra-terrestrials, UFOs, and the Creation of Man. These two were Dr. Zecharia Sitchin, writer of the *Earth Chronicles*, and Monsignor Corrado Balducci, a Catholic theologian appointed by the Vatican to deal with the issues of UFOs and Extra-terrestrials. Despite the worldwide differences of these two men they nevertheless arrived at common conclusions.

- Yes, ETs can and do exist on other planets.
- Yes, they can be more advanced than we.
- Yes, materially Man could have been fashioned from a pre-existing sentient being.

"If Extra-terrestrials were so involved," Monsignor Balducci said, "even by your own interpretation they had to do with Man's physics, body, and rationality; but God alone had to do with the soul."

On UFOs Balducci said, "There must be something in it. The hundreds and thousands of eye witness reports leave no room for denying there is a measure of truth in them, even allowing for optical illusions, atmospheric phenomena and so on. As a Catholic theologian, such witnessing cannot be dismissed. Witnessing is one way of transmitting truth." (From www.sitchin.com.

Tres: I am glad to see, Ida, that you take the Sitchin-Balducci conversation with such seriousness.

Ida: Oh yes! I do indeed. Sitchin also explains that his thinking evolved toward the spiritual or divine aspect. As he came to understand it, the Niburians were "emissaries of God".

Tres: How do you respond to that, Ida?

Ida: In observing the differences of opinion between Maez and Thoth — Maez as an ET from Arcturus and Thoth of the same lineage as Jesus — I believe the ETs are not emissaries from God, nor are they Godlike. My own experiences with them belie any Godlikeness. They are not straightforward and they interfere with our free will. They are tricky and evasive of the truth.

Tres: Perhaps because of the differences between you, and the necessary precautions they must take in their interaction with you, they only seem tricky and evasive.

Ida: I will gladly concede there are differences. But after more than twenty years of conversation and interactions during which they have been in constant surveillance of me, they should know me well enough by now to be honest with me. I won't call their *modus operandi* unethical but I will call it inhumane and belittling. Also in Sitchin's books those from Niburu whom he calls "gods" certainly do not act like anything noble. They are robbing, fighting, quarreling kin-killers. These are Gods? As bad as the Greek "gods."

Tres: Such Gods do not live by the rules of 21st century middle class housewives.

Ida: Maybe they should. Or why do they expect us to live by such rules as honesty, decency, forgiveness, generosity, responsibility, and ask us to raise our children by such rules?

Tres: They believe their special position and duties give them special privileges.

Ida: Horseradish! The higher the position the more care and concern should be given those less fortunate. *Noblesse oblige.*

Tres: I heartily agree with you. I only wanted your statement on all this.

Ida: I am only suggesting that we be more careful on whom we call our "Gods". The Niburians may indeed be emissaries of God but that does not make them Gods with either a big or little "g".

Tres: I agree on that also. You will not find God the first Creator among the Niburians, not even Anu. But they did engineer the Adamic race through the manipulation of their own genes and those of an Earth pre-human consort. (See Appendix.)

The only revelation lacking now is that the Niburians were not the only makers of *Homo sapiens* on Earth as well as elsewhere! But we will explore all that in your forthcoming book. You will be writing mainly of the Masters of Arcturus who themselves were offspring of the Niburians and originated on Earth in earlier times! Now there is a history for you to explore, and we will!

Ida: Then that would explain why people who originated in the Middle East and those in the Western Hemisphere could be genetically compatible. I wondered about that.

Tres: This conversation between Sitchin and Msgr. Balducci should wake up a few more people to the reality of UFOs and ETs. I believe it also opens the door for us to give you some more direct and important answers to your many questions. If the Vatican authorizes such statements (and we all know Balducci would not dare to make them unless they were authorized) the door is spread wide open for many revelations which have been waiting on tiptoe to bound forth.

But because these ETs have made enormous physical and technological advances does not mean they have spiritually evolved equally far.

Balducci: "So the idea of taking a pre-man or hominid and creating someone who was aware of himself is something

Christianity is coming around to. The key is the distinction between the material body and the soul granted by God".

Ida: Perhaps it would be wise at this point to recount our cast of characters for this study:

1. Mr. T., or Lee Trippett, a Bigfoot researcher for nearly forty years. He is well known among the pursuers of Bigfoot and his reputable name is in many of the best known books.

2. Bigfoot, a mysterious and elusive creature of characteristics that seem a cross between an animal and a man.

3. Maez, known only by his telepathic voice. He is from the Arcturus star system, a "little gray" but nearly six feet tall. He is head of the Council that monitors Bigfoot, and reveals that Bigfoot is a genetically altered creature originating from Earth's *Australopithecus* with a genetic input from the Masters of the Arcturian planet. (These were originally from planet Earth and of the Niburian strain of humanity).

4. Thoth, a current incarnation of the original Thoth of Egyptian and other historical fame. He is not Arcturian and not to be confused as a current Extra-terrestrial. He wants to be recognized as totally terrestrial. He is known only as a telepathic voice.

5. Tres, another telepathic voice, who does not reveal himself except as a highly placed spiritual being. Except for his telepathic voice the rest remains in darkness.

6. Ida, a very ordinary and puzzled Earth person. Why me? I must re-emphasize that Thoth and Tres are not to be confused as Arcturian and not to be considered under the current understanding of Extraterrestrial. Their entire and proper designation at the present time can only be thought of as "not known for sure."

My book *Project Earth*, published in 1995, follows and illuminates the stressful course of such telepathic relationships.

Is all this **real**? For one who reads with "the willing suspension of disbelief" as poet Coleridge advised, the mystery breaks up into swallowable pieces. To anyone who is undergoing a like event (and there are many) it all becomes coherent and logical, and yes, it is **real**! It requires a bit of gracious imagination and a lot of personal courage — or is it foolhardiness — I often wish I knew for sure. Happy reading!

I believe the conversation between Sitchin and Msgr. Balducci leaves the door wide open toward the acceptance of UFOs into an ever widening field. UFOs and Bigfoot have been reported in these later years to have been seen many times in close association.

Yes, I am afraid all this is very real, because that imposes many more questions that we are not prepared to answer, but with Maez's help we shall try to anticipate and answer some.

In the Bigfoot Co-op newsletter of April-June 1992, Mr. Albert Rosales admits that his personal area of interest includes UFO related humanoids.

"I concluded several years ago," says Mr. Rosales, "that there is a solid link between UFO phenomena and certain Bigfoot-like creatures. There have been numerous incidents mentioned in the literature that indicate a clear link. I am going to mention two cases of Bigfoot-like creatures seen in or coming out of a UFO type object."

1. From the MUFON UFO Journal #264 Near Tillamook, Oregon September 27, 1989

    A woman, alerted by her young granddaughter to something unusual, stepped outside and was confronted by an object resembling a toy top hovering just above the ground. It was maybe 20-30 feet in diameter and had a flat bottom and a bright yellow-white light shone at both ends. The woman approached the object to within 30 feet and a door opened revealing a blond human-like being of average height with fair skin and blue eyes, wearing a silvery coverall. The woman then noticed, at a window next to the door, a large, hairy, Bigfoot-like creature apparently seated, and visible from the chest up. The woman stared at the object and being for a few minutes, then the object suddenly vanished from plain view!

2. Humcat files #1844 (addenda)

    Between Mairieux and Maubeuge (Nord) France Joel Mesnard and Jean-Marie Bigorne November 26, 1973

    A man and a woman in a parked car on the Canourgue Road (apparently connecting both locations) noticed a white metallic looking dome-shaped object on a snow covered road about 100 yards away. A large, dark opening became visible and six beings of three different kinds emerged. There were small four foot tall humanoids ... behind these beings stood two human-like figures. Also emerging from the object was a large, squat figure with long dangling arms, covered with dark fur, "resembling a great ape". The ape-like creature re-entered the object first, followed by the two tall humans, and then the short humanoids. The object rose vertically, becoming orange-luminous, then bluish, then reddish before disappearing from sight."

Ida: These are only two of many reported incidents involving both a UFO and a Bigfoot type creature.

Maez, 4/20/2000: It is good to be in communication again. For the present we shall write only; no wild goose chases to annoy you.

Maez to Ida, 4/29/2000: We shall not waste time on chitchat, but get right to work on Bigfoot. I know your main interest is his relationship to *Homo sapiens*. Mr. T.'s main interest is in spiritual understanding and his intellectual development. Both of these themes can be integrated into the exposition I have planned.

It might help you to read over the notes we have made so far, it has been some time since these were given and I am sure you have forgotten some points.

For today I want to give you some interesting points that no one has given in any text that I know of.

First, the identity of each Bigfoot is not noted by a name as yours is but by a sound. Each, in a given area, has his own call signal. He gives it to attract another Bigfoot, or to identify himself when he is in a group, or if he is approaching another. We will go more deeply into its use later.

Another singular characteristic is his attention span. You can scarcely wait a half hour without getting restless. He can wait for twelve hours or more and scarcely move in that time.

Another characteristic that might be useful to know if you are trying to catch a glimpse of one, is that he can be so stationary you would think you are looking at a tree trunk. Try holding yourself absolutely still and you will see how different his action can be from yours. More tomorrow. This was just to break the ice.

Maez to Ida:

What Bigfoot Thinks and How He Acts

Now that you have reread all the information offered to date, we can proceed to amplify the short bits you were given previously. Since there has been considerable time lapse between that date and this, let us call this Part II and proceed as you and Mr. T. have suggested.

Let us start at the top and consider Bigfoot's idea of a God. He does have an idea of someone whom he considers a protector and adviser, very much as you do yourself, Ida. I, of course, am not privy to his innermost thoughts, in fact not as much as I am your own. You make me begin to question our policy of intruding into your thoughts. The reason for doing this is that we — us grays — have a collective sort of mind. This was given to us by the Masters for their own reasons. They do not have a collective mind and neither do you, but we have been treating you as though you do have, and it is our natural way of treating each other. Perhaps we should rethink our approach to you and find a way of interacting that is not so foreign and irritating to you. But then I cannot think of a way that would allow me to dictate information to you. Or Bigfoot could not do so either. We have been hasty and thoughtless in our interaction with you. If I can think of a better way (from your viewpoint) of interacting with you, I shall put it into effect immediately.

Back to Bigfoot. As far as I am able to ascertain, he does not think of God in any form but as a natural force, just as he accepts the activity of the wind. "It" is a power or force that can do things for him and has just naturally provided such things as food and water. He takes all this for granted, just as your people do.

Bigfoot thinks of God as a friend and companion and he sometimes talks to "It" just as you do. He does not think of God as a being like himself or like yourself, or even myself, although there are times when I think he confuses me and my place in his life as being equivalent to God's. We discourage this innocent picture and tell him we have never seen God either and cannot describe "It" any more closely than he already has. Bigfoot is pure innocence but not as a child. It is a mature and thinking innocence. It distresses him when he sees humans of your kind acting in a foolish and dangerous manner because he knows their actions can lead to trouble and danger. But he does not judge them according to any moral law; therefore he does not recognize the idea of forgiveness either for them or for himself. It is an idea totally unknown to him. He is not that sophisticated.

Bigfoot does not pray in the sense that your kind of humans do. He talks to God in a comradely sort of way and accepts whatever happens relative to his question as an answer. It is a very simplistic kind of "religion", a direct interaction with the force he accepts in the way you accept the idea of God.

I am glad there has been so long a time in between our correspondence because it has given me time to find out many things about Bigfoot and his way of thinking that I had not considered previously. You and Mr. T. have suggested a closer look at what makes Bigfoot "tick" as you say. There is so much I had just taken for granted that deserves closer scrutiny.

Bigfoot is not exactly the same as Adam and Eve in the Garden before they learned the conflict of good and evil, but he is almost.

Bigfoot is not malicious and any action he takes of a violent or destructive nature is a reaction to something that he has seen or that has been done to him. He can react in a violent or animalistic way to something that has horrified him, but there are many of your kind who do the same and with far less reason. I read your newspaper with you every day and am myself horrified at the violence reported from ordinary people, that you would never suspect of being capable of such actions.

I am not trying to make Bigfoot out a saint. He can show jealousy, particularly of a mate or to some interference into their lives. He can even plot some kind of savage rebuttal, but it is always in response to an interference. He does not initiate "hate crimes".

This is not to say that Bigfoot does not have a moral sense, but it is so much an inbuilt part of him that it is more a quality of his nature than any moral philosophy. To see a child of any species deliberately or brutally mistreated would arouse a fury I would not want to witness. Perhaps this is more from his natural gentleness than any real moral sense, but the result is the same. He does not judge the person, he judges the effects of the action and he takes steps to stop it.

In such an action as this, there is no time for judgment or forgiveness. His action is immediate and final, the extent depending on the severity of the crime. In severe instances Bigfoot has been known to kill the perpetrator. In all instances the perpetrator is made to wish he were dead. There are no courts of law in the Bigfoot domain. The monitors have no time to intercede.

No, Bigfoot has no thoughts of forgiveness, per se, nor any need to. If he sees an action one day that causes harm or danger to others, he will immediately take steps to stop it. And, as far as he is concerned, that is an end to the matter.

If he sees the same person the next day behaving in a good and proper manner, he will treat that person accordingly. There is no judgment, no grudge, and no hold over from the day before. Bigfoot may be a little more wary, knowing what that person is capable of, but that is only good sense and natural caution.

Bigfoot's demeanor in such a situation is so natural and complete he does not have any thought of "forgiveness" although in essence that is what it is, a complete and natural forgiveness.

Bigfoot does not see that his reaction or stopping the dangerous or harmful action is anything that requires anyone's forgiveness, not even God's. He reacted in a natural and proper manner. He has no guilt. He is totally innocent and without judgment of another, grudge, forgiveness, or guilt of his own.

If someone, or a group, builds a road, dam, too big a bonfire within his territory, he will think it calls for a warning action, perhaps some destructive act. Again, this is a reaction to what someone else is doing; it is not a self-initiated act of aggression. Do not threaten harm to anyone in any way that Bigfoot might resent and he will leave you in peace.

I think we have covered the ideas of forgiveness, guilt and judgment as well as we can at this point. Let us go to another question.

We have spoken some of Bigfoot's manner of "prayer". He does not pray as your people do, he talks to God as though to an unseen friend, explaining what his problem might be and mulling over what might help him. Whatever happens thenceforth, relative to that problem or question, he takes as an answer to his complaint. He accepts it and makes the best of it according to his understanding and abilities. He talks to his monitor in the same manner although he can hear an answer or even receive a visit to straighten out a severe problem. At least twice a year he is taken aboard a UFO for what you would call a "physical", and is tested thoroughly for any health problem. At the same time he is given oral tests to gauge the condition of his mental and emotional states. If help seems required in such matters, it is given. In rare cases he is kept in confinement for a period of time to work out his psychological and emotional difficulties. This is rarely necessary. Bigfoot is so much a man of nature that he maintains a consistent mental balance that your humankind could well envy. Without a sense of guilt and with very few natural fears, he keeps a mental equilibrium second to no one.

In this study we are talking about the Sasquatch type of Bigfoot that you will find in the Pacific Northwest. There are other branches of the Bigfoot species but in a much generalized way what we are saying here will apply equally well to most of them. If you do not appear as a threat to any of them, they will prefer to slip away into the forest and not let their presence be known.

Yes, we said oral tests. Bigfoot has vocalization abilities. We, however, hear him just as Og spoke to you, by thought vibrations that the receiver translates into his own kind of speech, no matter what kind of guttural or gibbering voice it has been uttered in. I think Hweig explained this to you as well as possible although he did not know exactly how it was accomplished. He accepted and used the facility as a natural phenomenon. We don't want to get technical in this but present it as a very natural part of existence.

And, incidentally, at his own request, Og is learning to speak as you do, in English type of words. It has been educational for all of us to teach him to use his vocal cords in this manner to learn words you will understand. A few others of his species have done so, but Og seems to be such an apt pupil, perhaps because he wants to so badly. We are making preparations to teach some young Bigfoot to speak in this manner. It should be easier for them while they are still young. Even among your people, if someone is not taught to speak until they are adult, it is extremely hard for them to do so, many times impossible. Og, as you named him, is incredibly intelligent.

Perhaps that is enough for right now. Go take your shower and get ready to go buy groceries. You have morning glories to plant and pansies to buy. We will talk more later today or tomorrow or whenever.

Maez, 5/8/2000: For his general spiritual understanding Bigfoot has much in common with the Native American way of thinking. There has been close interaction between them for years, indeed generations.

Ida: Once I was told by a lady Indian shaman that Bigfoot and her people had an on-going relationship for centuries.

"When one of our people is injured in the woods and cannot take care of himself," she said, "Bigfoot will come and carry the man to his nest and see that he has food and water and that no animal molests him until he is well enough to take care of himself. Then Bigfoot will take the man back to the exact spot where he found him and leave him there."

Maez: On your world map, Ida, you have pointed out the possible locations to expect a Bigfoot: mountains inaccessible to white men, a body of fresh water, such as a lake or fast-running river, and impenetrable forests. These are three requisites for his safety. He does not come down to the lowlands or farm country unless he is extremely hungry or in need of help.

Bigfoot does not understand the idea of private property. His essentials of life have always been derived from the areas just described which provide him and his brethren with everything they really need except in cases of distressful circumstances such as bad weather, earthquakes, volcanic eruptions, forest fires, or floods or encroachment upon his habitat in such a manner that renders it unfit for his use.

Bigfoot does not grasp the idea of theft as of a farmer's livestock or chickens. The forests, the mountains, and streams have always provided for him in a manner that he considers free for the taking. God put them there for that purpose. That someone should parcel off a piece of land and proclaim, "This is all mine," is a joke to him and not a very good joke. He freely shares what he has gathered with his family, his clan, even with strangers, or shows them how to collect their own, actually a more useful lesson. His down to earth living practices are more sensible and life serving than those of a city man sweating his life away on a job he loathes. Unfortunately, we cannot all take to the woods and become hairy philosophers with such an earthborn pristine knowledge.

Understandably his monitors cannot always reach him quickly enough to save him from the wear and tear of catastrophes. We send him what help we can as quickly as possible, and we have a dozen different ways to come to his rescue. We shall describe some of them a little later as we build up our rather complex revelations. So little is really known about Bigfoot's personal lives and tragedies, and his very lengthy history on earth. Native people in the areas that he inhabits could reveal a great deal, but experience has taught them not to talk too freely until they are sure of the person they are talking to. They have found it wisest to pretend ignorance of the whole subject.

Bigfoot feels a certain kinship with the Native Americans. They "speak the same language", that is they understand, need, and utilize the same things of nature.

The Anglos confuse him. He can see what the white man is trying to do in building roads and dams, but he cannot see that it is in any way a good or useful thing. To him it is all destructive, and he sometimes takes severe actions to express his displeasure. He realizes the overwhelming number of white people calls for different ways from his own in solving the everyday problems of life, getting food, creating shelter, etc. He wonders where all these white people are coming from and he wishes they would go back there. That is about as far as he comprehends the situation. He is intelligent enough that he could be taught to understand more if anyone could see the use of doing it. His monitors prefer to leave him the innocent that he is. Why try to make a white man out of him? That mistake was taken with the Native Americans. Leave Bigfoot alone!

To discover a Bigfoot, to make a friend or collaborator of him, you must first learn to think like a Bigfoot!

What does he value? First and foremost his freedom. Anything that would seem to limit or cramp his freedom would be repelled by him. If the action pressed too closely upon him, he would resist, violently if necessary. A bear will do that much.

Bigfoot understands far more than a bear, and the violence of his reaction depends more upon his fear of being pushed back than his anger at the intrusion.

Maez: We have been discussing the collective minds of persons like myself, the ones you call "the grays".

No, Bigfoot does not have a collective mind. His was the first instance of Species Homo that had an individualistic mind. However, such minds had immediate and constant contact with each other through telepathy. The Earth-born do not have the telepathic abilities to the extent that the Arcturus generated ones had, but the Earth-born are facile in learning and using telepathy. They learn from their parents or others, just as you learn to speak. Because they are so adept at telepathic communication they have not needed to utilize speech to any extent. They can use speech if they are taught and feel the need to do so. We have already discussed this.

Arcturians with collective minds, such as myself, use telepathy in several ways unknown and unreachable to you.

The Masters of Arcturus have individualistic minds like your own, but they also use telepathy in several ways.

Maez, 5/28/2000: Please forgive this hiatus in communication. Several events have occurred that cause us to reshape our plans. One of these you now know, your old friend (well, communicator) Hweig has returned and wants to work with you again. After considerable discussion, including your own negative input, a decision has been made against this. I am now delivering information directly to you myself, and I think we should leave it at that.

Ida: For six weeks Hweig has been playing that music in my head night and day, just short phrases repeated over and over. In no way is it pleasant or soothing. I do not find that conducive to want to work with him again. I don't know how he engineers the production of such jagged bits, but if his purpose is to drive me nuts, he is well on the way. I can't think. How can I work when my mind is being jerked about like this?

Maez: We shall try to silence the music.

Ida: I can't imagine what its purpose is, but it is too distracting. This is the third or fourth period of time that this has taken place. That's enough!

Maez: We shall try to find a remedy.

Ida: I do not consider anyone who treats me like this, despite all my pleas and remonstrance, to be a friend. Let's change the subject.

Maez: That is best. We need to get back to Bigfoot. I hope you will be patient with us and understand our problems in getting information and evidence to you. We have three factions to bring together in common understanding. 1. The monitors and Earth Supervisors of Bigfoot. 2. Bigfoot himself.

3. Your own understanding and wishes relative to Bigfoot. These are three unique factions who have totally separate and different ways of thinking and different knowledge of Bigfoot both historically and physically. And each has a different way of acting with little-known persons. It is much more difficult than a town meeting of friends and neighbors who have known and interacted with each other for years.

Ida: We seem to be the out-landers.

Maez: From our viewpoint, yes. For you, we are the aliens.

Ida: We are out-numbered.

Maez: We are thinking of you as representative of all your kind.

Ida: There is that collective mind approach again.

Maez: With the help of the Earth supervisors we will try to overcome that. Hweig can be of help here, also.

Ida: Just keep him out of my hair. I had twenty-two years daily and nightly of his games. Keep him in the background. I realize receiving information is a terrific opportunity for which I should be grateful. Believe me, I am. But I refuse to be harassed any longer. I won't play by his rules.

Maez: I promise to do my best. Now teach me some more of that card game. Solitaire?

Ida: Yes. Okay.

Maez, 5/29/2000: I think we have solved the problem of Hweig and his incessant scraps of music. We held a joint session of the Tribunal and the Council and it was decided to send him on a very desirable job with the stipulation he was not to annoy you in any way ever again. You may hear bits of music for a few days until all "installations" have been removed. Please do not ask questions. The less we talk about this and keep it in your mind, the sooner all music will cease.

Ida: Fine with me. My appreciation to the authorities involved! I can think better on the information about Bigfoot now.

Maez: Og has asked permission to speak to you a minute or two each day. He wants to show off his new way of talking.

Ida: We spoke for a few minutes yesterday. He asked me if I was lonely. This morning we spoke again. He is doing very well.

Maez: He doesn't want to talk long for fear of making a mistake. As he gains confidence he will talk longer. Do you still hear the music?

Ida: Now and then. If I start to read I do not hear it.

Maez: Good. Let us get back to our subject. The major point we want to make, so that there is no mistake or question concerning Bigfoot, is that the dominating species of humankind on Earth today is a complex variation of the Arcturian Master race and a species (*Homo erectus*) very highly evolved from *Australopithecus africanus* exactly as Bigfoot was from the original *A.a.* This makes your humankind and Bigfoot full blood and genetic brothers. Let there be no doubt about that. When the Native Americans say that Bigfoot is their brother, they know exactly what they are saying. They are not speaking sentiment. They are stating fact. The natives of the Western Hemisphere are closer than all others to Bigfoot both historically and genetically.

At the present time to try to elucidate the entire complex and confusing historical evolution of the various races of mankind on Earth would be sheer futility, both from the complexity of the inter-breeding and genetic altering *by several other planetary people* and because there are not enough true historical facts accepted by your people to make such an intricate and confusing story acceptable. It will take many years of study, research, and revelation to compose a background for such a story.

When you come again in your next lifetime, Ida, come as an anthropologist, and make the story of mankind on Earth your life study just as Sitchin has done.

Ida: That is my intention if we are allowed to choose so far ahead.

Maez: Oh, yes! All of the study and discoveries you have made in this lifetime will not be allowed to go to waste. You are already preparing yourself for your next life. The world is not ready yet for your discoveries. Come back in another fifty or a hundred years.

Ida: I am looking forward to it. You are taking some of the pressure and sense of urgency off my mind. Maybe now my blood pressure will go down.

Maez: Well, you are not about to leave this life yet, so why don't we get back to Bigfoot?

Ida, 6/1/2000: Maybe I can teach Og to play solitaire, too.

Maez: I doubt that! And I doubt the Council would permit it.

Ida: You are teaching him to speak words.

Maez: We may find that is a mistake.

Ida: Speaking may be an evolutionary trend that cannot be denied, if he has the idea of speaking, wants to do so, and has the vocal apparatus necessary.

Maez: He has all of that. There seems to be no way of stopping him.

Ida: Then don't worry about it. Let it happen. It will anyway, whether you worry or not. Don't push it if you don't want to, but don't try to stop it. You would only anger and

‌‌‌‌‌‌

‌‌‌

‌‌‌‌‌‌‌‌‌‌‌‌‌‌

---

frustrate him. I, for one, don't want to face up to an angry and frustrated Bigfoot.

Maez: Nor do I. I have seen what happens. He has the strength of ten men and the fury of a hurricane. That will be our Bigfoot lesson for today, don't anger or frustrate a Bigfoot.

You had better get the vacuuming done. Company is coming. That was a beautiful pie you made. I'm sorry I don't eat pie.

You called it a lemon — what?

Ida: Meringue. A lemon meringue pie. That was the white stuff on top. It tasted pretty good too, even after I upset half of it. I gave the good half to my daughter. It is too sweet for my diabetic diet.

Maez: Why did you bake it then?

Ida: I was bored and wanted something different to do. When I get bored I bake something.

Maez: I learn more about you every day.

Ida: Stick around. Sometimes I get really interesting!

Maez: I think you discovered the right culprit to blame for the continuous on-going of music in your head. The one called Roger has been letting poor old Hweig take all the blame.

Ida: Roger's purpose was to get Hweig in trouble and to make him stay away from me. Instead Hweig was given a terrific new job that he never would have gained otherwise, if he promised to stop harassing me. So Roger simply pushed Hweig into a tremendous professional advancement. Now Roger will be the one punished and also made to stop annoying me. Both fellows are supposed to never talk to me again. I apologize to Hweig for blaming him. I am greatly relieved to be free of their game-playing. I was the game board on which they were battling out their competition. This was not the first time.

Maez: Has the music stopped?

Ida: Mostly. It is not so frequent and not so loud.

Maez: You should never be troubled by it again. Roger will face the Tribunal. What I don't understand is why Hweig did not deny that he was the one making the music. He never defended himself but let everyone go on thinking he was the guilty one.

Ida: It was his lever for getting the job he wanted. It gave him something to trade.

Maez: The rascal! I knew he was clever.

Ida: He was using us all, and Roger the most. I am finding it very funny!

Maez: I'm glad you can laugh after all the torment those fellows put you through.

Ida: I can see now why Thoth and Tres let the music run on after I begged them to make it stop. They were giving Roger time to entrap himself.

Maez: So we have just witnessed an episode of competition between rivals, Roger and Hweig. Bigfoot would never plan nor engage in such a nefarious scheme to put an enemy in trouble with the authorities. His mind does not work in that way. It is not so complicated. It is not bitter.

Ida: I've been wanting to ask you, why did Og ask me if I was lonely? Was he seeing me?

Maez: Yes. When he talks to you we click on the visual in his implant. You do not have a visual, only an aural. He always sees you sitting alone at your desk. Bigfoot does not like to be alone. One always has a partner, either a mate or a younger one he is training. If one of a pair dies, a young adult is always provided within two weeks at the most. No Bigfoot is ever alone more than a few days. They are so accustomed to always having a partner they have never learned to be alone. If you see one Bigfoot in the woods, be very sure another one is close by. Remember to look for a second one. They may separate as far as a half mile, but very briefly. Their habitat for the most part is very wild and they must depend on their own resources. The partner plan was established in their very beginning as a safety device. It has become like a part of their nature. Even the female of a pair is usually somewhere close to the male. It is a safety element for both.

Maez, 6/5/2000: Enough time has been spent on cards, back to work. I'm glad the music is fading out. In a few days it will all be gone. Is that a monkey in your trees?

Ida: No, that is a red squirrel. We do not have wild monkeys in Oregon. Farther south in Mexico and South America they have many kinds of monkeys.

Maez: I understand you and Og have been having some conversations.

Ida: He said, "I love you," and I said, "You don't know me very well," and he said, "I know you are kind and good and understanding", and I said, "Oh, Og, that is the nicest thing anyone has ever said to me."

Maez: He said he made you cry. That worries him.

Ida: Oh, please explain to him it was because I was touched and pleased. Silly women sometimes cry when they are happy. I told him, "I love you too, because you are big and strong and tender hearted."

Maez: I am glad you two have struck a rapport. It will make things — our work — much easier. Was that all?

Ida: The rest is personal.

Maez: Fine. Let's get back to work. We were discussing the yearly meeting of Bigfoot at a place on the Olympic Peninsula. It is at a different place each year so as not to attract unwanted guests. It usually takes place around the middle of July, though the timing changes too.

Ida: Do all the Bigfoot attend?

Maez: About one-half to two-thirds try to go. They leave some on alert in the home area. And they come in and out; they don't all barge in at once. It takes place over five or six days.

Ida: What do they do at their convention? Have speeches?

Maez: It is not so formal. It is more like a family reunion. They visit with each other, discuss experiences, warn about new dangers, catch up on gossip, and eat a lot, just like you do at family picnics.

Ida: Wow! To walk into a gathering like that would startle a Bigfoot hunter out of his shoes.

Maez: Out of his skin more likely. It is unlikely this would ever happen. They post sentinels and do not gather in a tight spot. They scatter out and talk to a few friends at a time. If someone should approach too closely they warn each other through telepathy and just melt into the woods. There is little to indicate a gathering has taken place. There are no candy wrappers or tuna tins or dead campfires left behind. The area they meet in is very dense, almost impenetrable to a hunter.

Ida: What would happen if a hunter should stumble upon them?

Maez: It depends on the hunter and his reaction. He would probably die of fright, his hair would turn white, or he would go stark, raving mad.

Ida: Now you're making fun.

Maez: All right. I exaggerate. Since such a thing has never happened that I know of, I cannot really answer your question.

Ida: Olympic Peninsula, huh? North, south, west?

Maez: North, definitely north.

Ida: Sequim, Port Angeles, Forks?

Maez: Ask me no questions, I'll tell you no lies.

Ida: Boy, you do come up with some of the tritest expressions I ever heard.

Maez: I've been studying your vernacular for a long time. I like the breeziness, the good-naturedness of it. I really don't have a chance to use it often as I do not customarily converse directly with your people.

Ida: Why am I chosen specially then?

Maez: I'd rather not answer that at this time.

Ida: From how large an area does this convention draw?

Maez: They do not consider their area by states as you do although they recognize your pattern of states. They draw from very southern British Columbia and Alberta, from Washington, Idaho, the very edges of Montana and Wyoming, from Oregon and the upper edge of California, from about Eureka north. This is a very rough estimate of the area. Maybe a little from upper Nevada. I don't want to be too specific for safety reasons.

Ida: I appreciate that so I won't bear down too hard on the specific questions. In general then, we can expect a movement of Bigfoot toward the northern peninsula in mid-July?

Maez: For their safety I'd rather not discuss this any further.

Ida: Do other areas of the country have their own yearly gatherings?

Maez: Yes, usually once a year but in their own time and place. This has been the custom of their kind for thousands and thousands of years. They would describe it as Native Americans do as their "gatherings".

Ida: If Bigfoot is moved about periodically by their monitors, how do they keep track of their own clan?

Maez: In the first place they consider any Bigfoot of their own kind as a relative, a distant cousin perhaps, but as part of their "clan". And secondly we try to keep each one within a definite geographical area so that he is never too far distanced from his closest family. To send him away for any distance from his family would be for a very short time for a purpose to be accomplished quickly and then return to his own area. We try to be considerate of his own wishes and feelings. It keeps him happy with us and willing to do what we ask of him.

I think this is enough for today. Maybe we could have a game of cards and then it is your bedtime.

Maez, 6/6/2000: We were discussing Bigfoot and his senses of competition and possessiveness. He has very little of either. He can show a little jealousy over his mate, but otherwise there is almost no possessive or competitive spirit.

He does not stock up on groceries or buy new furniture for the "den". Everything he needs is procurable for the day he needs it. If it isn't we move him to another locality where nature provides his daily necessities. If he finds he has gathered in more than he needs for his own use, he gives it to another, even a stranger. He does not let provision turn green in his refrigerator, he finds someone to share it with.

Ida: I'm afraid you've been watching me clean out my ice box before garbage day.

Maez: A-hem. He does use rocks for several purposes but he does not carry them about with him. There are always more at hand for his immediate use. If not, he uses sticks. He has no pockets or knapsacks to carry things about. He may have a dozen different sleeping nests but he never uses one too frequently or any for too long a time. Again, this is to keep anyone from marking his place and making a stake-out or trap for him. His kind has learned the value of such precautions ages ago. That is why they are still with us.

Ida: With the watchful protection of Bigfoot monitors and supervisors, his own centuries-old tricks of the trade, his psychic ability to fade out of sight, the ignorance of our kind of people concerning him, it seems Bigfoot is very well protected from capture. Why, then, do you give me all of this information? Does this not make him more vulnerable?

Maez: Because everything is changing with great rapidity. The safety structures of the past will not serve much longer. We want your people to see and understand the simple purity and wonder of our Bigfoot, to recognize him as a brother human, and to protect and cherish him as we do. Look at what has been done to re-establish the American Bison. If they can do that for a buffalo, they can re-establish and protect a human brother, although he looks so different in appearance.

Ida: You put up a good argument, revelation rather, in their defense. I hope it will be listened to and taken under advisement.

Maez: The Council has given an enormous amount of thought to this problem. We do not lightly reveal so much information. But we believe the only way your people can ever come to a true understanding of Bigfoot and his nature is by telling you these facts.

Ida: I see the necessity of it. I hope my kind is wise enough and sympathetic enough to use these revelations for the purpose for which they are given. As you said, they did it for the buffalo; maybe they can do it for Bigfoot, and also help to re-establish the Native Americans.

Maez: Oh God yes! There are great efforts being made in that direction. But let us not take in too big a territory here. Let us just stick with Bigfoot for now.

Ida: You know I started this study out of curiosity. I'm afraid I am now becoming emotionally involved.

Maez: Well, don't be afraid, be determined. You are proof of this premise yourself. Once you know the true nature of Bigfoot and recognize some of his problems, you can't help getting emotionally involved. That's what we want everyone to do.

Ida: I understand. You know what you are doing. There is more to this than idle chit-chat. I will continue to be your scribe. Maybe that was why I was so fascinated with the statue of the Egyptian scribe in the Louvre. (I must learn to sit cross-legged.)

Maez: Stay light-hearted, Ida. That's the way we like you. No whimpering. No whining.

Ida: My mama wouldn't let me.

Maez: Your mama raised you right!

Maez, 6/8/2000: Just a note this morning to tell you we are re-positioning Og. He can finish his "school" lessons just as easily there as here. He, his mate and grown son are now living within a hundred miles of you as their permanent base, but it is not likely you will be ready to meet this year. There is much to be learned on both sides before a meeting is advisable. We will continue on this correspondence level for the present.

That is all for right now. Come back this afternoon or tomorrow and we will talk about stones and how Bigfoot uses them.

Maez, 6/9/2000: You were too absorbed in other matters yesterday but the subject of stones will keep. Stones are patient. We can talk about them anytime.

This morning we have been talking about Bigfoot's knowledge of such things as fire, hot water, ice, earthquakes, volcanoes, floods, and other outrageous acts of nature. Each Bigfoot has been well advised of these although they may not occur in everyone's territory. He is not an ignoramus concerning problems of nature. No, he does not attend school as you do, of course, but part of his young adult training with an older partner has been to inform him of such acts of nature. He may, in his future, be transferred, even temporarily, into an area of such natural destructive violence. Thus we have a body of workers well prepared to cope with such disasters to be of aid, usually quite inconspicuously to local people.

The secrecy with which Bigfoot must act for his own safety from detection makes him less valuable in rescue operations where he might be seen.

During a spring flood the owner of a valuable herd of horses or of cattle, might find that somehow his livestock managed to escape out of their expensive pasture holdings and onto high ground in time to preserve their lives. "It was a miracle!" exclaims the rancher. No, it was Bigfoot, who destroyed that three hundred dollar locking device or tore up the "impregnable" fencing itself. With his strength and intelligence he can destroy any such barrier to freedom. He was taught about locks so that he might break into his own freedom if impounded like an animal.

Suppose Bigfoot has taken a friendly liking to a young couple honeymooning in a remote cabin? He has been drawn to them by the affection and caring they exhibit for each other. With his extended senses Bigfoot detects underground movement and rumblings that would presage an avalanche or rock slide or other earth movement that would endanger the cabin. He does everything he can think of to scare the young couple out of their cabin in time to escape the catastrophe. Showers of rocks against the cabin side at night would be his most potent warning. Anything left outside at night would be found a distance away in the morning, intact, but moved just enough to make them nervous. Heavy, pounding footsteps, as though wanting to be heard, would tramp around the cabin at night. Woodpiles would be rearranged in a conspicuous manner. Strange animal-like calls and hoots would be heard from close by within the forest. These manifestations of mischief would grow more ominous until the young couple would flee just before the avalanche would break loose and bury the cabin.

"It was a miracle that we escaped just in time," the young couple would say forever after.

Bigfoot is ingenious in his manufactured schemes, but they are never intended to hurt or harm, only to warn.

Ida: I was once told a rather lengthy story by a man who had a juvenile Bigfoot playmate when he was about ten or eleven years old. This was in Washington State I believe near Walla Walla.

The two boys would toss a ball back and forth and play simple games. Sometimes they would wrestle, as boys do. Once Bigfoot broke the boy's arm. He did not mean to, but he did not realize his own strength or the comparative weakness of the boy. Once they had a bit of disagreement, as boys do. The boy ran into the outside basement door and slammed it shut. He shot the bolt in the lock. The juvenile Bigfoot retaliated by slamming to the outside hatch and snapping the padlock through the hasp. Then Bigfoot ran away leaving the boy to find his own way out. (Of course there was a basement stair into the upper house).

When the boy tried to tell his Dad about Bigfoot he was severely beaten for lying.

Maez: I am sure the boy (and the man) was telling the truth, every word.

Ida: The circumstance under which the story was told guarantees its accuracy. I do not want to say more or betray confidences.

Maez: Here we have touched upon the favorite use Bigfoot has for stones — that of ammunition — as when he pelted the cabin of the honeymooners. You remember in your family story, Ida, where your brother was teasing you and you threw a stick at him and broke his glasses?

Ida: Can I forget?

Maez: Bigfoot would have done exactly the same, only he would have used a rock instead of a stick.

Ida: So would I, if I had one.

Maez: I believe you would. No wonder Og finds you kindred souls.

Ida: That pleases me. I am proud to be a kindred soul to Og!

Maez: Actually Bigfoot and your kind of human share the same soul pool. You could be a Bigfoot next time if you chose.

Ida: The lifestyle does not tempt me. I am not a happy camper. I have already put in my bid to be an anthropologist, remember?

Maez: Oh yes! Perhaps for you that is better.

Ida: Could Bigfoot choose to be an anthropologist next time?

Maez: I am not sure where Og is in the line of progression. But he certainly could be a your-type of human if he chose.

Ida: Wow! That will make some hairs stand on end. Even on bald heads!

Maez: Shall we get back to work?

Ida: I've got to get ready to go to the grocery store.

Ida, later: O.K. while I eat my angel food cake and send my blood sugar up, let us get back to Bigfoot and his stones.

Maez: More about his use of them as ammunition first. Sometime back we mentioned him rolling large rocks, small boulders, through campfires he did not approve of. Rolling or throwing them across trails to deter persons from taking that path is another obvious use. He will roll some downhill in such a fashion as to start little rockfalls when he wants to turn someone back from the path they are taking. Very seldom, almost never, has he been known to hit someone with a rock. There would have to be the most extreme case of foolish or harmful behavior to make Bigfoot use a rock as an actual weapon. Once two bully boys were tormenting a younger one making him cry and be afraid. Small rocks, not much more than pebbles came whizzing out of the underbrush, striking the two tormentors across the back and shoulders, proving that Bigfoot can take pretty good aim when he wants to.

He also uses rocks as temporary tools. He does not shape them, only very casually, nor does he carry them about or keep them for another time. There are always more rocks available for levers or weights or aids in preparing food, and if not, sticks will serve temporarily.

The one surprising use to which Bigfoot puts stones has to be seen to be believed. We mentioned previously his "aesthetic" sense and his "art work." It is all done with stones. He stacks flat rocks to make columns, or mounds round stones to build "monuments," or surrounds larger boulders with a circle of rocks.

It is difficult to tell his production from accidental works of nature unless there are too many of them in one place to be anything other than intentional. To come upon a hidden area of forty or fifty such constructions would suggest at once that human intelligence had been at work. The size of the rocks used in such arrangements — and there are some — would suggest a "modern art" at its most bewildering. Once constructed, Bigfoot does not like his art work disturbed and therefore such fields are in the most inaccessible places on earth. There are two in the Pacific Northwest. They cannot be reached on foot, horseback, vehicle, helicopter, boat, or plane. One of our smaller scout ships could take you there only because we know exactly where to go.

These areas are not likely to be found accidentally. Some future day when all the giant forests are cut, all the rivers are drained, and all the lakes have become dead swamps the people of that future will exclaim over the towers and mounds and wonder what kind of people had constructed them. That is millennia into the future. In the meantime whenever Bigfoot feels the need to leave his mark for the future he goes to one of these areas.

Ida: Does he realize what he is doing?

Maez: To some extent, yes, or why do it?

Ida: Do they consider these grounds sacred?

Maez: Not in those terms, no. But they consider them to be private and personal and do not want them disturbed.

Ida: I am finding it very difficult to get my mind into conjunction with Bigfoot's.

Maez: That is why we are writing all this, to put your mind and others into a deeper understanding of our hairy brother.

Ida: One minute I find I am giving him too much credit for "cultural" behavior and the next minute I am giving him too little. I can't find the right level.

Maez: Before we are through you will have it laid out exactly. That is what we are attempting to do.

Maez, 6/10/2000: Perhaps we make Bigfoot sound too benign, too goody. There are plenty of opposing reports, enough to make us cautious. He is also disturbed by witnessed effects and capable of rage.

Read your local newspaper for one month. How many of your countrymen have committed acts that send shivers down your spine? Granted many of these were done under the influence of drugs or alcohol (Bigfoot does not imbibe). Basically these actions we read about were promoted by hate, anger, rage, jealousy, and long-time seething of these less admirable feelings. And you are supposed to be "civilized" and "cultured" people!

I'm not trying to point fingers as an excuse for Bigfoot's occasional outbursts of violence.

It is only fair and caution and good sense to remember such "crimes" as he has been reported capable of committing. It is also fair to realize he has a reason for his actions. He is not just a wild beast that has gone berserk. His viewpoint and understanding should be given respect. Bigfoot cannot call upon a local constabulary with his grievances. He must be his own arresting officer, jury, and executioner. He judges only what he sees himself. He does not depend on the veracity of other witnesses who may be biased or compromised. He reacts only from the purity of his own nature.

Let us bring in a new topic, Bigfoot's physical well-being. I have told about his twice yearly physical exams when any illness or injury can be remedied. We have mentioned here and there how he responds to elements, storm, heat, cold. He takes great glee in sitting out in a hard pelting rain, just as children do playing under a sprinkler. Cold weather and snow do not faze him but he finds any degree of heat distressful. He is cautious during high winds as any old growth timber can come snapping down with very little warning. You have watched great limbs and saplings break down in your little bit of woods, you know how unexpected this sort of thing can be.

You would be surprised at Bigfoot's appreciation of bright colored flowers. He will stand and look at a yard full of brilliant blossoms and think nice things about the people who live there. He has a true aesthetic appreciation. If you are in a camp, hang your brightest colored garments on a line outside. He may come to admire the colors. Don't think you can entrap him with this, he can read your intentions like a book.

Bigfoot would be intrigued in watching people dance in smooth swaying movements like saplings in a breeze. Any movement sharp, coarse, jerky would repel him. The same with music. Try playing a mellow flute, or a recording of one, to entice him near with sweet, dulcet sounds. His curiosity is enormous. We've touched on that before. But remember he can read your intentions. Any ulterior motives would drive him away. If you want to share a nice experience and make him happy, he will know the difference. Examine your motive honestly before you make such overtures. If you plot with the wrong intentions he will not respond.

Food, of course, is always on his mind just as it is yours. A-hem. Some prefer certain foods over others, but all like fruit and vegetables, particularly root vegetables, berries, and fish.

These are the mainstay of his menu in the Pacific Northwest. He will not turn down an offering of poultry or small game, raw, of course. He does not eat cooked food readily; too much would make him ill. A nice fresh catch of fish is almost irresistible to him. Don't let your cat run wild in the woods. If a raccoon doesn't eat him, Bigfoot will, unless he is well acquainted with you and your cat.

Maez: Well, Ida, I know you will find this awfully abrupt but I really believe it is time to bring this written conversation to a close. Our plan has always been to end on June 30th. I know you have expected more. We have touched, briefly I admit, on all of the vital questions and information that it is wise to expose at this time. Most readers will demand evidence. We can't provide you with that while you are sitting at a desk. We can't demand that Bigfoot walk up and ring your doorbell. You have established a good rapport with Og. From time to time I will bring you news, or Og may speak to you, but there will be no more of this writing for publication at present. This is not the end of our relationship by any means.

You and Mr. T. have at least a hundred more pages of notes to add in here and from time to time. I will be available to answer questions. By the time you get all of your notes assembled and have written in various explanations you will have a full paged book. If anything exciting comes up while you are assembling this, you will be the first to know. Mr. T. has found a splendid rendezvous place to meet Bigfoot and plans to go out once a week in hopes of seeing him.

You have done enough in here to give other people insight into Bigfoot and his idiosyncrasies. Even if they don't believe, they will find this contains many, many useful hints.

We spoke once of trying to find a Bigfoot baby that had been born with problems that would not allow it to live the rugged life of its parents. There has been great aversion to giving up such a child to us, both from Bigfoot and the Council. We have had to put that idea aside for some time in the future. We do not want to arouse distrust of ourselves. There is a great complex of fears and sentiment and general suspicion woven into this negativity. But we will wait patiently for any future possibilities.

And so we say thank you for your patience and time and somewhat erratic typing. You know you type too fast.

Ida: I know I do, but I can't seem to slow down. Anyway, this has been a pleasure. I can see it is more important now to get out into the field and find some evidence of the reality of Bigfoot.

Maez: Don't worry. We are not abandoning that idea. Acquiring evidence is the next important step. Your friend, Mr. T., will be the active one here. He has spent many years studying and taking steps in that direction.

So take care, and thanks to you both. Maez, Og, and Others

P.S. Og is busy getting acquainted with his new territory. As soon as he feels safe and comfortable in that situation you will hear from him again. M.

Thoth, 6/14/2000: Yes, Ida, you guessed correctly. I did ask Maez to bring his discourse to a close. He was beginning to let those pranksters play on your nerves too much, for example the on-going music.

Maez is much too busy a fellow to keep a tight rein on such details.

You will be given evidence of Bigfoot's reality. That has been promised, and it is needed to put a solid foundation under your story. The Arcturian's intervention with Earth people is based upon their own belief in their ownership because of their genetic intervention from time to time. They overlook the fact and that this is a physical/mental intervention only. They do not touch upon or even consider very much that the soul that animates humans, and Bigfoot also, is the real human identity.

So we have to step in from time to time and bring their activities to a closure. You were loaned for a definite period that is over at the end of this month. You have a different agenda. You will put these notes together for a book about the true nature of Bigfoot and you will find evidence of his reality; that is all. Another project is waiting for you. In the meantime we have to work on bettering your health which has been allowed to deteriorate. You have other book manuscripts to find publishers. Don't think you will be idle.

To Tres and me the book about Bigfoot is important to prove that he has a human soul. Therefore we will be helping you to get your notes in order and ready for publication. We do not want you to become too much embroiled in Arcturian schemes.

The reason all those researchers have not been able to find patterns in Bigfoot's activities is because they have been collecting and studying data based on him being a curious animal with a big brain only, and carefully listing all the characteristics that would make him so. Until they consider his human traits, and study his higher mind and soul, they will never prove him anything.

They are afraid to discover his humanness. It raises too many questions about their own.

That is why your and Mr. T.'s book is important. If Bigfoot is to be saved from extinction these facts must be brought out. His extinction would only presage your own.

Thoth, 6/17/2000: I see you have a full report written up regarding your fossil head. I don't think it is necessary to include that all in the book right now, but keep it on hand. It may come in very useful. Add every detail you can remember.

Ida: Does all this have a purpose? Is it important?

Thoth: It may be in the future.

Ida: O.K. I'll have to do a little brain dredging. All this happened over ten years ago. I guess I should buy another bottle of Ginko Biloba.

Thoth: If it helps.

Ida: Og wanted me to name the fossil "Ruthie." How come he knows a name like that?

Thoth: "Witherso e'er thou goest, I go also."

Ida: He seems to know a lot about our Bible. He asked to be called "Og" also. That was a giant, the king of Bashan.

Thoth: Before the Bigfoot are sent into an area of a country, they are given a certain amount of orientation concerning the inhabitant's major spiritual beliefs, a background of history, politics and culture. Bigfoot is no ignoramus. He understands all this on a different, simpler level than you do but he understands where the people he is to be near are "coming from" as the saying has it.

When you were just starting school you mentioned, rather boastfully, to a playmate that your grandmother had shaken hands with Abraham Lincoln. She asked, "Who is Abraham Lincoln?" You were surprised that she didn't know.

Bigfoot would have recognized the name as one who had been the leader of your country, was considered the personal hero of many (including yourself) and who had freed the country from owning slaves. Bigfoot has been cultivated to understand your basic and vital historic beliefs and attitudes, in a very limited and basic way of course.

Ida: How about his own history? Does he have any sense of where he came from or his relationship to other Bigfoot?

Thoth: He understands very little. He has been told that all Bigfoot are brothers and sister created by one God. I don't believe he thinks about it, just accepts it as he does when someone tells him those are clouds up there and they bring rain. Such simple explanations satisfy him and he does not question further or argue. His monitors keep him dependent upon themselves in this way in order to keep rein on him. If they were to educate him, and he is capable of much more education than he receives, he would become less dependent, more self-willed.

Ida: That's sensible as far as their purposes are concerned. So are we protected from the truth in many instances, for our own good, of course.

Thoth: Do I detect that sarcasm again?

Ida: Certainly!

Ida, 6/19/2000: Why did you pull me away from Maez's conversations?

Thoth: Because you were doing exactly what you said: getting emotionally involved. We do not want you going off in tangents from your real work. You are not here to promote thoughts about Bigfoot. You are here to study, understand, and illuminate ideas about humans like yourself. That is why you came into this lifetime, for you and me to work together on the question of where *Homo s.s.* originated, how and why. As soon as you finish with Bigfoot you and I can start on this long awaited project.

Ida: I'm looking forward to that. But I don't want to leave the story of Bigfoot half told.

Thoth: It won't be, but I will help you to finish it in such a manner it will lead directly into your next book — ours! Maez understands and consents. He has many problems to work on besides giving you information. In fact, he seemed greatly re-lieved. He says you always wrung more out of him than he meant to tell.

Ida: It seems that to really understand Bigfoot we must first understand his levels and capabilities of consciousness.

Thoth: Exactly. As your friend and co-explorer Mr. T. has pointed out. You and Maez have touched upon this briefly with many a hop, skip and jump. Perhaps that is enough to start on. Bigfoot researchers who consider only such things as footprints, hair samples, and brief sightings are doing a great job of gathering evidence of his reality, but they are not analyz-ing evidence of his humanity.

Ida: I was appalled when Mr. T. mentioned the well-known researcher who has put together a database of thousands of such physical evidence reports but has consistently thrown out any report that might hold the slightest hint of Bigfoot resembling humanity. What an incredible waste! He calls them apes. He has spent forty years discarding the most vital data.

Thoth: More will be found once researchers are made aware of what might be important. Then they will reshape their reports.

Ida: I should think anything that might indicate Bigfoot is aware of a hunter's or camper's intentions, if not actual thoughts, and of his telepathic abilities would be important. You can't get that from collecting physical notes, only from analyzing his actions.

Thoth: That is very important. That is where Jack Lapseritis has opened a pathway for more scrupulous interpretations with his book *The Psychic Sasquatch*. It points out many human aspects and the great understanding abilities of Bigfoot. This is probably the most important Sasquatch book ever written. It opens new dimensions into the whole research program. It has opened the way for our own discussion. Besides enumerating many telepathic contacts with Bigfoot, Jack also relates instances in which UFOs were observed in conjunction with them, and also times when Bigfoot used his disappearing techniques. All of this is of extreme importance to be understood before there can be any major contacts with Bigfoot. That's where you come in.

Ida: Hah! No one is going to listen to me, especially when I start talking about aliens and genetic altering, or if I say Bigfoot has a soul comparable to our own, he just is not as far along in his evolution. People don't accept the basic truths of such talk and here we are beginning to fly a little high.

Thoth: Don't worry. You will be listened to by those who matter.

Ida: I'll do my best, but I have little hope for a favorable response.

Thoth: You may be surprised! Now that you have read most of the Bigfoot books provided by Mr. T., what do you think?

Ida: About what?

Thoth: The books. Are they useful?

Ida: To me they are. I had not read much about Bigfoot and other varieties of Yeti before.

Thoth: Do you think the books are accurate?

Ida: Ninety-nine percent of them as far as they go. They give only descriptions of physical facts. All such material is necessary to establish a base so we know what kind of thing we are observing and can agree on many basic facts such as physical characteristics and emotional reactions.

Thoth: That much agreed. Anything else?

Ida: I think Jack Lapseritis has filled in the missing quotient — his contacts with Bigfoot on the psychic level. I know the psychic level or dimension is very real. I have been there, done that. It is only on a different level of reality than our everyday lives.

Thoth: You trust Jack's story then?

Ida: Absolutely. I trust Jack 100 percent. He is totally sincere. He would not have devoted so many years of his life to it if he had not believed that it is all real and true.

Thoth: Good! That is all I wanted to clarify today. Go on with your studies.

Ida: If one of those inspired hunters would go out and shoot a Bigfoot and bring it to some medical research facility and they dissect every bone, muscle, and cell, what would that prove? They obviously have nothing to compare it to. They can write hundreds of pages about its various parts but the thing is dead meat. What can that tell us about the other living ones out there, or about ourselves? We need someone like Diane Fossey to go out and live with the creatures, whatever they are, and to study them in relation to each other. You can't study their lives and social and cultural habits from their pancreas and liver. This is why Albert Ostman's story is of such importance. He watched four Bigfoot in their interactions with each other and with himself. He was very observant and articulate in telling his story.

Thoth, 6/24/2000: We cannot continue with our writing until July 1st, so put all this aside unless there is something you want to bring up to date.

Ida 6/28 and 29/2000: If Maez wants Bigfoot protected, let a few be seen unmistakably. If deemed animal, then turn on the Endangered Species Act. If declared human, the ESA would not apply, but murder would. Why do we have to go to such tremendous lengths, as all of these good people have done, in order to settle a question that could be settled so easily and comparatively quickly? People have spent 20, 30, 40 years in pursuing Bigfoot. This sounds like another of Maez's cat and mouse games.

Maez seems to get his jollies by sending us on wild goose chases, and now-you-see-me-now-you-don't sort of games through the means of his 400-500 pound hairy will-of-the-wisp.

Can't we have a little straight-forward, down-to-earth interaction between Maez and ourselves, and Bigfoot and ourselves? Perhaps resorting to these games is our fault because we refuse to consider Bigfoot other than flesh and blood incompetence. Maybe if we considered him in a different light we would get a different interaction and different answers.

Let us review briefly several of the outstanding stories of Bigfoot's interaction with our kind of humans.

1. Foremost we must consider Roger Patterson's film of a Bigfoot female. This film has been exhaustively taken apart in every conceivable manner of study, even in Russia. The prevailing opinion among all these scientists who have studied it is a cautious vote of authenticity.

2. Second place must go to Albert Ostman, who reports having been kidnapped while in his sleeping bag and transported to the nest of four Bigfoot. He was kept there for six days before he managed by a ruse to escape.

3. The story told by Fred Beck, one of five miners whose cabin was attacked by irate Bigfoot after having been shot at and one of their members possibly killed.

4. Theodore Roosevelt in his book Wilderness Hunter told of two trappers in the Bitterroot Mountains on the Idaho-Montana border. One, in the absence of his partner, was killed by an unknown creature. This is now included in Bigfoot stories.

5. In 1958 a road building crew at Buff Creek in N.W. California had a merry round-about with Bigfoot tossing heavy equipment around and making wonderful footprints from 13 to 18 inches long.

These are some of what we might call the "classics" of our Bigfoot lore.

One would think that the various printed stories of Native American women who had been kidnapped by a Bigfoot for mating purposes and who had produced babies from them would indicate the creatures have to have some human DNA or reproduction would not be possible. There is one story of two native women who tossed their Bigfoot babies overboard from a Puget Sound ferry boat.

Then there is the story of Zana, an Alma female of the same species as Bigfoot but in the Caucasus region, who was captured by a local village, trained to do chores, and had babies by four village men. That would certainly indicate a close genetic relationship to our kind of humans. Not only were these children also able to bear children, but these grandchildren of Zana are reported to be human in appearance, able to speak and live normally.

A very recent story published in the Akron (Ohio) Beacon Journal (January 18, 2001) tells of a man who was able to record Bigfoot's speech on a voice activated tape recorder. The sounds were translated by a man familiar with ancient Native American dialect to: "We are watching," or "We are being watched."

You can check this out on Rich LaMonica's website: http://www.geocities.com/saqatchr/index3.html.

Ida, 6/30/2000: Just because we, as what we call a human species, use language, fire, and tools, does not mean that all human species need do so in order to call themselves human. The "human" element is based, and should be so recognized, on the creature's comprehension ability.

One who giggles and sheds tears and teases others certainly is one who comprehends such human susceptibilities as humor, grief, or sadness, and has the capacity to make jokes. Our Bigfoot has been observed engaged in all of these very human activities.

Does an ape or any known animal act in this manner? Does an ape swim under water? Do female apes have breasts?

How does Bigfoot think, act, and respond to stimuli? Questions such as these cannot be answered by obtaining bones and guts, only by observing the actions of a living creature.

Ida, 7/2/2000: Bigfoot has been turned loose to some extent by his supervisors to evolve at his own rate according to his nature. He is no longer necessary to Maez and his council, other conveniences have taken over his former tasks; that includes watching us.

On his own, Bigfoot is trying to make some advances to us, to convince us of his reality and his nature so he won't be shot.

His bodily nature is trying to comprehend the meaning of his human soul. Isn't that what we are doing? We are only a bit, a very little bit, further along.

Thoth said that Bigfoot is capable of learning a great deal more than his monitors are willing to teach him.

This is exactly the opportunity for us to make an ally of Bigfoot!

Ida, 7/5/2000: When I first became interested in learning something about Bigfoot (October 1998), I was amazed at how much back-biting went on among the major adherents to the study. No one seemed to really give credence to another's approach, to the various problems of gaining information, or of any information gained.

One approach was through the assertion that Bigfoot was an Ape and the only recourse was to kill a specimen for examination.

Another approach was that Bigfoot was in some manner or extent a human, or sub-human, or borderline human and should be helped and preserved.

Another approach was that the consideration of any mention of UFOs was anathema to the cause and would destroy any credibility the subject has gained.

Another approach was that any type of psychic connection, or telepathy, or unearthly abilities of Bigfoot was simply fantasy and unmentionable. Which leaves us with four important questions: Is Bigfoot Ape?

- Is he human?
- Has he connection to UFOs?
- Has he extra-sensory or psychic abilities?

After two years of intensive study of the best known literature and other informative input, I can sincerely answer: No, yes, yes, yes.

1. No, he is not Ape, and if you kill one you may find yourself answering to a charge of manslaughter although his type of human may not be precisely your own.

2. We might believe that border-line *Homo sapiens* is as clear a distinction as we are able to make. Border-line does not mean he is not *sapiens*. He is a hold-over from his beginnings hundreds of thousands of years ago.

3. When the proponents of number three worry about the credibility of their approach to the research of Bigfoot if they dare mention UFOs, they are more worried about their own reputations than about the honest research of Bigfoot. To maintain our integrity in any study we have to state what we see regardless of what hole that drops us into. The study subject is the criterion of what we report, not our ego.

4. When the Ape prospector refuses to note anything pertaining to human factors, he is throwing away three-fourths of Bigfoot's reality. Can you make a reliable case-history of only one-fourth of the facts? We have to factor in all four of these approaches because Bigfoot lives, breathes and thrives in all four elements. Leave out one and you will never know Bigfoot for what he really is, a very complex, and living, intelligent, comprehending creature.

5. And by that word comprehending you will find the key to approaching the reality of Bigfoot. Every time someone makes a move in his direction Bigfoot is aware of their intention because he is psychic, because he is connected to UFO people, and because he is an intelligent, comprehending, borderline human being.

Ida, 7/6/2000: Only now, after all these months of intensive study in the Bigfoot literature do I begin to see a pattern in the information garnered about Bigfoot's reality. In the literature I find that no such pattern is discernible. To find a pattern one must consider all the evidence whether some of it conforms with one's personal ideology on the subject or not.

Besides the four mentioned "approaches" and the questions derived therefrom, one must include the historical and geographical factors of the study and some of the books available have done that very well. This gives us six threads to begin weaving our pattern.

1. Is Bigfoot Ape or solely animal?

2. Is he to any extent human?

3. Has he any connection to UFOs?

4. Has he psychic or extra-sensory abilities?

5. What is known of his history?

6. What are his geographical occurrences and differences?

From all of these we can form our pattern. Only when we are willing to explore the full depths of all these types of information can we find any pattern. These ARE the pattern.

There are some superb books written about Bigfoot, but not one of these covers in any detail every one of these approaches. Each writer has his (her) particular points to emphasize and his particular points to throw out the window.

First to go out is the UFO connection, second is the question of Bigfoot's psychic abilities. Third is his historical connection with the Natives of any country. Fourth out is the geographical coverage in any detail. (This covers all types of Bigfoot and Yeti also). That leaves two factors and the big question and the big battle — is Bigfoot all animal or to some degree human?

What makes a human? Not language or use of fire or tools and artifacts, but there is one major necessity to be a human being. Does he have a human soul? Throw the question of a human soul out the window and the whole value and mystery of Bigfoot goes with it.

Why are these scientists so bashful in mentioning the human soul? Are they ashamed of it? If it exists — and it does — it must be one of the most important factors of any study of a human being, even a potential human being, even a borderline human being. What makes him human? We don't need here to go into great argument about what is a soul and what is not. A human soul is what makes you sad enough to weep, happy enough to laugh, joyful enough to sing, sympathetic enough to help, caring enough to protect. Bigfoot has been observed engaged in every one of these performances.

Bigfoot has a soul that speaks to and responds to our own. Bigfoot is human, not as fully developed as ourselves in the physical sense, but one of us in the Spiritual sense.

Thoth, 7/7/2000: I know you and Mr. T. are very disappointed at my abrupt cut-off of Maez's and Og's conversations. They have both contributed vital information to this book and we are duly appreciative. Maez's forward plans would have included the same modus operandi — mind games, wild-goosechases and cat-and-mouse play that you have so complained about in Hweig's twenty-two years of correspondence with you. To be quite blunt, you are now nearly eighty-six years old. Your life span is much less than a third of Maez's or Og's. It is hard for Maez to believe that you do not have forever to respond to his "testing and training" such as he gave to Hweig and Hweig gave to you for so long.

Ida: If these fellows don't know me quite thoroughly by now, they never will. Yes, I object strenuously to any more "testing". It exhausts me. I won't play by those rules. I will pick up my marbles and go home.

Thoth: There is no reason why it (testing) should be necessary. I am trying to reach a compromise with Maez; either allow Og to continue or to find another Bigfoot to continue informing you and answering your questions.

Ida: That would be most welcome. Thank you.

Thoth: It is now time to include Mr. and Mrs. T's helpful and important work.

Ida: Lee has been in Bigfoot pursuit for nearly 40 years. He has given some valuable observations and some questions of his own. I've been eager to get it all in here.

Thoth: Good! It is time to use the excellent material he has suggested.

Ida: Without these two there would be no book. I consider them to be full collaborators.

Thoth: Get some sleep now. You have all day tomorrow to work on this. I am glad you were able to get the black ink cartridge for your copier so quickly. You will need it.

Ida: Thanks to my faithful daughter and her pretty white car.

Lee:

Examples That May Relate to a

"Human" Nature of Bigfoot

I discovered this information during my forty years of interest and research:

Robert Morgan, co-founder of the American Anthropological Research Foundation, and Steve Jones, host for "Outdoor Sports" on WAOH TV, join to meet Bigfoot under the cover of dark and stormy conditions. After overcoming some radical intimidation by Bigfoot and avoiding the remarkable Bigfoot imitation of other animals, these two men meet face to face with two Bigfoot. Both sides show outstretched arms with open hands. Robert has trained others who have accomplished similar results. The technique is dependent on attitude. The procedure is outlined in an audio tape titled: "Bigfoot! The Ultimate Adventure!"

Jack "Kewaunee" Lapseritis, M.S., published author and longtime researcher of Bigfoot, has had numerous encounters with Bigfoot. Jack has seen Bigfoot physically and has very real and powerful encounters with some aspect of his "spiritual nature." Bigfoot has helped Jack and a number of his friends with a variety of physical and mental health problems. Jack feels that Bigfoot are human and spiritual. In his book *The Psychic Sasquatch*, there are numerous references to the occasions of Bigfoot mentally communicating with others in our society.

Richard Ireland of Phoenix, Arizona was a very successful minister and businessman who had been the subject of studies by universities on the varieties of unique talents of the human consciousness. While traveling through Oregon for the first time, he related to me that he had a distinct feeling there were a number of Bigfoot residing in the Three Sisters region and the only way to get close to these "beings of a different human nature" was through the tactic of patience, curiosity, and respect for them and the environment. He felt they had a highly developed instinct which allowed them to know our intentions and that we could not trick them with any kind of mask.

Ida K., 86 years old, published author, had been writing about the characteristics of Bigfoot in relation to their possible mental and spiritual nature. One day, quite suddenly and powerfully, a Bigfoot whom she has come to call Og, started speaking to her through her mind. Og seemed to be fully aware of her home surroundings, her replies and her feelings. This first communication was very impressive to her and since then Og has initiated communication several times.

Morna B., U. of O. candidate for MS degree in education, in 1964 was suddenly and inexplicably impressed by some kind of "powerful light of knowledge" after an evening of discussion about Bigfoot. She got out of bed and wrote as fast as she could and sent me a copy of her insights. In that rare revelation she describes how Bigfoot, as a human, had taken a different line of evolution. The Bigfoot developed what we might call the subconscious mind and by this internal "tool" of consciousness they developed a sensitivity to "know" their environment by some extension of perception. They use this in terms of their needs for food, safety, and shelter. (See text of Morna's letter to Lee and Marlys in the following pages.)

Betty McCaleb of Selma, Oregon, told me of a report by a local Boy Scout troop leader that a smoke jumper[1], who had become seriously injured while falling on a smoldering stump, was carried by a large, hair-covered, human-like giant to the edge of a road. Betty lived near the southeast portion of the southwestern Oregon's Kalmiopsis Wilderness Area between 1927 and the late 1980s. She was a strong person with consistent integrity who could see into your heart. (Note: [1]A smoke jumper is a firefighter.)

Joe Mayberry of Cave Junction, Oregon was a gold prospector who had spent time with native Mexican people in the northwest region of Durango, Mexico. He told me that these natives spoke with Bigfoot and that Bigfoot would use fire when in the deep remote canyons of that region. Joe also spoke of seeing drawings of strange craft on the walls of some caves and seeing furniture which would fit the needs of giants.

Two deer hunters, Edwards and Bill Cole, had a very close and unexpected encounter with two Bigfoot in the Mt. Ashland area of southern Oregon. Bill was picked up and carried for a short distance. He lost control of his body and mental functions and had to remain under medical supervision for many years, even though there was no physical evidence of harm. The other hunter had a clear and close view of both creatures and was not adversely affected by the occasion.

A minister of a small church in Eugene, Oregon had become very intrigued with Bigfoot stories that I had related. Because many of the stories centered in the region of the Three Sisters of the central Oregon Cascades, he later went to that region and came back with the notion that Bigfoot spent considerable time in lava tubes during the winter. He also had a very strong impression that these Bigfoot were incredibly curious as to why we made "straight narrow high clouds in the sky" and why we would "slip down the mountains on wooden sticks".

While camping in an isolated area of the Chetco River in southwest Oregon, I heard a very peculiar bark, call, or sound of something with powerful lungs. Not much to worry about, except there was a similar sound from the other end of the canyon, and we had no way out but to travel the river bottom on foot past either source. The walls of that portion of the canyon were steep and covered with thick underbrush. My partner was an experienced outdoor person who did not recognize the strange character of the sound and soon started feeling deeply and internally terrorized (not scared) while I felt completely calm. He was carrying a side arm. I carried no weapon. We were there specifically to look for Bigfoot based on earlier evidence. (Lee Trippett, June 2000)

From Mr. T's Notebook:

A Hypothesis by Richard Ireland

July 1962

Phoenix, Arizona

These creatures are of human aspect and nature, possibly of a lost civilization. They are definitely physical entities but with a much higher instinct of E.S.P. that civilization has not taken from them. They are able to communicate with one another by thought. They are sort of like a clan of people — they don't live together in a social order but do have a government, so to speak, where there is a leader. There are probably many more of these creatures than most of us think. It is well to search them out and bring the matter to the attention of others as the creature might have much to offer in certain areas.

These creatures know what you are thinking when you are in their country and this makes it so easy for them not to be there and so on. The better approach would be one of friendship, kindness, and love. To approach them from the view of science would send them away. They are ahead of us in some respects.

Their greatest significance to us is not of the physical but of the mental.

From Mr. T's Notebook:

Hypothesis by Jose del Kapote (Joe Mayberry)

Cave Junction, Oregon - April 1966

Are the Giants of America the same as the Yeti of the Himalayas?

There are many places on Earth where there are the creatures. As among the known peoples of the Earth so among the creatures there are groups of so-called different races in various stages of evolution. The creatures are referred among themselves collectively as the Waukleglan.

How should the Waukleglan (Bigfoot) be approached?

It would be better to concentrate on a particular group in a particular area as each group is different. Do not think that you can go and take pictures and show the Waukleglan to others. It is not possible. It must be remembered that they have abilities of which most of your sciences are unaware. They have developed along entirely different lines of evolution, but remember they are still a people and are just as human as you. Any approach will be greatly enhanced if the Waukleglan are considered as a people to be respected. They are only different, not above or below any other people.

What is their way of life?

Their way is strange and different and presently beyond the normal understanding of most. So too, the ordinary known people have a way of life that appears without useful purpose and strange to the Waukleglan. They are not as close to the animal as it would appear. The method and place of living does not determine the scale of living things. They have a much greater appreciation of the One Father Creator than most of us. Their mind functions just like ours but they have learned to control free will.

What is their form of communication?

Thought transference; however, they are not mute, and do have in some cases a language. Only a very few groups, very far removed from America, have not developed this thought transference. Normally it is a very easy thing for them to know the thoughts of one who represents a possible hazard to them.

Do the Waukleglan use tools?

Yes, but not in the usual sense. Their highly developed thought transference is a very powerful instrument in providing their needs. Then, too, their way of life in our terms is very, very simple. They would desire to have fire, and it is within their ability, but they dare not for reasons of safety from our pursuits. They would like to have other conveniences but these too would attract attention to them and they know very well from experience, and because of their far inferior numbers, that it is not safe. Our people have not treated them kindly.

Are the Waukleglan dangerous to us?

No more than we are to them. It depends on the nature of the meeting. In most cases they have a tolerance that almost defies description. Jose del Kapote (Joe Mayberry)

Lee:

Encounters With Bigfoot by John Green

This 1994 3rd printing of a 1980 copyrighted book by John Green has a section about "Apes and Men", on page 63, which makes several statements which need to be challenged.

First paragraph indicates that Bigfoot is not human. This statement is made without defining the term "human".

Second paragraph: It is true that humans seem to identify themselves by their shape but that is both inappropriate and incomplete.

Third paragraph: Contemporary research shows that humans are NOT the only ones to have a complex communication system.

Fourth paragraph: Scientific research shows that animals have extensive communication abilities. It is wrong to say that they cannot communicate "ideas" when we do not understand the content of animal communication.

Fifth paragraph: The list of similarities and differences between Bigfoot and human does not answer whether something is human until the fullness of the "human characteristics" are defined. One must go beyond physical, social, and verbal communication characteristics.

Sixth paragraph: Cooperative effort and tools do not make a creature "human" even though that view may be generally accepted in our culture.

Seventh paragraph: The brain's size and development does not necessarily relate to reasoning, memory, inspiration, mind, emotions, spirit, etc.

Eighth paragraph: Some universities of Asia have had scientific teams in the field looking for Bigfoot evidence. Science is wrong in its definition of what constitutes reasonable proof or evidence. The volume, character and consistency of both soft and hard evidence are often ignored by science without valid justification. They often put too much emphasis on the need for replication and the need of consistency within a particular frame that is only "theory".

Lee:

The Reality of False Truth

June 2000

Throughout recorded history the evidence points to intellectual scholars leading humanity into believing illusions. And indeed, more than a few societies have allowed themselves to be so led.

It is our thought along with many others that makes something "true" when it is in fact false. Here are three major examples:

Once, we believed the Earth to be flat. This kept most of humanity from exploring the full geography of the planet.

Once, we believed that the sun revolved around the Earth — and indeed we let that belief penetrate other aspects of our life. It was okay because all of our evidence proved it! So certain were we of the "truth" that we developed a comprehensive science of astronomy around it.

Once, we believed that everything physical moved from one point to another through Time and Space. All of our evidence proved it! So certain were we of the "truth" that we built an entire system of physics around it.

Now the real wonder of this "science" and this system was that it seemed to work!

The astronomy that we created out of our belief that the Earth was the center of the universe worked to explain the visual phenomena we saw in the movement of the planets. Our observations supported our belief, creating what we then called "knowledge".

Our belief about particles of matter worked to explain the visual phenomena we saw in the physical world around us. Our observations supported our belief, creating what we then called "knowledge".

Only later, when we looked more closely at what we were seeing, were we able to change our mind about these "scientific facts". Yet the change of mind did not come easily. The first ones who suggested such a change of mind were sometimes called heretics. Their ideas were often called blasphemy. They were discouraged, denounced, and some of them were put to death.

It is our beliefs that are "true', the majority of us insisted. After all, were they not supported by every observation?

Yet, which came first, the belief, the perception, or the observation? That is the central question. That is the inquiry we resisted. And this point is crucial to the nature of the world at large and our own personal world.

Is it possible that we see what we want to see? Could it be that we observe what we expect to observe? Or perhaps more to the point, we look right past what we do not expect to see? Perhaps we would rather be "right" and "comfortable" than alter a foundation of "truth".

Even today when our modern science vows to observe first, and draw a conclusion later, still those conclusions cannot be trusted. That is because it is impossible for us to look at anything objectively. All things are considered within the context of what we think we already understand or perceive. Generally, in the secular world, which ignores the possibility of inspiration, we do not know any other way to proceed.

To put this another way, we are looking at the world from inside the world. Every conclusion we come to about the world is based on our perceptions of the world. And so, every conclusion could be a "false truth" or illusion.

How can we recognize a false truth when it seems so real? We have just learned that the reason it seems so real is not because it is real, but because we believe so firmly that it IS. Therefore, to change the way we see a "false truth" is to change the way we think about it. Thoughts are powerful and changing them can be upsetting.

We have thought that "seeing is believing," but in reality our believing governs our "seeing". This turns our world upside down, yet in truth, we might be turning it right side up.

If, when we confront an accepted idea and we believe it as a truth, it is possible even though it may not be probable, that we can readjust our viewpoint. Of course this means that we may be able to create a "truth" as we wish it to be, rather than simply watch it present itself as we imagine.

This is the secret about a "false truth": we are already creating it as we choose it to be.

Unfortunately, much of the time, we are not even making choices at all but accepting the choice of others. When we can stop choosing what has been chosen before, we may be surprised and experience liberty.

The "truth" will indeed set us free to discover a better way, greater possibilities, and a real reality. Just a few major examples:

Inventors struggled against the prevailing inertia of society to develop the light bulb, the airplane, the telephone, the computer, the TV.

The major religions of the world claim one god and yet within each main religion there are many factions or denominations.

As we explore our own consciousness we struggle to understand the difference between mind and brain, intuition and logic, inspiration and chance discovery.

Our universities have studied for decades some issues relating to expanded states of consciousness. Despite our reverence for science we have resisted accepting outstanding discoveries of the so-called paranormal faculties of the human mind or consciousness. The understanding of the interconnected nature of the subconscious mind is literally exploding but only being accepted within small circles of our culture.

Therefore, to say that Bigfoot is not human by making judgments based only on physical observations is yet another failure from being governed by limited perception rather than the possibilities of expanded knowledge.

Letter from Morna Bowman to Lee and Marlys Trippett

October 18, 1964

Note: Morna was a graduate student at the University of Oregon working for her Ph.D. in the field of reading and counseling. We (the Trippetts) met her through Hugh Lynn Cayce and have become good friends since her arrival from California in September of '64. We have talked only occasionally of my hobby (Bigfoot) and this letter completely surprised us as we had no idea this girl was either extra-sensitive or interested in this subject, which was new to her when we first met Lee T.

Morna Bowman

Many thousands of years ago — long before the dawn of written language — man lived in direct contact with his natural environment. He lived largely by instinct, and the seat of the thought process was not as it is now located primarily in the head but distributed more throughout the entire body, but especially in the body trunk. When Man began gradually to make weapons and tools, the life pathway between the "giants" and the rest of mankind began to separate, for the giants began to develop psychic power. This is not to indicate that the psychic development of the giants and the tool development of Man took place at the same time in history. Actually what happened was that the giants lived much longer in their historical development than primitive Man without highly developed tools or psychic abilities.

Thus it was the artifact which primarily separates the "giants" and Man. Modern Man however, with his artifacts, is a child lost in the dark. Instead of a mature being, he is a frightened child. In the development of the artifact, Man has developed that part of his consciousness which is called the brain and located in the head. He does not usually realize that this is but a part of his total consciousness. Modern Man is thus overbalanced and can fall. The main danger in contacting the giants is that the huge part of Man's undeveloped consciousness, sometimes called the unconscious, will over-balance the consciousness thus making the person "crazy". This cause is partly due to the fact that these latent areas of Man's consciousnesses are wanting to be self-conscious and therefore are encouraged into greater service activity by the presence of entities in whom there is a greater development of these aspects of life. But the cause is also partly due to the fact that these "giants" use Man's unconscious power against him in order to protect themselves. The giants have developed psychic powers to protect themselves.

The strongest psychic powers are those which

use an element of the enemy against itself.

Attempts to contact the giants without artifacts have failed mainly because Man is frightened without them and the giants pick up the fear and have no respect. They are not likely to harm such a person, but they certainly will not make themselves known. Attempts to contact the giants with artifacts have failed because the giants hold the possession of artifacts as a sign of psychic weakness much as we regard a crutch as a sign of physical weakness; thus again, they have no respect for Man. They are also afraid of artifacts. Remember that these are not fully formed human beings any more than Man is. There is a tendency for you to think of them so because of your inner need for a teacher. Man is over-developed in his brain. These creatures are over-developed in what we call the unconscious, but what is conscious to them. (A true teacher is developed in both areas.) These creatures are afraid of artifacts because they represent an undeveloped side of their nature. However, their fear of the artifact is not a fraction as great as Man's fear of his unconscious.

Thus, if contact is to be made, it is not likely to be done by a naked man, full of fear, for these creatures dislike fear far more than artifacts. It is also not likely to be made with a gun and camera in hand, but rather with a man dressed as he would in the outdoors when he has no fear. It would be wise, however, to wear on the person, next to the skin, something which brought a feeling of psychic security and spiritual focus. This thing which is worn should be as close to the natural state as possible.

The greatest weapon which Man has to protect himself from these creatures, and also the greatest means of attracting them to him, is an attitude of respect, is love. This love, however, must be an outward giving and not an inward seeking. The necessary mental attitude is a combination of humility and self-respect.

One should approach these creatures with the attitude that they are neither inferior nor superior to Man. They are another development of Man from which modern man has much to learn.

Therefore the attitude should be similar to a student who has become a great silversmith in his own right, who now goes on a journey to seek teaching in the cutting of gems — a subject about which he knows nothing. It is difficult for modern man to maintain an attitude of outward-going love. But when an adult takes on the joyous seeking of a child he is close to it. Therefore, the love felt toward these creatures must be of the kind that makes you feel "happy".

Sincerely,
Morna Bowman

"P.S.: The moon is the focus of the lower level of psychic forces, but not of the higher levels which are more spiritual and focus in the sun. These psychic forces which focus in the moon are very powerful when used with knowledge and insight. However, since your unconscious development is not as focused as theirs it is to your decided disadvantage to meet them at the full of the moon, even though it is easier to find them at that time because they feel safer and stronger, and therefore do not hide so much. It would be better for your psychic health to meet them in the morning on a sunny day. If this cannot be done, it is better to meet them by starlight on a moonless or even a new moon clear night, even though you will have the disadvantage (not so in their case) of not being able to see. If you must meet them at the full of the moon and cannot meet them by sunlight, I would recommend dawn rather than evening. There is a time when the moon is still bright and the first faint light can be seen in the East. This might be your best compromise. If you make a contact with them at that time, time itself will be to your advantage and you will soon be standing in the sun. Morna B.

Thoth: Ida, I wish to intersperse an admonition here. Do not skip lightly over these words of Morna Bowman. I cannot say precisely where her information originated but it is valuable. It gives you an insight as to how Bigfoot thinks, an invaluable clue as to how he is likely to behave and why. He thinks from what we would call in ourselves the Unconscious, that is, the buried residue of all his past experience. (And that past is a lot longer than our own.) This clue is the basis of our differences and if studied deeply and carefully it can help us to anticipate and plan for any confrontation with Bigfoot. It gives us a fantastic insight into the character of the real creature. He is much more complex and intelligent than is generally realized at present.

Ms. Bowman's character sketch is worth ten years study in the field. Don't worry about the source, just give it proper credence. You can soon prove to yourself its veracity.

Ida, 7/21/2000: I am permanently confused about the use of the word "Unconscious". Everyone who uses it seems to have a different definition of what it is. At this point I am wondering if it concerns what I have called a "species trait". Or is that the Collective Unconscious? Dr. Carl G. Jung defined it very succinctly but everyone else seems to have his own definition. I shall have to study.

Letter from Mr. T. to Ida

July 27, 2000

Many thanks for the recent large package of notes and copies. I appreciate your gentle nature and approach to the overall Bigfoot issues. And I appreciate your high quality of integration of the many aspects of the Bigfoot situations and nature. I am looking forward to exposing the world to your comprehensive viewpoints about Bigfoot.

In your discussion about the "human nature" of Bigfoot, I am wondering if there might be some ideas within your book about *Reconciliation* that would help in defining the nature of Bigfoot and their "human nature".

I have one area of concern about your thoughts expressed in your "sleepy notes" of July 6. It would seem to me that to define "human being" by having a "human soul" is a bit redundant or circular. A basic fundamental difference between human and animals is the issue of the human being created in the "likeness and image" of God. This does relate to "human soul" but the basic fundamental essence of "human soul" needs expansion and clarification. Animals have a soul, so how is it different? It, too, is created by God, but how is it NOT like the "image and likeness" of God"?

It probably would not be appropriate to introduce a discussion about the nature of God, but I do believe that a secular approach can be made about "soul" that brings into play some of the "spiritual" and "creative" qualities that make up the difference between "human" and "animal" souls. Much of this relates to the nature of "consciousness" which we have already discussed.

Ida, 7/19/2000: Mr. T. has asked a pertinent and important question. "What is the difference between an animal soul and a human soul?" Answer: Very little; the major difference is that one with a human soul is cognizant of God, even though it may be a limited understanding. An animal does not have that comprehension.

We have discussed Bigfoot's recognition of God as being someone or something, a power that has provided forest, rivers, trees and food in various forms for him.

Maez remarked that he thinks sometimes Bigfoot confuses him with God. But essentially Bigfoot does understand that there is a greater and loving someone who cares about him. No animal gives a darn where its sustenance comes from as long as it comes on time. Bigfoot not only recognizes that there is someone who provides everything he needs, but more than that he feels intimations of a contact with that Power. He resonates to it and is aware that he is doing so. In short, he FEELS God. If he were permitted more education he would turn to that Power with his questions and petitions. That is why he is not given that education.

Bigfoot's practical value to his monitors lessens as they discover new means to get their wanted information that Bigfoot has heretofore gained for them. Perhaps now they will consent to let him expand his mind to greater realities than he has been allowed previously.

There are reports, especially from the Caucasus, of Bigfoot or Yeti types, called there Almas, being trained to do simple farm and household chores. They are capable of learning.

Bigfoot is capable of understanding the role of God in his life and to respond to the urges of his soul. He is aware of a God Power. He is a primeval Human. No animal can be so aware. A human soul is aware, responsive, and seeks for more. Doesn't yours?

The small conversations I had with Og, most of which are not included in this writing, were filled with questions. "What is this? What is that? Why did you do that?" Many reports in the books have remarked on his intense curiosity. He wants to know, to be informed.

An inquiring mind shows a soul struggling to get out of the cage of ignorance where it has been entrapped by lack of opportunity or fear. A youngster tagging at our heels and asking a thousand questions, until our tongue grows dry answering, can exhaust our patience, but it is one of the most exhilarating experiences we can have if we pay attention and perceive it rightly. It revives our own curious soul.

And so is Bigfoot's curiosity when he peeks in windows at night or creeps about a campsite looking into everything loose. He is not just looking for something to eat, but for something to understand. He is looking for answers to his own questions. That is what he was generated to do, gain information. That certainly shows a degree of intelligence that no animal possesses, although some animals (cats and monkeys) are extremely curious for what seems to be the pure sake of mischief. Such as Lord Spike constantly stopping the pendulum on my little antique clock, until I taped the door shut.

So back to Mr. T's question: What is the difference between an animal soul and a human soul? This can be answered in two words, comprehension and cognizance.

We must thank John Green's *Sasquatch, The Apes Among Us* for describing an activity that fairly indicates Bigfoot's sense of artistry. A report was given by a man who had observed a family of Bigfoot searching in an area of loose, flat sharp rocks, lifting rocks that must have weighed from fifty to 100 pounds and bringing up small rodents which the male, female, and their young one ate on the spot. The Bigfoot did not toss the removed rocks helter-skelter back into the deep hole their activity had created. He stacked the rocks carefully atop each other from 3 to 15 to 20 in a heap, leaving tall towers of rocks behind them as they gathered their lunch.

What had begun at one time as a simple gesture to get the rocks out of the way continued beyond that to become an activity for the sense of pleasure in producing what was a budding art form. The fact that Bigfoot builds towers instead of tossing the rocks about, that he seems to enjoy doing that, and that he leaves the towers intact and does not disassemble them, indicates his appreciation of their effect. He values his towers for their own sake.

I have seen "art displays" by our own serious and well-accepted artists that have less merit and character than Bigfoot's towers. He, however, is not ego-centric about it. He seems to do it for sheer enjoyment. Perhaps it is unconsciously a way of saying, "Bigfoot was here." Then it becomes a matter of communication and true art.

Thoth: Previously you were told about two "fields" which displayed Bigfoot's sense of aesthetic appreciation. They cover several acres each, but they are like this small area with many, many towers, some 15 feet high. Some are very ancient. When they are found — in time — I hope it will be remembered that Bigfoot built them for sheer artistic pleasure.

Ida: We were told previously of Bigfoot's fascination with colorful flowers. He will stand outside a yard for a long time contemplating bright blossoms.

Perhaps Jack Lapseritis' book will encourage observers and prompt writers to include more of such matters in their reports. To toss out certain observations is a disservice to one's readers. It falsifies Bigfoot's true nature. EVERYTHING must be told or the reports become propaganda.

Bigfoot is **not** an ape, no matter what authority tells you so. A complete and honest evaluation of him, if only from sightings, and without distortion of appraisal, would reveal that. Bigfoot was genetically derived from an Earth basis of *Australopithecus africanus*, and *A.a.* is not considered an ape.

A quote from *Lucy to Language*, a recent and well-illustrated book by Donald Johanson and Blake Edgar, page 136 (slightly abridged):

"On August 1, 1947, paleontologist Robert Bloom and his assistant, John Robinson at Sterkfontein, South Africa, recovered from a cave breccia a portion of a thigh bone, several vertebrae, and both hip bones of an Australopithecine. These were vital elements to prove that A. were indeed hominids. The partial skeleton indicated the bipedal nature of Australopithicines which assured them a place in the family hominidae."

(Additional fossil pieces confirmed they were more humanlike than ape-like.)

Of course the above is not the final work on anthropological information. The scientists change their minds along with their socks as often as new fossils are found.

I am not denigrating any honest researcher's efforts to find truth for all of us, or discounting the countless hours of toil they have put in, years and years of it. But I do despair of the cages they build around themselves with their limited paradigms.

Whether we believe Bigfoot developed from *Australopithecus africanus*, or whatever stem of evolution he came from, we have to admit our studies and observations by this time evidence that he is NOT an ape, and he is not *Homo s.s.*, but as Hweig told us years ago, "a biological creation halfway between the two". Our main concern at this point should be how to get closer to him and bring him under the umbrella of our honest protection and aid.

Yes, Bigfoot and his brothers and cousins have done things that we cannot praise, that we abhor, but let us remember, "Let he among ye who is without sin be first to cast a stone." Our sins toward Native Americans are called to mind.

We believe we had "good cause" and a "moral right" to drop atom bombs on Hiroshima and Nagasaki. God help us! Bigfoot would cringe in horror if such actions were explained to him. The day those terrible events took place I lost faith in many things I had venerated before. But back to Bigfoot.

Lee Trippett shared his outline of "Examples which may relate to the human nature of Bigfoot", with a friend whom he signifies as a professor of physical science from a Northwestern college. Herr Professor questions our knowledge of "human" characteristics; therefore I insert here, at Mr. T.'s suggestion, some pages from my book *Reconciliation*. This is not in print yet at the moment I write, but should be by the time this book on Bigfoot is published.

Reconciliation

"I have absorbed the following from several helpful and personal sources:

"The essence of humankind is self-reflective consciousness. The higher primates are self-aware, but cannot reflect on it. They use no verbal language and cannot plan ahead or analyze the past. They have no sense of consequences for their actions except for the immediate effect of which they are the cause. Humankind has always, from its inception, had self-reflective consciousness.

"The animal primate was abandoned as the carrier of evolution, although it came very close to succeeding. Its most fatal flaw was its inability to appreciate the meaning of time, to remember yesterday or to anticipate tomorrow. There is no missing link unless Mankind is the missing link between physicality and the divine.

"A model to carry evolution was needed that was constructed on a different blueprint, one that could communicate verbally or in an equivalent manner (telepathically?) And one who could recognize that yesterday, today, and tomorrow required different approaches or patterns of thought and action.

"Such a model existed but not in the physical mode. This non-physical, other dimensional, volunteered to take on physicality and to populate the Earth. We call these volunteers 'souls'. All of the great myths of the world recognize them by different names: the mythical ancestors, the gods and heroes, first man and first woman, etc. Such souls enter into bodies at some stage of birth. Encased in humankind they experience separation and relativity. At birth they forget the past from which they came. These brave pioneers had to learn from the very basics how to survive in a material world. The first souls had no experience in physicality to guide them. It was a matter of trial and error all the way. Human beings are not superior primates; they are superior souls. These souls are immortal and are recycled from lifetime to lifetime. They are our identities. We do not have souls, we ARE souls."

Tres: Humankind has been human from the start. Man did not evolve from animals, but from a proto-human, physically scarcely distinguishable from the most evolved ape-form. But different. The ape-form was not given the essential ingredient that was given to the proto-human: that was the all-essential recognition of self-identity, the seed of Ego, of independent self-will. It was a trust that was not given to any other physical being.

Ida: Didn't God make a slight error of over-confidence in Mankind?

Tres: Not at all. If you plant a packet of flower seed do you expect every seed to make a perfect plant?

Ida: No, I would say an expectation of about one-fourth would be optimistic.

Tres: God's expectation might be measured, if He did such things, as about one in a thousand or less. Even that would make a rejoicing in heaven. The finest anthropoid specimen was chosen and its evolution interrupted by genetic altering — this went through centuries of perfecting. The result was a created specimen of proto-human. You did not evolve from an Ape. The human line was a deliberate creation. The soul that was brought into this perfected specimen was totally different from that given an anthropoid. The human soul is from the highest hierarchy, a direct extension from the Supra-Consciousness.

Evolutionary consciousness was one of the results. No anthropoid has, or could ever attain, the dimensions of consciousness given to humankind, not the moral sense, or response to beauty, to creativity, to the arts, and most of all not the resonance to the calling of God, and not a voice nor a language with which to answer Him. You are not an evolution from the ape, nor a handful of mud from the riverbank.

In the beginning of Humankind the soul had so recently come through the inter-dimensional, or psychic, world that it was still able to endow early humans with great psychic ability. After the soul went through many physical lifetimes on Earth it became easy for oppressors to deny this ability to common man; the clarity of the psychic sense was diminished, repressed, denied, and eventually all but lost.

Ida: After we hear of the multi-dimensions of Space (coming up) this will be more plainly seen.

Ego has been given a bum rap, as though it is something immodest, almost obscene, and should be squashed.

We are sparks from God's anvil. Each spark is a personal ego. Ego is what gives us presence. Ego is self-will.

We should accept and cherish our ego, our individuality, try to understand it and keep it under control within limits of common sense and not let our personal self be swallowed up in a group, a cult, or an incorporated interest.

If we give ego a chance it will lead us to our purpose coming into this world in this lifetime. As a soul we have each come with a purpose. We are not here by accident.

Ida: I try to give everyone's opinion a fair hearing. The cast-iron rigidity of "scientific" thought is a little bruising. Assuredly there have to be rules and parameters to any study or it becomes messy and ungovernable. It is the double standard of scientists' private thoughts and public statements that irks me.

How can knowledge go forward if today's discoveries are cramped into the molds of yesterday? Knowledge is a precious commodity. It is a living thing and must be allowed to grow. The knowledge of Bigfoot can be tested and grow only if honest and courageous people come forward with detailed reports of their experiences. Every report offers a precious observation. It counts.

If someone laughs at you for your report, just say, "I am glad I was able to make you cheerful. We need more laughter in the world at any cost." One person who ridicules another over something he knows nothing about only proves his own ignorance and stupidity.

Perhaps we should not look to hard-shelled and left-brained science to reveal the mysteries of Bigfoot. Perhaps we should turn to the more soft-shelled such as psychology and the life sciences, or studies that reflect the right brain modulations.

So we can list some of the more obvious aspects of Bigfoot's human nature:

- Self-reflecting consciousness
- A verbal or equivalent language (pictorial telepathy)
- A sense of consequences beyond the moment
- An appreciation of the meaning of time to remember yesterday
- To anticipate tomorrow (to plan for tomorrow)
- Recognition of identity
- Ego
- Independent self-will
- Evolutionary consciousness
- Dimensions of consciousness

- A moral sense
- Response to beauty
- Creativity, arts
- Resonance to God (a God sense)
- A voice or language to answer Him
- Psychic abilities
- Individuality, individual recognitions and thinking
- Reactions showing individual thought, not species instinct.

We have seen that Bigfoot is so controlled by his monitors that he has not been permitted to develop his individuality to the extent that he would be capable of if left to himself. He is capable of learning a great deal more than he has been given the freedom to do. Nor is he prepared to be self-governing. He could be a threat if just turned loose without his monitor's guidance.

Marlys Trippett:

Notations on Human Aspects of Bigfoot

(Various Sources)

From, *Do Abominable Snowmen of America Really Exist?* by Roger Patterson (before his film), page eleven:

"After the Bluff Creek sighting a Hoopa Indian merely retorted, "Good Lord, have the white men finally gotten around to that?"

A reference from *Sasquatch Hunter* by Dahinden, page forty-two:

"It is not big news that Indians were very familiar with the subject of Bigfoot."

We have already told of the lady Indian shaman's reaction to the question of Bigfoot. "We call him brother," she said.

These three incidences uphold the usual Indian designation for Bigfoot as "The Wild Man of the Woods."

Marlys' report from John Green's book, *Sasquatch, the Apes Among Us*, page sixty-five and continuing:

"The Bluff Creek, California crew of road builders entered an area completely wild and buried in a closed canopy forest, totally uninhabited. Work started in August 1958, twenty miles north of Klamath River. Big tracks started appearing overnight."

"In the Bluff Creek area a sustained campaign against the road crew was carried out.

"Bigfoot picked up a trailer loaded with culverts, turned it upside-down and dropped it. At other times he had thrown culvert pipes, too heavy for men to lift without machinery, from the road into the creek without any damage to the bushes on the slope below the road."

Another time and place, "Bigfoot picked up a twenty foot section of a sluice-way and smashed it against a tree."

Marlys' references to the several Bluff Creek sightings are incidences that indicate Bigfoot's understanding of a situation in ways that an animal would take no cognizance of. Bluff Creek gave many footprints and casts thereof to give proof of his reality.

The fact that several creatures returned more than once and in several different incidents shows their understanding of this invasion into their territory. They did everything they could think of to discourage further invasion. Such continual tampering with the road progress indicates Bigfoot's understanding of consequences beyond the moment. It shows planning and cooperative effort.

The road construction continued for more than a year and then was halted because of many rock slides. We do not know that Bigfoot was the cause of the rock falls, but who else had a possible reason to do so, and who uses rocks better than Bigfoot in moral persuasion? The overseer of the work would not announce it if he knew. He could never have kept any worker on the job.

From Roger Patterson's book Marlys extracts the account of the five miners who were attacked by rocks thrown against their cabin at night, by at least a pair of Bigfoot and maybe more.

Marlys says, "It sounds like the attack was precipitated by one of the miners having shot at a Bigfoot four times that afternoon. He thought it had fallen and was killed."

The rock attack appears to have been an act of moral indignation. Seeking retribution for a previous act is a human trait. It shows a reflective delay that is not an animal trait.

From John Green's book Marlys quotes, "There are no reports of Sasquatch killing humans anywhere in Canada or the United States east of the Rockies." To what may we attribute this dispensation? Certainly they had been shot at many times and suffered countless other aggravations. Their reserve was certainly not from fear or weakness. Was it disdain for our puniness, or compassion, a feeling of kinship? We can't really know without more reports. Any pure animal like a bear would have turned on the aggressor on the spot, at least sometimes. Such a restraint indicates an understanding beyond animal instinct, whatever the reason might have been.

Marlys again quotes John Green's book about Bigfoot chasing humans in a bluffing manner, throwing rocks, shaking cars, and tossing one woman over a fence. Bigfoot can and will take action but it is limited by caution, thoughtfulness, and restraint such as no pure animal would exhibit.

"Bigfoot looked in total amazement at the fallen trees the crew had cut down."

Would a bear or deer or any other animal of the forest register the slightest interest or concern?

"Bigfoot had the power and speed to kill the people he occasionally chased if that was his intention." And on page 344 Green says, "Bigfoot could have torn the car to pieces if he wanted to." It is John Green's belief that Bigfoot is good at putting up an excellent bluff at times.

From Patterson's book (pages 102, 103-110, and 112), Marlys derives the story of the miner on vacation, Albert Ostman.

"This tells the story of a miner who was carried in his sleeping bag to a location where a family of Sasquatch seemed to dwell, a male, a female, and two children, a young boy, and a girl. The miner had a chance to observe them carefully before he escaped. He thinks he was captured to be a "mate" for the girl Sasquatch.

"The Bigfoot family gesticulated and talked in 'gibberish' among themselves. The 'old man' tried to make himself understood to Ostman."

This episode indicates intention and planning for the future in Bigfoot's mind. This also shows they do have language.

Marlys tells of a report, also in Green's book, in which an observer saw three Bigfoot, a male, female and child turning over rocks to locate rodents for food. After turning the rocks over, the male did not toss them helter skelter but stacked them in neat towers in an artistic manner showing Bigfoot does have artistic impulse.

Patterson is also quoted by Marlys in the incident where Bigfoot seemed to knock at a cabin door, and opened the door inward. "The man asked, 'What do you want?' Bigfoot did not reply but somehow made the man understand he wanted food. He was given a candy bar and went away mumbling something."

"Several incidents are of Bigfoot wearing scraps of clothing or things fastened around him." The desire for ornamentation is not animalistic.

Marlys describes a juvenile appearing at a woman's window and accepting an apple, but first looking back and getting its mother's approval. Seeking approval before accepting food is not an animal trait.

"A man thought he shot a bear and then realized it was Bigfoot. He saw two Bigfoot companions crying over it as humans would".

"Many hunters have drawn a bead on Bigfoot and then resisted shooting. 'It seemed too human to kill'".

Once you know what to look for you can find many human actions within the reported observations of Bigfoot. Here is another story from the Albert Ostman incident:

"Ostman made a dipper-type cup for the boy from a milk can and a small tree limb. It seemed to please the boy and he made gestures that he wanted another one for his sister. Ostman made her one from a vegetable can."

This is certainly a very human request on the part of the boy Bigfoot. I cannot imagine any animal replicating it.

Of course we recognize that "One swallow does not a summer make." But these incidents that seem isolated as given are representative of observed and repeated characteristics.

This is why it is so important to report sightings and experiences of contacts and interactions with Bigfoot in great detail without self-editing. Only by collating repetitious behavior can we accept an incident as representative of a specific species trait.

If one Bigfoot is observed building rock towers, that could be only an idiosyncrasy of an individual Bigfoot. But when Maez tells us there are acres of such constructs, built over a long period of time, we can safely believe such creativity is a definite species trait.

We can't make one Bigfoot replicate his activity in a laboratory or before a jury, but we can be observant if his actions and reactions, whatever they might be, has been repeated in some way by his fellows.

If a number of Bigfoot (Bigfeet?) show up wearing a scrap of clothing, a vest, a belt, a bit of leather it indicates a species trait. If we have only one report of such an activity it proves nothing except an individual prankishness. This is where the value of statistics is shown.

So when one researcher admits that for forty years he has tossed out every report that hints at anything that might be construed as a human-type action, he has done an incredible disservice to the earnest and sincere researchers who notate every scrap of information whether it serves their personal agenda or not. I find such an action noticeably unscientific and selfish. The same may be said for those who toss out any mention of UFOs or psychic manifestation. We cannot know Bigfoot until we have considered all the details of reports. We must encourage reporters to give such detailed accounts.

What exactly are you coy researchers trying to do, serve yourselves, or serve the study of Bigfoot?

Ida, 7/20/2000, middle of the night: I am writing this in the dark actually. I only hope I can read it in the morning. It is written in the dark about Bigfoot also, but with great hope for further enlightenment.

Mr. T. has dug out of the dictionaries splendid definitions of such words as "self, consciousness, soul, and spiritual". We can digest these definitions and then retranslate them into our own understanding.

I will insert Mr. T's definitions here, abbreviated in part, and then add comments of my own.

Lee:

How Is the "Self" or "Consciousness" Of Bigfoot

Unique, Common, or Different In Relation To Us?

June 2000

Possible meanings for "consciousness" etc.: Specifically, how is the 'self' or 'consciousness' of Bigfoot unique, common, or different in relation to us? Definitions from *The American Heritage Dictionary of the English Language*:

Consciousness

1. The state or condition of being conscious.
2. A sense of one's personal or collective identity, especially the complex of attitudes, beliefs, and sensitivities held by or considered characteristic of an individual or a group.
   a. Special awareness or sensitivity: class consciousness; race consciousness
   b. Alertness to or special concern for a particular issue or situation; "a movement aimed at raising the general public's consciousness of social injustice".
3. In psychoanalysis, the conscious unconscious. From the *Concise Columbia Encyclopedia*: In Psychology, that aspect of mental life that is separate from immediate consciousness and is not subject to recall at will.

Unconscious

Sigmund Freud regarded the unconscious as a vast portion of the mind including the instinctual drives and repressed residue of unacceptable experiences and desires.

Jung added the concept of an inherited unconscious, known as the collective unconscious, to the Freudian view.

Although some psychological schools reject the idea of the unconscious, most modern psychologists accept that a person has latent, or unretrieved, memories and ideas.

Self
1. The total, essential, or particular being of a person; the individual.
2. The essential qualities distinguishing one person from another, individuality.
3. One's consciousness of one's own being or identity, the ego.
4. One's own interests, welfare, or advantage: "thinking of one's self alone".

From immunology: that which the immune system identifies as belonging to the body, and tissues which are no longer recognized as self.

What are the possible meanings for "spiritual"? Specifically, how is the "spirituality" of Bigfoot unique, common, or different in relation to us?

From the *American Heritage Dictionary of the English Language*:

Spiritual
1. Of, relating to, consisting of, or having the nature of spirit;
2. Of, concerned with, or affecting the soul.
3. Of, from, or relating to God; deific.
4. Of or belonging to a church or religion; sacred.
5. Relating to or having the nature of spirits or a spirit; supernatural.

Some think or believe an individual is spiritual if they:
1. Attend to some ceremony with consistent devotion and integrity, (this is regardless of the religion, but some think the issue of which religion is extremely significant),
2. Or if they meditate long hours for years (regardless of the religion or cult or philosophy or illusion or truth),
3. Or can heal by any number of different non-physical modalities,

4. Or they attend some "church" (temple) type building on a regular basis,
5. Or they can see past all of our surrounding illusions,
6. Or they have a persistent denominational language pattern,
7. Or they demonstrate daily acts of patience, forgiveness, tolerance, love, etcetera,
8. Or they study or memorize matters relating to all issues of theology,
9. Or they have visions of spiritual beings who have long ago passed on.
10. All of the above may relate to any number of different periods, cultures, or material advancements.

Soul

From the *American Heritage Dictionary of the English Language*, specifically, how is the "Self" or soul of Bigfoot unique, common, or different in relation to us?

1. The animating and vital principle in human beings credited with the faculties of thought, action, and emotion and often conceived of as an immaterial entity.
2. The spiritual nature of human beings, regarded as immortal, separable from the body at death, and susceptible to happiness or misery in a future state.
3. The disembodied spirit of a dead human being; a shade.
4. Soul. Christian Science. God.
5. A human being.
6. The central or integral part; the vital core.
7. A person considered as the perfect embodiment of an intangible quality, a personification.
8. A person's emotional or moral nature.
9. A sense of ethnic pride among Black people and especially African-Americans, expressed in areas such as language, social customs, religion, and music.
10. A strongly, deeply felt emotion conveyed by a speaker, a performer, or an artist.
11. Soul music

Many New Age viewpoints express the meaning of soul as the "Basic essence or Self" of a human.

Some consider the soul as the Light of God or the essence of Christ (Son of God) that **is** the essence of Life for any and all humankind. Of course, this brings up the need to define the meaning of 'God' and 'Christ'.

Everything has a soul which is Divine Energy placed within any material form which carries the vibration of Life.

Soul is the sum total of every feeling, attitude, impression, thought, etc.

The Soul has **no** specific location in any form or body. It **is** the expression of God (Universal Creative Spirit) behind the form and can be 'seen' in every cell, organ, and function of any form which expresses Life.

Ida, 7/11/2000: To put my own spin on the definition of Self:

The recognition of the Power of Self was an evolutionary burst of consciousness that came into an already budding humanity. Now the Self could break away from the collective consciousness that the telepathic form of communication permitted and become distinctive and individual thinkers. Now one could make decisions for himself, recognize his own being, and learned to take time to analyze a situation before he took action. He came logically to delayed action rather than relying solely on reaction. Bigfoot is being held by his monitors in a mostly reactive stage, but he is capable of analytical action when Maez and the Council turn him loose.

Somewhere along our evolutionary line the idea of independent Self was given a jump-start. The idea of self appears in our own children around the age of seven, indicating that the human line did not start with it. Was this idea of self-power, the Fall from Eden? Mankind had to take over his own Providence?

When Bigfoot went on a rampage at Bluff Creek and started tossing heavy equipment and supplies around to show his giant displeasure at this invasion of his homeland he was reacting through the Power of Self. How much of this was a reaction from pure anger? How much was calculated and analyzed action? How much of it was instruction from Maez? If we knew the answer to these three possibilities we would know how far Bigfoot's consciousness extends.

Consciousness means to be aware of what exists outside the Self and separate from it, and one's experience of that outside, and one's reaction to it.

Ida, 7/2000: Are you there, Thoth?

Thoth: Always, my dear. Or if I can't answer, Tres will. He is always here.

Ida: He doesn't talk much.

Thoth: He has many ways of letting his thoughts be known. What was your question?

Ida: About this fossil head and the artifacts. Is it really worthwhile to present this?

Thoth: Why not?

Ida: No one will believe it. I've been trying for ten years to get someone interested. They only think I am nuttier than usual.

Thoth: Does that bother you?

Ida: It did at first. But the damage is already done. I might just as well continue if you think it is useful to do so.

Thoth: If you are satisfied that you have presented something you really believe is of value to knowledge, what does anything else matter? You are still skeptical yourself that this is really a Bigfoot head, is that it?

Ida: A little. It doesn't seem possible that I should have found it. I didn't know anything about Bigfoot then, or fossils either. I just thought it was a funny looking rock.

Thoth: Think of all the steps that led up to finding it. Remember what led you to being in that place at that time.

Ida: I have. It all adds up, step by step, too tedious to write it all here. It began really in 1982 when my daughter and I left the Laramie conference early and made a roundabout trip through Wyoming. I've mentioned that. I found some sandstone concretions that were the exact shape of a large human hand. I sent them to the Smithsonian and was told they were only one of Mother Nature's jokes. I said, "If I ever have the opportunity, the time, and the money I am going to come back to Wyoming and hunt up more stuff like this." After my husband died in 1988, I had all three, opportunity, money, and time all of which I have spent ecstatically. I have more sandstone concretions, but of animal bones. I think I was sent back purposely to find this fossil. A longer story but it will keep for later.

Thoth: Doesn't it all seem somehow planned for you?

Ida: I have thought that.

Thoth: Then stop squawking and get on with your work. You have two, possibly four more books to write before you can call it quits. Get busy.

Ida: I have often heard, "There is no rest for the wicked."

Thoth: As long as Lord Spike is not nagging for his lunch you can put that off for a little while. This note won't take long. You have pretty well caught up on your writing tasks, all those notes worked in fairly well. Now it is time to take off on a new line. There is no need to repeat all of the old Bigfoot stories here. Anyone who has the least bit of sensitivity to Bigfoot has already read them, probably a dozen times. We need to pump some new information into the story.

I am still working with Maez on a new approach to Og as I know you would be most comfortable talking to him rather than someone new.

Ida: Yes, I would.

Thoth: I will keep suggesting ways to Maez to make this contact worthwhile for both of you. Meantime let us get on to other matters. Someone has suggested that there are at least 10,000 Bigfoot on the North American continent. There are not 10,000 of the entire species in the whole world. This is a wild assumption and irresponsible. It makes a man with a gun think, "Oh, there are lots of them. Let's just bang away one or two."

We have located a little fewer than 500 on your map. There are more, as we said previously, maybe five or six times more, but nothing like 10,000 in the whole world. A too generous estimate would be 3,500. Your map shows you where they are most likely to be seen, not where they all are. They are moved about regularly.

If twenty sightings are reported in one locale it does not mean there are twenty Bigfoot. It could mean four very active ones. Or even only two.

There are no longer "a lot". Their number has been terribly decimated by the poisoning of their habitat. Do you remember when you baked the eggplant without paring it? All the scrubbing you did on it did not remove the pesticide that had permeated the skin. You took one bite and collapsed on the floor. When Bigfoot borrows his supper from the fields, he does not wash it too well unless there is a prominent lot of mud. More than one Bigfoot has fallen just as you did, but did not rise again. So where are the bodies? I told you Bigfoot is seldom alone. A companion is always within a half mile. This one removes the body to a hidden place and telepathically reports to the supervisors who send for it to be picked up by a UFO. That is where all the bodies go.

Ida: There have been reports by someone who sees several Bigfoot bury a body and roll huge boulders over it.

Thoth: To keep predators like cougar or wolves from it. If that person would later take a shovel and dig under the side of the boulder, he would not find a body. It is only concealed until a craft can come for it.

Ida: Sounds logical, I suppose.

Thoth: I'm afraid Maez's games have aroused your skepticism again. Unfortunately.

Ida: I know you do not lie.

Thoth: Thank you. So much poisonous stuff has been dumped into rivers and ponds that they take the toll of Bigfoot year by year. They are not prolific enough to keep up the species. They need protection in many different ways. Guns are one of their greatest dangers. They have developed many different ways of avoiding hunters, but to tell you their secrets would leave them vulnerable. This is enough for today.

Ida (thinking), 7/2000: For the last several days my mind has been circling around the thoughts of Maez, the Councilman from Arcturus who monitors Bigfoot. Why does he treat us as he does, obviously with little respect?

He treats us as do adults, who, from their superiority often treat small children in an unintentionally unkind manner. It reminds me of the time I told my small niece in a disgusted tone, "You're eating ice cream? I wouldn't eat that stuff, it has vitamins in it!" She almost gave up eating ice cream. I had made vitamins sound like bugs. Afterwards I was ashamed of myself.

Maez treats us in the same way. Out of his superior knowledge he makes us worry and scramble our brains to make sense of what he is doing.

Then it hit my head hard. Of course! He was treating us the same way we treat his precious Bigfoot. No respect! We think of Bigfoot as merely animal, ignorant, without sensitivity, with fewer rights of humane consideration than we give our dogs, cats, and canary birds. Maybe when we learn to respect the humanity in Bigfoot, Maez will respect us a little more and desist his merciless and arrogant teasing and games. I will concede Maez is more knowledgeable than we, but we have some human virtues also.

Maybe if we take a more humane and compassionate approach to Bigfoot; Maez will take a more understanding and respectful approach to us. It becomes a problem of ethics on all sides because we are all three human, though of various aspects.

We are all three Children of one creator God, regardless of how much the Masters of Arcturus fiddled with our genes by adding some of their own. Bigfoot, as Maez has told us, was a start from *Australopithecus africanus* with an induction of 20% of their genes from the Masters. We were interrupted (this time) at about the *Homo erectus* stage and given an 80% induction of Master genes. Maez and his Council of "Grays" were 100% from the Masters, who changed some of themselves in a series of genetic experiments that, we perceive from their actions, went rather sour.

So we were originally brothers and sisters, children of one Creator God, until we were messed about with genetic meddling. For us it meant a larger brain and a quickening of our projected evolution.

Of course that leaves us asking, "Who are these Masters?"

Where did they come from? They were from Earth, of Niburian descent. It will take another book to untangle this web of history. It is too lengthy and complicated to unravel here.

Maybe if we stopped trying to be so almighty "scientific" (which are only the guesses of today) and became a little more humanistic in our approach to Bigfoot, we would have a better chance of meeting up with him. No doubt he views us with considerable suspicion and anger; he has been shot at so many times. We have not given him much humane consideration, as a human being with a soul equal to ours.

"My brother is a hairy man," says it all.

Once we change our attitude, our experience will change.

And Maez's contempt and arrogance toward us will change. And Bigfoot's cautious avoidance of us will change. For a large part he takes his cues from Maez. With their almost constant contact by telepathy Maez can guide him instantaneously in what to do.

Someone has to take the first step toward understanding each other and this is my first step.

Thoth, 7/2000: I am still trying to get Maez to allow Og to continue his conversations with you. Maez imposed such demands and restrictions that I could not accept. If he will lessen the severity of these, you may be able to continue.

Ida: What's his beef?

Thoth: He is afraid your influence on Og will turn him away from the control of Maez and the Council. Og has already shown an inclination toward rebellion. He is something of a renegade.

Ida: What's his beef?

Thoth: His powerlessness under the existing control structure. He is ripe for a revolt. He would make an excellent leader.

Ida: Yow! I don't want to start another war on Earth! We've got enough going now.

Thoth: No, revolt is not the solution.

Ida: Education is. Let the Bigfoot be educated to the best of their abilities. Then they will not feel so powerless.

Thoth: Maez is afraid too much knowledge is the very action that will trigger a revolt.

Ida: That makes me suspicious of the quality of their control. However, this is not something for me to deal with. I'm a stranger in these parts myself.

Thoth: Yes, but I thought it best to let you know what was really behind all this fiddle-faddling around.

Ida: Thank you. I feel better now. I was worried that I had done something wrong to make the break-off with Maez and Og come so suddenly.

Thoth: Nothing wrong.

Ida: I admit I am not wise enough to want to help instigate such a revolt. I think everyone is better off if Bigfoot continue under the control of Maez and the Council, at least for the present.

Thoth: Maez plays his Bigfoot like a champion chess player.

Ida: Bigfoot is not ready to govern himself. Maybe he will be in the future, if there are any left in the future.

Thoth: We are hoping to help that happen. That is why you have been called upon to write this book so that people will understand his character and conditions and want to help him continue his race. The wonder and mystery of the whole world would be lessened without him.

Ida, 7/13/2000: I am told we have come to the last two weeks of solely note taking. Starting August 1st we put the notes together into a book which is scheduled to be finished (in first draft) on or before December 31st, 2000. We can, of course, add in any additional information that comes to hand or any conversational information that is given. But the form of the book must be outlined beginning August 1st.

We have left so many things only mentioned, always with the saying, "Later we will explain this more", or "Later we will extend this." Always "later".

Thoth: Guilty as charged. We will do all the extending we are able to do as we write the book itself. By courtesy we cannot override the decisions of the Council. We are receiving any information at all through their generosity and trust of us. We have planted the seed of many ideas. Anyone actively interested can find the extension of these easily enough in the general literature on Bigfoot, in anthropology books, and yes, in the Bible.

Ida: Dr. Leo Sprinkle has called my attention to a book that describes the original Og's participation in the voyage of the Ark, and many other tales. *There are Giants in the Earth*, by Michael Grumley (Doubleday, 1974).

Two other good sounding books that mention Sasquatch or Bigfoot are also in the article sent by Leo: *Lost Mines and Buried Treasures*, by Leland Lovelace (Ace books, 1965), and Charles Berlitz's *World of the Odd and Awesome*.

Ida, 7/13/2000: If my explanations and definitions are sometimes so basic and simple they make me sound like an ignoramus and simpleton, I would like to tell you how many years I have studied to do just that — simplify! There have been at least 60 years of consciously trying to find the bottom line of a subject and state it in clear, simple terms. I may lose literary qualities (fluff) in doing so, but I am understood.

Thoth, 7/22/2000: So we wind up the written notes for this book. Now you can start getting it all in order and writing the first draft. We still have some outside exploring to do which will be more interesting to some of your readers.

Let's get all of the chatter out of the way first.

We have examined most of the ideas concerning Bigfoot's history, past and present, and read many accounts of contacts. There is not much more to be learned from these casual contacts and hasty glimpses than we have already squeezed out of them.

A few more stories like Albert Ostman's or a few clear photos would add to our knowledge of Bigfoot enormously. Unless we can shake something loose from reluctant and shy experiencers we shall have to find new evidences of our own.

I know you feel we have not kept certain promises but dangled them before you like carrots before a donkey to keep you interested and writing.

The point of this long delay in allowing you a closer experience of Bigfoot himself was to give you and Mr. T. time and opportunity to come to a better understanding of the creature. I am sure Maez's, mine, and Tres's exposition has given you deeper insight into Bigfoot's character. This delay has also promoted his understanding of you. He had more qualms about meeting you than you had to meet him. I think his reluctance has been considerably assuaged.

Tell Mr. T. to keep a good camera at hand and in his car at all times. When the time is right he will have a sighting long enough to get a photo or two. It may not be Og, but any Bigfoot that is in the area he travels can allow himself to be seen for a few moments.

The creatures are scarce and wary and we cannot force them to do something if they are reluctant. (I would like to see someone force a reluctant Bigfoot!) We will do our best to arrange such a contact soon. You have all been so patient and so willing to do what we say.

No, Ida, you will probably never see a Sasquatch. You would probably want to take him home with you to play with Lord Spike.

Actually I am afraid you would want to spend too much time on the subject thereafter and I want you working on different topics. Bigfoot was only a lead-in to your real work.

Ida: When I finish putting this book together may I please have some months off before I begin another? I need to rejuvenate these little gray cells.

Thoth: I was going to suggest it. I know you will get bored and not stay away from writing long.

This is all the writing we will do until your first draft is in place. I am saving something for a grand finale. As you say, Ida, we want to end with a bang, not a whimper. We will have a big bang to end. Now take a few days rest; then jump into the arrangement of your notes. I am going on a cribbage tournament and will see you August 1st to begin the actual writing of My Brother is a Hairy Man. (Tres is always on hand if you need someone.)

Think Like a Bigfoot

Email from Ida to Lee
August 18, 2000

Honestly, I agree with just about everything you mentioned but I have a little different perception of it thanks to out Bigfoot friend "Og". He has visited me twice this week, on Tuesday, and again after I received your email on Thursday. He seemed recognizant of everything you said. I came to believe he must not only be not exceptionally telepathic but he must have some kind of implants from some mental contacts.

Og's first visit on Tuesday was mostly a friendly "hello, how have you been, etc." But the second one was very informative and helpful. I won't try to remember word for word what was said but will paraphrase en total.

Og's greatest concern was that "We must learn how to think like a Bigfoot." We have been making all our plans and decisions without considering his different way of evaluating a situation.

First and foremost in Bigfoot's thinking is Self-Preservation. "How is this plan, if carried out, going to affect the safety of me and my people?" This is why Bigfoot does not allow his photo to be taken. He destroys all photo traps and refuses to "pose". Og pointed out that the minute a photograph (or any device) proved to the world that Bigfoot was real and in a nearby wilderness, every man who owned a rifle would be on the hunt and they would shoot anything in the woods that made a dark shadow or moved.

This is where I broke in to say wistfully, "Maybe they will shoot each other."

Bigfoot laughed. I had been wondering if it was really Og or someone pretending to be him. His English had improved considerably since we last talked. But that laughter convinced me it had to be a Bigfoot. No full human could laugh like that! If I heard that out in the woods I would have been terrified. I pulled in all my fingers and toes as if I could close up for safety like a trapped oyster. He laughed again later but I was prepared for it that time.

Og also pointed out that no Bigfoot would go near an electric or microwave tower. I had been warned of the same thing because of my implants. That's why I thought Bigfoot, at least some of them, might have implants of some kind also. (I forgot that warning once while in Laramie and played around a microwave tower for about two hours while hunting for some black jade that was supposed to be there. Result: I had a blackout and spent four days in the hospital.)

Og also said that no Bigfoot would go near a parked car for fear it would start up suddenly. People had tried to run down some of them. He said the only things on the ground that could run faster than Bigfoot was a train or an automobile and they were very fearful of cars, even parked ones. They knew trains stayed on the tracks.

Think like a Bigfoot!

My implants allow those entities who put them there (in 1940 on the craft) to "see through my eyes and hear through my ears" whenever they choose to. If Bigfoot's implants do the same for him, maybe that is why he is so often forewarned when danger is approaching and knows how to get out of danger.

Og says they are afraid if photos appear the rifle hunts in their home territories will drive them deeper and deeper into the wilderness. They will lose contact with those few people they consider friends who will help them if they are in trouble. If some disaster strikes they will have no friendly place to go for help. In the wilderness they will not have access to farmers' barns and the dried food stored up to feed farm animals during the winter.

To Bigfoot a published photo means disaster and he can't be talked out of that notion UNLESS THE HELP AND PROTECTION ARE IN PLACE FIRST. And we know that is not likely.

Driven deep into the wilderness in the winter any available food supply such as rabbits or small rodents or fish under frozen streams would not last too many Bigfoot very long. Bigfoot can hibernate some but the intricacies of hibernation have been mostly forgotten as they have not had to do it too much in the past. There will be a few, very few babies born who will need their usual nourishment, mother's milk. A brand new baby simply will not hibernate. Maybe the bears could teach them how to do it!

Thoth, 9/14/2000: This is going to knock your socks off!

In the beginning of your interest in Bigfoot, October 1998, we did not intend to go so far in explaining him to you, but since you have pushed your way into his major "secrets" we might as well tell you more important details. Maez will do the honors in this.

Maez: Thoth is not sure how much we want to reveal at this time and this is the reason for his hesitation in giving you the information. It is probably best that I do so.

Bigfoot is far more intelligent than you imagine. His animalistic front gives him a cue to act as you might imagine an animal would. Actually he behaves much more humanlike when he is not under observation.

The Big Bang

<u>Nearly every sighting has been planned, staged, and executed for the effect on the person or persons involved!</u>

Each sighting has had a big effect on those person's lives. You can follow this up if you like by interviewing those who have reported a sighting, preferably some years ago so that the effects have had time to register. In fact some of this has been done and written into some of the books.

Thoth does not want you, Ida, to go any deeper into the life of Bigfoot. You have other work waiting for you that is more in your intended direction. Let those who have made Bigfoot a life study follow that lead.

<u>No sighting is an accident</u>. Did not Hweig tell you dozens of times, "There are no accidents"? There have been very few unplanned events. Bigfoot is a great actor and he loves doing it. It tickles his inclination to be prankish.

Those who do follow up interviews will find in the recitations of the effects on the lives of the percipients that certain items on the reports are repeated over and over:

1. Those interviewed will say they became more interested in and compassionate of all living creatures from Man to rabbits.

2. They will confess to a new belief in, or understanding of, or desire to get closer to God.

3. They will tell of new habits in reference to their environment and things of nature, such as trees, rivers, wilderness, and will tell they have taken some steps to aid in programs of conservation.

4. They will say they became more interested in studying the history of the human race other than wars and kingships.

5. They will profess a greater desire or ambition to be of service and value to their species and to the world.

In other words the impact of their Bigfoot experience has shocked a change of direction to their lives.

Thoth: These few points, of course, are only a smidgeon of what a dedicated interviewer can discover.

Let us leave that pleasant chore to someone who has spent decades enwrapped in the obsession of unraveling Bigfoot's mystery.

Your chore, Ida, is calling you in another direction, so say "Thank you" to Maez and "Good-bye" to your audience. We have other work to do.

P.S. There are incidents of Bigfoot struck or brushed by a moving car. These were certainly not planned to that extent but were the result of Bigfoot misjudging the speed of the car or the driver's intention.

Ida: Yes, I would like to express our appreciation to Maez and the Council for giving us this deeper insight into the character and personality and background of Bigfoot.

There will be skeptics and scoffers. That's all right. If only a few aficionados of Bigfoot learn something useful and of value to them from this book, it will have served its purpose.

Maez has given so much of his time and good Spirits to this enterprise. I apologize for getting mad at his *modus operandi* sometimes. He has his way of doing things; I have mine. I'm sure I must make people gnash their teeth now and then. I am notoriously stubborn.

And Thoth and Tres have my consistent appreciation as well. I wouldn't know what to do without them. (That is more poignant than you know.)

Now to find someone who can type!

Tres to Ida, 12/6: We have already gone over the subject of this writing, but I am going to dictate it word for word as your short term memory is quite, quite short.

We have been discussing the key to understanding Bigfoot. Certainly it is not to be found by chasing him endlessly over many years to take a photo or to grab a handful of hair, although these items are useful and perhaps necessary as proof of his physical reality. Much good work has been done in this area by all those obsessed researchers. We must not underestimate the value of their relentless pursuit of physical evidence. Such facts are basic. But a true in-depth understanding of Bigfoot's qualities can only be found by "trying to think like a Bigfoot", as we have admonished you from the beginning.

This morning you punched the right key. "He wants to be accepted as part of the human race," you said. Quite so.

At one time he was so accepted. If you had time to read all the books in the libraries about "giants of old," you would discover Bigfoot in many of them. He was once much closer to acceptance as a brother than he is today since he has retired into the wilderness for safety's sake.

Bigfoot's main everyday conscious wish is simply to obey his monitors and follow their suggestions and to be true to his nature. But deep underneath that hairy exterior beats a heart that more or less unconsciously, or subconsciously, longs intensely to be accepted and appreciated among the full humans around him. When you put your finger on that longing, you are touching the soul and core of Bigfoot.

That is why he peeks in people's windows, a loneliness of soul, and why he obeys his monitor's instructions to appear in unexpected places before selected witnesses. As we have said previously, "No sighting is accidental". The sighting, at whatever age of the percipient, marks that person for future work toward the discovery of Bigfoot. It often becomes a life obsession.

Have you wondered why certain persons become so entranced with the pursuit of Bigfoot? Because they were selected at an early age whether they remember it or not. The memory may be wiped out but the urge is renewed and remains. A hypnotic regression might help recall the original impetus, the marking of the person.

Once marked, the life of the to-be researcher is followed by Bigfoot monitors to see if they become the kind of person needed/acceptable to carry out the monitor's plans.

The most desirable researchers are the most independent; they do not belong to organizations or social or political groups that have an in-built rigidity of thought, but are free-thinkers and free-doers. There are no social or commercial or intellectual ties that hold them back from devotion to their cause, to find Bigfoot. They must feel free to commit absurdities if that is what it takes. It means it also takes self-confidence and courage.

Courage is seldom lacking or they would not even consider doing such a thing as chasing a hairy giant "monster" through the dark forests on moonless nights.

It is self-confidence that is so often turned aside by other considerations. The final spark needed to fan the flame of obsession is lacking: self-confidence.

Ida, 12/20/2000: For a long time I could not understand why Thoth had cut off my conversations with Macz and Og so abruptly. "I do not want you to become so emotionally attached to Bigfoot", Thoth explained.

I confess that in following Maez's historical explanations and expectations for Bigfoot that I was becoming sentimental over the creature's current plight and his future. Was he destined to become extinct?

I put my sentiment on a par with the possible extinction of the African elephant and the Siberian tiger. The Australian aborigines, it is reported, have chosen not to have children, thus planning the extinction of their own kind. That may be very wise and courageous but it hurts to think of humans so miserable in our world that they willfully choose extinction and plan for it. Can that be our future? Evolve or die, seems to be the dictum.

Can Bigfoot evolve into a more human being or is he lost on the fringe? Yes, I am getting emotionally involved. Bigfoot seems to understand that future. He seems to want to become one with full Humankind. As long as he lives under the command of his monitors, he is not free to set his own course. He lives now with one or two partners and very little communal spirit. Earth humans resist and resent him. His monitors live very far away and do not encourage any real social activities of an everyday nature. They keep Bigfoot dependent upon them in every way possible.

Will Bigfoot plan their own obsolescence as the aborigines are reported to have done? Or will he rebel against his monitors and try to join up with humankind? Or will he go berserk with anger and destroy everything in his path? Or will he sink down in apathy and do nothing? There is a mighty force of change throughout the land. How will Bigfoot react?

The last thing the monitors would want is for Bigfoot to become a social creature and join together for concerted action toward greater freedom. It is only Bigfoot's lack of social unity, the communal spirit, which keeps them from becoming wholly human.

Bigfoot is in a cage more real than one with iron bars. Yes, I am emotionally involved with Bigfoot, but I don't know what to do about it. Except to write this and plead for more understanding of Bigfoot and his problems.

12/21/2000 Happy Solstice! As we have already mentioned, Mr. T. shared some of the information given herein with one of his friends, a college professor. The learned Gentleman's reaction was, "Maybe Ida is just making it all up!" He wishes to remain incognito, so he shall. His credibility and his livelihood depend upon his discretion and his innocence. Let it be so.

We have two choices, to believe to our individual extent, or to repudiate it. Believing in Bigfoot is somewhat like believing in God. Many books and newspaper and magazine stories have been written about Bigfoot sightings and other indications of his reality; many books have been written about the reality of God, under His various names. How do we decide whether to believe, yes or no? By what gives us the most in return. What is our gain in believing? What is our loss in not believing? Our choice.

Compare the stories of contact with Bigfoot with the information given here. Does an analysis of the sightings qualify with this information? There is your documentation.

Here we have to depend on the integrity of the book's writers. I don't believe they are all "just making it all up". Most of them have spent years and years pursuing the stories and looking for evidence. Can we not accept thousands of incidences of Bigfoot's reality and information as to his personality and characteristics? It has all been told hundreds of times and verified over and over, his curiosity, his elusiveness and all the rest. And remember many facts have not been told out of fear of derision and disbelief or for personal motives such as the well-known and prolific writer privately confessed he threw out every report that even hinted at a human aspect of the creature. And like the timid professor who fears it may all be made up. Now he can laugh and turn away. Now he doesn't have to deal with it. I suspect his main scoffing was directed toward my part of the story and the inclusion of Maez, Thoth, and Tres. This means he does not accept ET's influence in Bigfoot's life. It means he will never really understand any part of Bigfoot's story. His choice.

Ida, 12/24/2000: What do we really have on Bigfoot so far?

1. Bigfoot is real. There is a long history of giants in the past, including the Bible. Many stories are told for truth in many literatures.

2. Bigfoot is borderline *Homo sapiens*. He probably could be on a par with Neanderthal, if he were not held back by his monitors.

3. No contact or sighting of Bigfoot is accidental. There is a plan, or intention, behind it all.

4. Bigfoot is more important to us than we realize.

5. Bigfoot is in danger of becoming extinct. It is to our advantage to help that this does not happen. (Can the activities of the Nature Conservancy Group be directed toward areas beneficial to Bigfoot?)

Up to now we have been asking, "What do we want from Bigfoot?

His picture, a handful of hair, a piece of hide, his head. Let us now ask, "What does Bigfoot want from us?" To be accepted by humans as a fellow creature, to be allowed to live in peace, not pursued by rifles and threats to his peace of mind and safety to himself and family. He asks only what we ask of our fellow man, "Life, Liberty and the Pursuit of happiness".

Let us give him a chance to show his mellow side, the friendly, helpful, useful reality he can bring into a closer relationship. As long as he is pursued with death threats, he can only react with acts of self-defense.

Try to think like a Bigfoot!

Ida, 1/1/2001: Yes, Thoth has returned from his Christmas project, not entirely happy.

Thoth: It is too difficult to change the minds of mature men.

If we want to sell Bigfoot we shall have to go to the young men who retain a spark of imagination and wish for adventure. Our audience in our next book will be the 18 to 24 year olds who live and will live in a world we can hardly comprehend, old fuddy-duddies that we have become. A lesson learned; we shall profit by it.

I am happy to be back, Ida, working with you and Tres and Mr. T. and others. We can edit this book we have so far and to finish in a short time. You were right to wait for me to make changes. Starting tomorrow, January 2nd, let us get busy again. Now go to sleep, it is 3:15 A.M.

Ida: Welcome home. And I am sleepy.

Lee:

A Striking Contrast

February 2001

Shortly after my return from one of many attempts to find Bigfoot in a remote wilderness area this fall and winter, I found myself being entertained in the local community concert hall. There is nothing much unusual about that except the sudden and unexpected awareness of the contrast between the lifestyle of two different forms of bipedal creatures.

My six decades of close familiarity within a living style of Western world society had numbed my senses to the fact that a totally different reality and viewpoint in living could exist.

The incredible elusive nature of Bigfoot provides a deep sense of challenge to many in our society. That challenge is to uncover the mystery of the contrast between abundant physical evidence and the total omission of consistent reliable validation by acceptable forms of evidence.

Unconsciously, most people of our world are intimately involved with some aspect of an artifact. The form of art in a concert hall relates to space, energy, matter and aesthetic perceptions that can be measured in many ways. The concert hall itself has been built and serviced by an elaborate financial commercial industrial complex that can be measured in ways that can be replicated and approved by others.

However, artifacts and form do not need to dictate the style of consciousness or awareness. In our society we relate only to human or animal forms of consciousness without fully understanding the many details of that consciousness.

It is entirely conceivable that a friendly hair-covered giant could have a character or style of consciousness that is unlike either animal or human. Extensive research over the past few decades indicates there are elements of intuition and instinct that are far beyond measurement or total analysis. Our customary reliance on perception by the five senses and an analysis of those perceptions by common views of our society is limited. We often do not wish to admit that our beliefs, logic, knowledge or understandings are limited. We often do not wish to admit that some of us have an uncommon but very extraordinary form of perception.

To explain the elusive nature of Bigfoot implies that we have been ignoring a dimension of consciousness that is under our very nose. The research of the past few decades indicates there are some forms of intelligence and perception that are quite extraordinary. There is a distinct possibility that Bigfoot could have a sense of perception or style of awareness that provides the tools they need for finding food and protection without the need of artifacts or animal-like instincts.

It is our exclusive dependence on the artifact style of living that is keeping the majority of us from understanding a means of approach that would work for Bigfoot. Even those pioneers of research in the study of primates in a remote wilderness would undoubtedly be at a loss in approaching a consistent meaningful contact with Bigfoot.

Part Three

Saving Bigfoot

Ida: Bigfoot is a prime example of the indiscretion of interfering with the genetic evolution of a race. Although his "composition" is altogether on the hominidae line, its components were chosen so far apart during evolutionary development that they have made a creature of scant adaptability. He is a hominid orphan. There is no other species, or sub-species on Earth to which he could adapt himself. It would be difficult with his own first cousins; he is too unique. Bigfoot is alone, wanted neither by animals nor today's *Homo s.s.* He is a curiosity born of galactic meddling with Earth's nature. But he is partly, indeed borderline, human and directly related to us. We cannot abandon him.

Why should we concern ourselves with all this? Oh, but we must! What happens to Bigfoot happens to us. We have been genetically engineered from the same gene lines. Our joint evolutionary line was interrupted further along in time after Bigfoot had long gone off in his own direction. Our interruption was just about what we now call *Homo erectus* plus the genetic input of the Master line of Arcturus. We are blood brother to Bigfoot, although far apart in physical inheritance.

I would not know how to solve all the problems of Bigfoot. I would not know where to start. Leave the species problem to Maez, the Council, and the Masters of Arcturus. But the Earth problems that we have helped to concoct we can do something about, things like guns and poisons. **We are dying ourselves, killing ourselves daily with them!**

The only reason any of us are still here is because we breed so readily; Bigfoot does not do so.

If we can't solve such problems for Bigfoot, we won't solve them for ourselves. And eventually *Homo s.s.* will dwindle and die as Bigfoot is currently dying.

Six billion people sound like an awful lot to worry about dwindling very fast. With diseases like cancer and AIDS, for which we have no cure, it won't take as long as you might imagine. What we do for Bigfoot, we do for ourselves, help him or kill him one way or another.

234 | IDA M. KANNENBERG AND LEE TRIPPETT

Bigfoot was manufactured and stuck into a crevice of evolution and expected to stay there. Currently the energy of change surrounds him as a denizen of the Earth equally as it does us. He, too, is becoming restless. As long as he depends so much on the instructions of his monitors, he will remain as he is. When he begins to demand to know, to be told, he will advance from his crevice into a proper human evolution. Bigfoot is stirring with questions and the monitors of Arcturus will eventually lose control. Without their guidance, Bigfoot will be confused. He has not been prepared to be self-governing. How much time do we have?

Very little.

The monitors are teaching Og and some of the children to speak our languages. That is a first step in our direction. Maybe we can take a step in theirs by trying to understand them as human beings, although very "primitive" ones by our standards.

I don't mind if you call me crazy. My ego simply steps to one side and lets the slings and arrows go futilely by, then steps back into place and keeps on working. I am not here to be pampered and petted. I am here to make a statement and I am making it.

Back to Bigfoot.

One of the most compelling characteristics of Bigfoot is his unappeased loneliness. He was constructed to live in isolation with only a partner and a few of his fellows to meet with from time to time. This is one reason why he peers in windows. One of the most basic human needs, next to food and warmth, is companionship. Bigfoot sees our families and gatherings in romps on the beach, camping in the woods, or picnicking in the park and his heart swells with loneliness.

If we can think of him with such human characteristics, we can feel an honest empathy and friendship, and our desire to meet and understand him will be sincere. Change our present intention and Bigfoot will come to us. We won't need to take a photo or get a bone or a piece of hide, everyone else will be meeting him also. We will all be convinced together. Bigfoot will know without a doubt if our intentions are only to exploit him and he will not come. We have experienced that.

Bigfoot's one-upmanship on us is his ability to read our intentions, or to have them interpreted for him by his monitors. They know that our attitude for him must change if he is to survive the poisonous wasteland we are making of his habitat. That is why they are giving us this information now, so that we can use it before it is too late. Bigfoot was prepared from Earth stock for Earth life; he would not survive for any length of time on Arcturus.

Does Bigfoot have a real value for us today? Oh yes, he gets people out into the far corners of the forests and mountains where they otherwise would never go, and they can see for themselves what is happening in our wild places, and he nudges us to reexamine our sense of brotherhood and decency. (Guns!)

If Bigfoot is poisoned by our fields, pesticides, our cruddy rivers and air, can we be far behind? I doubt we are behind, we are right in step!

Why are people so stricken with the idea of him that they spend decades trying to prove his existence? What is goading them on until the research becomes an obsession? Once you become emotionally involved, obsession is next. What is that emotional involvement? Is it the sub-conscious knowledge that once the riddle of Bigfoot is solved, so will be the riddle of humankind?

The scientists' fear of offending their peers and scarring the sacred tenets of their science will hold them back 100 years from any public commitment to Bigfoot. By that time he will be extinct, if there is no help, and we will be well started in that direction. It takes a few unblessed philistines like myself to get the message out there directly to the people.

Mr. T. has already tested the "scientific" reaction to our tale. If we were writing for scientists we might just as well fold up our figurative tent and go home. But the academic scientists are not the ones who are going to solve the problems of Bigfoot. We are, and the good people who do something about the poisoning of all outdoors, the Environmentalists, the Ecologists, yes, even the tree huggers. Then even if the reality of Bigfoot proves to be a hallucination, we still will have cleaned up the mess for our own sake.

And even if he prove to be something less than what we want to accept for a human brother, we have done no one any harm and ourselves good. He becomes a common cause for our own welfare.

The Summing Up

Ida: The Pursuit of understanding Bigfoot has meant the excitement of adventure and the undertaking of solving a puzzle with an elusive solution, and always with a shifting horizon. It has been a learning and developing experience, stumbling across unstable sands of the unkept promises of Maez, until Thoth, as irritated as ourselves, has cut off our direct contact with these self-described monitors of Bigfoot. If Maez wants us to activate a relief program for his hairy charge he must cooperate with us in our clumsy endeavors to reveal the reality, the description, the character, the identity, and the needs of Bigfoot. We do not have collective minds as he and his co-workers do. As individuals we tumble over each other in our earnest attempts to find answers to our many questions. Maez must try to understand us and what are, from his viewpoint, the short-comings of individuality.

I believe Maez has given us altogether valid information about this mystery, but very little we could not have discovered for ourselves if we analyzed the core of the sighting reports at a psychological and human level. It is all there.

Maez has led us through an amazing maze of secrecy, pointing out just the bare tips of information but never actually delivering Bigfoot to us. I doubt he had any real intention of doing so, at least not yet, not at this time.

Thoth stopped Maez's game playing before any real deception could take place, but deception was tentative, it was quivering on the edge. Maez can't help himself, he so delights in making playthings of us from his superior ranks of knowledge.

Listen, galactic friend, knowledge is not the peak of human endeavor. Believe it or not! Decency — just plain, humble decency is!

If Maez wants us to spend our time seeking various kinds of aid for Bigfoot — which I would love to do — he must stop giving us valuable information while at the same time disempowering our credibility. How can we convince our compatriots of Maez's veracity when every one of the projects he sends us out on slams up against a brick wall?

I firmly believe Maez is who he says he is, the head of the council that monitors Bigfoot, and that he is on a planet in the Arcturus system and that Bigfoot is a genetic product of the Arcturian masters.

Thoth and Tres are **my** monitors from planet Earth. I have recognized their help and guidance for far too many years for me to have any doubts as to their total honesty and goodwill. Many times their intentions for me are hampered by my own free will, ignorance and negativity. If I don't understand a situation and say, "No!" instead of "Yes," they cannot override my choice. Not even God can! Earth is the planet of absolute free will and that is not always a blessing.

So we must pick out the goodies from Maez's information and leave the rough shells too hard for us to crack with our limited understanding. Maez has had surely a discouraging task, how to wake us up to the difficulties of Bigfoot without exposing him to more of the traditional dangers that we represent. Let's try to view, the Bigfoot problem from Maez's viewpoint no matter how much Maez himself exasperates us with his modus operandi.

Essentially, all we have wanted to do is to convince people that:

Bigfoot is Real; he exists.

Bigfoot is borderline human.

Bigfoot needs our goodwill and protection.

There are too many "Others" trying to keep Bigfoot free of the dangers that we, ourselves, have presented to him in the past. We must take each of these "Others" into account because Bigfoot historically relies on them and is swayed by their opinions.

Bigfoot himself has little faith or trust in our good intentions. We have not proven them to him, but instead have shown ourselves to be undependable, deceitful, and erratic.

There are the Masters of Arcturus who genetically created him from developing earth stock, the council that monitors his life on Earth, Maez who plans the directives for watching over his welfare, and the Earth Supervisors, whom I suspect in this area, are Native Americans. In other parts of the world also the supervisors are probably the natives of that place. Few of them trust such persons as ourselves based upon their observation of our past activities.

Is it any wonder that we find it almost impossible to even catch a glimpse of Bigfoot? (Only when they want us to!)

Perhaps if we had a well-devised **cooperative** plan, instead of our competitive approach to finding and interacting in a genuinely helpful manner with him, would we find Bigfoot waiting for us under the apple tree? We mean well, but we have no concerted effort or plan to actually help him, only vague notions that we would like to.

Bigfoot and his advisors know, and may in some manner even attend our meetings in which we discuss plans and actions to **catch** him and subject him to **scientific analysis**. This is the best course possible to make Bigfoot distance himself from us. We are defeating our own purposes. When we change our approach and try to humanize our understanding of the Bigfoot problem maybe we can make some appreciable headway. Otherwise we haven't a chance of helping or even seeing our hairy brother.

In October 2001, I will celebrate my 87th birthday, delightfully on the same day as Jack Lapseritis. And that will be close to the day Jack introduced me to Marlys and Lee Trippett three years ago. Their friendship (and Og's) has been, for me, the best thing to come out of these years of large hopes and small adventures.

We do owe a vote of thanks to Maez and the Council for the information given us. It will guide us in our struggle to understand Bigfoot's needs and to interact with him "when the time is right".

I think I have brought the situation with Bigfoot down to some sensible facts and laid it all out as well as I can.

At my age, time becomes doubly precious. I have other duties, commitments, and hopes for whatever time remains to me. And so I retire into my dotage. Thank you for listening.

Appendix

Appendix

Adamic Race East,

True Human West

KRSANNA DURAN

In popular media, the Adamic race refers to descendants of Adam and Eve and assumes all humans descended from a single progenitor. This assumption echoes in the scientific hypothesis that all humans came out of Africa, where some theorists locate the Garden of Eden. The assumption that all humanity originated in one creation garden is decisively refuted by a Russian DNA study of the male Y chromosome, which finds DNA changed in different places and times with no central point of origin.

The Y chromosome is the male contribution, the "Adam," of the Adamic race. Adam's origin is vital in the religious history of Abraham in the Middle East but not in indigenous cultures that are commonly matriarchal. Spider Woman is attributed with creating the world in some Hopi and southwestern Native American accounts.

> The Arcturian representative for Bigfoot, Maez, described himself as a tall gray in 1998. In 2017, nineteen years later, a three-fingered mummy with a head resembling the gray race was discovered in Peru, an area Arcturians were anciently active.
>
> *Maez did describe himself. He has the appearance of those whom we have come to call "the grays" but is much taller than those usually seen on UFOs. He is nearly six feet tall and is considered a star example of his kind.*
>
> *Oh, he did say the Master humans on his planet, Arcturus, are like us but large people, seven and eight feet tall.* (Ida Kannenberg)

> *The Annunaki of the "Twelfth Planet" established their Adamic race in what you call today "the Middle East" — Sumeria (today's Iraq) and the lands between there and Egypt and into Africa.*
>
> *We, the Arcturians, established our race in the West. You call it Lemuria and the western areas of the United States, although it spread rapidly into what is now Canada, Mexico, Central and South America. (Maez)*

DNA from opposite sides of the world -- Europe and Native America -- was identified in a child who died in Siberia 24,000 years ago, no less than 1,200 generations ago. Interbreeding among humans in 24,000 years is so extensive that finding a pure line of extraterrestrial DNA directly linked to the Adamic race is impossible.

An account that Adam and Eve were created in the Lord's garden was passed down in Berossus' Babylonian history, which Hebrew scholars copied when compiling the Hebrew Bible from earlier sources circa 270 BCE. The Hebrew version that assumes only one God created all humans is disproven in classic literature of the world and strong evidence in UFO/ET contacts.

> *You will not find God the first Creator among the Niburians, not even Anu. But they did engineer the Adamic race through the manipulation of their own genes and those of an Earth pre-human consort.*
>
> *The only revelation lacking now is that the Niburians were not the only makers of Homo sapiens on Earth as well as elsewhere! But we will explore all that in your forthcoming book. You will be writing mainly of the Masters of Arcturus who themselves were offspring of the Niburians and originated on Earth in earlier times! Now there is a history for you to explore, and we will! (Tres)*

In the ancient Middle East (Eastern Hemisphere), the Anunnaki were aristocrats from the planet Nibiru and the Igigi were scientists of extraterrestrial origin that primitive humans viewed as gods and sons of God. The lord and governor of Mesopotamia, Enlil, had Adam and Eve created to work in his garden when the sons of God, i.e., extraterrestrial scientists (Igigi), rebelled against laboring to irrigate his garden. Some accounts relate that an Anunnaki scientist from Nibiru, Enki, used his own DNA to create Adam. One story reports an extraterrestrial Igigi scientist was sacrificed to create Adam, whose genetic material was mixed with a pre-human animal to create the Homo sapiens Eve.

When Enlil regretted creating humans, he devised Noah's flood to destroy them but saved Noah in Genesis 6-9. Of Adam and Eve's many descendants, only Noah and his family survived. The Adamic race was destroyed for displeasing the Lord, Enlil, and only Noah's descendants lived to inherit the world.

Strains of Homo sapiens different from the Adamic race were introduced in Lemuria with its own creation-knowledge gardens and extraterrestrial Arcturian progenitors in the Western Hemisphere. In Lemuria, human species were introduced when souls incarnating in ape (animal) bodies and required greater range of expression the human species provided. Their developing but unrefined intelligence was often a nuisance to the arrogant Anunnaki, but the Laws of Nature entitled them to the same exploration of human consciousness the Anunnaki had long ago taken. Exterminating early humans expressing soul qualities because they are a nuisance is genocide by all humane values.

Conflict among extraterrestrial races raged around the question of whether humans were animals jump-started with Anunnaki DNA but lacking godly qualities, or were an ensouled species entitled to develop potentials the soul endows in their home of birth, the Earth. Hyperboreans allied with Lemuria interceded in the Anunnaki's weaponized flooding to destroy humanity. This war resulted in the last island of Atlantis, Poseidonis, sinking 11,564 years before 2000 (9564 BCE) with massive tidal waves.

In George Van Tassel's UFO/ET contact in the 1950s, he stated that Eve was the animal creature hybridized with the extraterrestrial Adamic race, which can come to this planet only by incarnating among humans. This was a remarkable comment in the dominantly Christian McCarthy era of the 1950s. DNA science was in its infancy after the DNA molecule was discovered in 1953.

When military remote viewer Lyn Buchanan viewed 2050 he found three main branches of human hybrids: Nordic, Gray and Reptilian. He said the hybridization was ancient and not recent. As Helena Blavatsky wrote in the nineteenth century, new races and subraces will eventually populate the world.

Ida M. Kannenberg

A pioneer researcher of UFO phenomena, Ida Kannenberg sponsored with Dr. Leo Sprinkle the First Rocky Mountain UFO Conference in 1980 at the University of Wyoming. She introduced the time travelers that contacted her in 1940 at the historic conference.

"Like most UFO abductees or contactees, she [Kannenberg] sees herself as an unobtrusive, unimportant, 'everyday person,'" wrote Dr. Leo Sprinkle. Kannenberg wrote about UFO encounters as she experienced them, information conveyed by the time travelers, and observations about them. She puzzled over composite human nature, humanity as a species, how the species came to its present evolution, and the individual as an existential filament of physical and spiritual worlds. Yet, Kannenberg puzzled in down-to-earth terms and called herself a little old lady in tennis shoes. She extended a steady hand in support of fellow contactees and abductees, and her first book was a manual for UFO experiencers.

A tireless researcher, she wrote seven books about UFO contact, psychic development, ultraterrestrials, extraterrestrials and time travelers.

Ida Kannenberg was born October 27, 1914 in Iowa. She passed from this life on May 17, 2010.

Lee Trippett

Veteran Bigfoot researcher and scientist Lee Trippett contributed his wealth of knowledge about the Bigfoot species as well as scientific protocols in the search for Bigfoot. He had served with a team that monitored the electromagnetic compatibility of complex electronic equipment for an automatic guidance control of a nuclear defense system; and as an instructor in physics, automation control and calculus for electronic engineering technicians. In the 1970s and '80s he spearheaded the application of micro-computers for public education. And in 1967 he pioneered development and manufacture of scientific demonstration apparatus for the national consumer market. He invented the original Swinging Wonder™ illustrating Newton's third law of motion: For every action there is an equal and opposite reaction.*

Mr. Trippett resides in Oregon with his wife Marlys, who retired from public education instruction in the field of reading specialist.

*http://www.eugeneweekly.com/2007/12/13/news2.html